African American American Heritage

In the Upper Housatonic Valley

James VanDerZee photographs © Donna Mussender VanDerZee

Cover photos courtesy of: Sheffield Historical Society, Mark Dewey Research Center, Carrie Smith Lorraine; Mrs. Frances Persip Duval Collection and *Berkshire Eagle*; Wray Gunn Collection; John Garrett and Ann Rollison Penn Collection; Massachusetts College of Liberal Arts, Freel Library, Local History Archives; Special Collections and Archives, W. E. B. Du Bois Library, University of Massachusetts, Amherst, Ruth D. Jones Collection, W. E. B. Du Bois Memorial Committee; and Gary Leveille Collection, Great Barrington Historical Society.

Upper Housatonic Valley African American Heritage Trail
113 Division St., Great Barrington, MA 01230
www.uhvafamtrail.org

Published by:
Berkshire Publishing Group LLC
314 Main Street, Great Barrington, Massachusetts 01230
www.berkshirepublishing.com

Printed in the United States of America

Library of Congress Cataloging-in-Publication Data

African American heritage in the Upper Housatonic Valley : a project of the Upper Housatonic Valley National Heritage Area / David Levinson, editor ; Rachel Fletcher, associate editor and photo editor ; Frances Jones-Sneed, associate editor ; Elaine S. Gunn, contributing editor, Bernard A. Drew, contributing editor. — 1st ed.

   p. cm.
 Includes bibliographical references and index.
 ISBN 1-933782-08-0 (alk. paper)
 1. African Americans—Housatonic River Valley (Mass. and Conn.)—History. 2. African Americans—Housatonic River Valley (Mass. and Conn.)—Biography. 3. African Americans—Housatonic River Valley (Mass. and Conn.)—Social conditions. 4. African Americans—Housatonic River Valley (Mass. and Conn.)—Intellectual life. 5. Historic sites—Housatonic River Valley (Mass. and Conn.) 6. Housatonic River Valley (Mass. and Conn.)—History, Local. 7. Housatonic River Valley (Mass. and Conn.)—Biography. 8. Housatonic River Valley (Mass. and Conn.)—Social conditions. 9. Housatonic River Valley (Mass. and Conn.)—Intellectual life. I. Levinson, David, 1947– II. Fletcher, Rachel, 1947– III. Jones-Sneed, Frances. IV. Upper Housatonic Valley National Heritage Area (Mass. and Conn.)

 F102.H7A35 2006
 974.4'10496073—dc22

                                                                    2006023921

African American Heritage

In the Upper Housatonic Valley

**A Project of the Upper Housatonic Valley
National Heritage Area**

David Levinson, Editor

Rachel Fletcher, Associate Editor and Photo Editor
Frances Jones-Sneed, Associate Editor
Elaine S. Gunn, Contributing Editor
Bernard A. Drew, Contributing Editor

BERKSHIRE PUBLISHING GROUP

Berkshire Publishing Group Staff

Marcy Ross
Project Coordinator

Tom Christensen, Joseph DiStefano
Photo Coordination

Sharon Wirt
Copy Editor

Mary Bagg
Proofreader

Heather Hedden
Indexer

Toelke Associates
Design and Composition

Upper Housatonic Valley National Heritage Area, Inc., a private nonprofit
organization established in 2000, manages the national heritage area encompassing
twenty-nine towns in western Massachusetts and northwestern Connecticut.
Its overall goals are to celebrate and preserve the region's historical, cultural and
natural attractions. Visit www.upperhousatonicheritage.org.

This program is funded in part by the National Park Service; the Massachusetts
Foundation for the Humanities, state-based affiliate of the National Endowment
for the Humanities; and by grants from the Great Barrington, Pittsfield, and
Stockbridge Cultural Councils, local agencies that are sponsored by the
Massachusetts Cultural Council, a state agency. The findings of this guide
do not necessarily represent their views.

Contents

List of Maps ii

Preface iii

Introduction iv

What Should We Call Ourselves? vi

Upper Housatonic Valley African American Heritage Trail Mission viii

Advisory Council ix

Acknowledgments x

List of Contributors xi

Timeline of African American History in the Upper Housatonic Valley xii

Business and Professional Life 1

Black Entrepreneurs 2

Warren H. Davis, Entrepreneur 4

Sylvanus Grant, Hewer of the Pittsfield Elm 6

Men's Work 1863–1946 7

May Edward Chinn, Physician 9

Florence Edmonds, Public-Health Nurse 10

Henry Jenkins Roberts, Physician 11

John Garrett Penn, Federal Judge 12

Sources 14

Civil Rights and Social Activism 15

Slavery in Northwest Connecticut 16

James Mars, Community Leader and Activist 19

Slavery in the Berkshires 20

Cuffee and Nana Negro, Pioneer Blacks in Berkshire County 23

Mum Bett (Elizabeth Freeman), Antislavery Pioneer 23

Underground Railroad 25

William Edward Burghardt Du Bois, Scholar and Activist 30

James Weldon Johnson, Essayist and Activist 33

National Association for the Advancement of Colored People (NAACP) 35

W. E. B. Du Bois Memorial Committee 37

W. E. B. Du Bois Boyhood Homesite Photo Essay 40

Ruth D. Jones, Preserver of the Legacy of W. E. B. Du Bois 45

David Graham Du Bois, Scholar and Activist 47

Activist Orators 48

Sources 50

Education   55

Struggles and Achievements   56

Lucy Terry Prince, Author   59

Dorothy Amos, Educator   60

Eugene Brooks, Educator   61

Margaret Alexander Hart, Educator   62

David Lester Gunn Sr., Coach and Community Leader   63

Teaching Black History and Culture   65

Sources   68

Military Service   69

American Revolution   70

Agrippa Hull, American Revolution Veteran and Caterer   71

Civil War: The 54th Massachusetts Volunteer Infantry Regiment   72

Milo J. Freeland, First to Fulfill His Term with the 54th Massachusetts Regiment   76

Edward Augustus Croslear, Civil War Veteran and Farmer   77

Civil War: Other Massachusetts Units and Service   78

Civil War: The 29th and 31st Connecticut Volunteer Infantry Regiments   81

World War I   85

The Persips in World War I   86

World War II   87

Berkshire Women in World War II   90

Sources   91

Religion   93

Religious Institutions   94

Women as Religious Leaders   97

Freeborn Garretson and "Black Harry" Hosier in Northwest Connecticut   98

Lemuel Haynes, Pioneer Minister   100

The Second Congregational Church, Pittsfield   101

Samuel Harrison, Minister and Activist   105

Samuel Harrison and Harrison House Photo Essay   107

Thomas Nelson Baker, Minister and Philosopher   110

Clinton A. M. E. Zion Church, Great Barrington   111

Willard H. Durant, Pastor and Community Leader   114

Sources   115

Society, Arts and Ideas   117

Kinship   118

Guest Homes for African Americans   121

Entertainment and Social Life   123

African American Literary Societies	126
Robert A. Gilbert, Photographer and Ornithologist	127
The Harlem Renaissance	129
James VanDerZee, Photographer	130
W. E. B. Du Bois, Native Son	132
Du Bois Williams, Professor and Sole Granddaughter of W. E. B. Du Bois	136
Jacob's Pillow	138
Local Black Children as Norman Rockwell Models	140
Sports	142
Frank Grant, Baseball Player	144
Billy Hart, Athlete	145
Larry King, Athlete	146
Sources	147

Personal Essays — 149

Elaine Gunn	150
Mae Brown	157

Community Guides — 163

Massachusetts

Gulf Road/Wizard's Glen	164
Pittsfield	166
Lenox	174
Lee	179
Stockbridge	184
Great Barrington	189
Honoring W. E. B Du Bois in His Hometown Photo Essay	198
Sheffield	200
Mum Bett and Ashley House Photo Essay	204

Connecticut

Northwest Connecticut	206
Salisbury	207
Norfolk (Canaan)	210
Sharon	213
Cornwall	216
Kent	218
Warren	219
Barkhamsted Lighthouse	220

Local Resources — 223
Index — 226
About the Editors — 230

List of Maps

Alleged Underground Railroad Stations in Massachusetts	28
Pittsfield	172
Lenox	178
Lee	183
Stockbridge	188
Great Barrington	196
Sheffield	203
Northwest Connecticut	222
Upper Housatonic Valley African American Heritage Trail	Insert

Photograph of the Berkshires by James VanDerZee. Copyright Donna Mussenden VanDerZee.

Preface

In 2002, Bernard Drew and I had the honor of working with David Graham Du Bois to dedicate the Housatonic River Walk's W. E. B. Du Bois River Garden. It was a proud moment for the River Walk's creators who nonetheless realized that the small park, the first accessible place in Great Barrington to bear the Du Bois name, could hardly represent the scale of his legacy. And so we vowed to join Elaine Gunn, Robert Paynter, Homer Meade, and others in their quest to realize a fitting memorial at his boyhood home, the National Landmark property in Great Barrington that has languished since efforts to create a park there were thwarted in 1969.

As of this writing, the site remains virtually invisible. But until the beloved House of the Black Burghardts is recognized, Great Barrington—indeed the Berkshires and all New England—will not have sufficiently honored the Du Bois legacy.

Meanwhile, work was underway to recognize other African American landmarks—the Samuel Harrison House in Pittsfield, Clinton A. M. E Zion Church in Great Barrington, the Hoose House on Gulf Road in Dalton, Mum Bett's importance to the Ashley House in Sheffield, to name a few. And so a plan evolved to create a heritage trail that would locate such places on a map.

Quickly there emerged a rich and remarkable story of freedom, perseverance, and achievement in the courts, business, the arts, education, religion, the military, and civil rights. It chronicles a rich and compelling story of a small population of ordinary citizens, many of whom achieved national and international prominence. All are rooted in this place we know as the Upper Housatonic Valley.

The advisory council that formed in January 2004, with Frances Jones-Sneed joining as co-chair and David Levinson as editor, first presented *African American Heritage in the Upper Housatonic Valley* in June 2005. The draft coincided with the debut of an African American studies colloquium and a fifteen-month program of curriculum development in our region's schools, and benefited from public comment and review, especially among African American communities. The publication of the present volume is timed to conclude the curriculum project, together with a national conference and inaugural bus tour of key trail sites.

The book is largely a volunteer effort, the result of an unprecedented sharing of research and knowledge among academic and local historians, community activists, and the people whose story it tells. We have tried to tell it from the perspective of the African Americans who lived here. Until now, their history has been largely ignored, concealed in the shadows. This is a modest beginning.

We are fortunate that much can be related in photographs and other visual documents. One such photograph reveals a Berkshire landscape through the eyes of the great African American photographer and Lenox native James VanDerZee, that he named "Road to Home." The image, and its title, speak volumes.

With this volume, we know so much, yet know so little.

And we continue to ask—what is it about this place that makes makes these stories possible?

Rachel Fletcher

Introduction

Discovering the Upper Housatonic Valley's African American Heritage

Tucked away in western Massachusetts and northwestern Connecticut is a treasured place. Bound on the east by the Berkshire Hills and on the west by the Taconic Range, the Housatonic River gives it life. This place has played a pivotal role in the political, religious, industrial, and cultural history of the region and the nation.

The first stirrings of the American Revolution emerged here in the Upper Housatonic River Valley, with the Sheffield Declaration of 1773. During the fight for freedom from British rule, the furnaces of Salisbury provided vital iron for weapons and armaments. In the decades following the war, discomfited farmers took part in Shays' Rebellion and influenced the writing of the U.S. Constitution.

As the decades passed, agriculture ceded to industry, which ceded to cultural attractions and tourism. Today people flock to this area to luxuriate in what was once Giraud Foster's Bellefontaine, now called Canyon Ranch. They visit author Herman Melville's home Arrowhead or Edith Wharton's estate, known as The Mount. They learn of history at Alexander Holley's house in Lakeville.

What has largely gone unrecognized is a rich history of African Americans who played pivotal roles in key national and international events and made significulture. They spent their lives defining the tenets of freedom and democracy, hoping to claim the "inalienable rights" our founding fathers deemed "self-evident."

"Road to Home, Lenox Massachusetts," c. 1903. Photograph of the Berkshire landscape by James VanDerZee. The picture shows Hubbard Street, looking westerly from a point near the VanDerZee home and up Hubbard Street Hill. Copyright Donna Mussenden VanDerZee.

Several dozen Blacks served in the Revolutionary War, among them Agrippa Hull of Stockbridge. Elizabeth "Mum Bett" Freeman of Sheffield pioneered the fight against slavery and her lawsuit in 1781 contributed to Massachusetts' decision to abolish the practice statewide. In the Civil War, more Blacks from the region enlisted in the famed 54th Massachusetts Volunteer Infantry Regiment than from anywhere else in the state, among them Chaplain Samuel Harrison of Pittsfield and Milo J. Freeland of Sheffield and East Canaan—the first volunteer to complete his term. Modern times brought James VanDerZee, the famous Lenox-born photographer of the Harlem Renaissance; NAACP leaders such as Mary White Ovington, who had a summer cottage in Alford; poet and journalist James Weldon Johnson, a summer resident of Great Barrington, who also wrote the words of the "Negro National Anthem;" and Williamstown native Frank Grant of professional baseball.

The loudest voice for African American equality still resonates today. W. E. B. Du Bois of Great Barrington, the father of the modern civil rights movement, single-handedly awakened America's understanding of the Reconstruction period and the meaning of freedom for everyone. Along with others, he challenged and clarified what it means to be an American.

African Americans in the valley began to define their role in society very early. Several Black churches were established in the mid-1800s. In 1895, participants in the national African Methodist Episcopal Zion Sunday School Convention in Great Barrington, warned:

> What we need in this critical condition of public affairs is just what we needed in the dark days of slavery—men to "stand on the wall." As did Garrison, Phillips, Sumner and Douglass, hurling their thunderbolts at the citadel of injustice, and swaying the rulers and people of the American nation into a recognition and practice of the principles of the constitution of the United States.

Those who penned their names to the Declaration of Independence and the Constitution could not possibly have envisioned how literally African Americans of the Upper Housatonic Valley would take these words. So many have come to "stand on the wall." As Du Bois later wrote, they wanted freedom, justice, and equality, "not in opposition to, but in conformity with, the greater ideals of the American republic, in order that some day, on American soil, two world races may give each other those characteristics which both so sadly lacked."

Du Bois died in Ghana the evening before Martin Luther King Jr. spoke at the Lincoln Memorial during the historic March on Washington in 1963. In that monumental speech, he echoed Dr. Du Bois's understanding of the meaning of American citizenship:

> When the architects of our republic wrote the magnificent words of the Constitution and the Declaration of Independence, they were signing a promissory note to which every American was to fall heir. This note was a promise that all men would be guaranteed the inalienable rights of life, liberty, and the pursuit of happiness.

The clarion call of the churches, the prophecy of Du Bois, and the revelations of Dr. King can clearly be observed in the stories of the people in the Upper Housatonic Valley, as Blacks and whites cooperated to bring about social change from the time of the Revolutionary War to the time of the modern civil rights movement. Although small in number, African Americans here made a significant impact on the moral and social fabric of our country.

In the shadow of the mountains and beside the river, African Americans in the Upper Housatonic Valley thrived and prospered and made their mark. Very little is known about most of these people, even within the valley, yet their story is an important part of the national story of freedom, democracy and equality of which all Americans can be proud.

While little is known, there is much to learn about African American history in the region and people's lives and much material to be drawn upon for that story. Libraries, historical societies, churches, town halls, and people's homes are filled with records, letters, photographs, and accounts detailing African American history and culture from the 1700s to the present. Regional newspapers such as the *Berkshire Eagle* and *The Berkshire Courier* contain thousands of articles and reports—most short but some long—documenting African American life. The entries that fill this volume are a first systematic attempt to locate, search through, and categorize this mass of material. The entries cover individuals, organizations, places, and movements. Several of the articles are guides that provide an overview of African American history in each community and a guide to key sites. We hope this volume will inform and illuminate. We also hope it will stimulate more research and writing.

Frances Jones-Sneed, PhD
Professor of History
Massachusetts College of Liberal Arts

What Should We Call Ourselves?

"What's in a name? That which we call a rose by any other word would smell as sweet." From Romeo and Juliet (II, ii, 1–2)

"If a thing is despised, either because of ignorance or because it is despicable, you will not alter matters by changing the name. If men despise Negroes, they will not despise them less if Negroes are called "colored" or Afro-Americans. . . . The feeling of inferiority is in you, not in any name. The name merely evokes what is already there. Exorcise the hateful complex and no name can ever make you hang your head. . . . A Negro by any other name would be just as black and just as white; just as ashamed of himself and just as shamed by others, as today. . . . It is not the name — it's the Thing that counts." From W. E. B. Du Bois, *The Crisis,* 35 (March 1928), 96–97.

The old childhood rhyme, "sticks and stones will break your bones but words can never hurt you," has never held true for people of African descent. We have been trying to find a name for ourselves since the earliest migrations out of Africa. The problem is that as slaves we were rarely allowed to name ourselves, rather we became known by the names of our masters. As soon as slavery ended, one of the first things that happened was that ex-slaves changed their names, sometimes selecting fanciful titles such as Queen Esther or surnames of kind masters or famous people. Throughout their history in this country, they were divided over how to designate themselves as a people. *Africans, colored Americans, Blacks, Negroes,* and *Afro-Americans* all enjoyed some popularity at various times. It is no wonder that the quest for self-identification continues into the twenty-first century.

When the debate surfaced in 1989 over what we should call ourselves, Black or African American, *Ebony* magazine interviewed several prominent Black leaders for their views. There was not a consensus but Dr. Benjamin L. Hooks, Executive Director of the NAACP said the group would not take a position, noting: "This does not indicate a lack of concern about the issue, but rather an abiding respect for the sound judgment of our people, who, on their own, will reach a consensus about what to be called, just as they have done in the past." He concluded his remarks by saying ". . . the dialogue about what we call ourselves should not be permitted to overshadow the more immediate and pressing problems that afflict our communities."

In this guide we sometimes use terms that are historically accurate, so you will see a variation on all of these term. The word *colored* will be used when referring to non-Whites in the early census records, while *Negro* will be used when referring to Blacks before the 1960s, when the term was popularized and embraced. The term *African American,* although introduced long before, was popularized in the 1990s. The terms *Black* and *African American* are used interchangeably in this guide. We hope that the contents of this guide will lead to a greater knowledge of people of African descent in the

Upper Housatonic Valley and the economic, political, and educational systems under which they developed. As writer Gloria Naylor said, "Those things are more important than the debate over what you call me."

Frances Jones-Sneed

Sources

Hooks, Benjamin L. "Afro-American or Black: What's in a Name? Prominent Blacks and-or African Americans Express Their Views." *Ebony* 44, 9 (July 1989), 76.

Litwack, Leon F. *Trouble in Mind: Black Southerners in the Age of Jim Crow.* New York: Alfred A. Knopf, 1998.

Editors' Addendum

The issue of what general name or names to use for the people and communities that are the subject of this guide has been discussed at length by the Advisory Council. We are not of one mind on this, although by the end of our several discussions a near consensus emerged that we use *Black* as the general name along with *Negro, Colored,* and *African American* in their historical contexts. Most discussion centered not on picking among these names but instead on whether Black should be with an uppercase "B" or with a lowercase "b." Du Bois himself was quoted by board members in support of both positions—Black because it is a proper noun; black because names mean little in defining who people are.

One problem we had was that there has never been any agreement in the United States as to what generic label to apply to people defined as being of African ancestry. This very diverse category of people has at times been labeled *Colored, Negro, Black, black, Afro-American* and *African American.* All of these labels have been at times acceptable to some and unacceptable to others. This was also true of the individuals who make up the Advisory Council. Some suggested that we use the label most common at the relevant point in history. Others limited this idea a bit by arguing that the label, *African American,* is appropriate only after 1866 when all Blacks became citizens. Others suggested that African American be limited to the last few decades when it came into common use.

But, as we said, uppercase B or lowercase b was the issue. Supporters of *black* argued that using *Black* places too much emphasis on skin color and suggests that color is the basic, defining attribute of the Black "race." One advisor was careful to note that the distinction of White, Black, Red, and Yellow races is in fact a distortion of human biology, often to ill effect. But human culture endows this set with potent societal and cultural meaning, which the capital letter recognizes and affirms. As another advisor put it, "I am not a black man in the sense of the adjective denoting color. I am a Black man no matter what my skin color is." Supporters of *Black* argued that it is a matter of status and respect that puts the population on equal discourse footing with other defined populations such as Latinos and Jews. It is insulting to use "black." In the end, we agreed to disagree about ways to express dignity and respect, then adopted the capital B.

Upper Housatonic
African American Valley Heritage Trail
Mission

To identify, preserve, share, and celebrate our African American heritage in the Upper Housatonic Valley, through the creation of a heritage trail and related interpretive materials.

We support: the protection of heritage sites in the area; the collection, compilation, and preservation of historical materials; and educational initiatives and related curricula.

In accord with our mission, this volume is the first attempt to bring together in one publication information about the African American history and culture in the Upper Housatonic River Valley. This volume provides information about African American history and life in two sections.

The first section contains six chapters, each containing several articles. Each article provides a general overview or history of the topic and/or describes and discusses the significance of an important person, place, event, process, or organization. Some are significant locally, others regionally, and a few nationally or internationally. What is covered here is a beginning; it by no means exhausts all that might be covered, and future editions of this work may well include additional people, places, and events.

The second section contains community guides to African American history and life in towns and cities in the region. These guides and accompanying maps are the first step in producing a series of stand-alone community guides that direct people to African American sites along the African American Heritage Trail and provide interpretive material. These entries provide an overview of the history of African Americans in the community and provide a list of sites with locations. Each guide also provides a *See also* cross-reference which directs readers to relevant articles in the first section.

The volume is largely an original and collaborative work. The authors of the articles relied heavily on primary source material in researching and writing their entries. These sources include newspaper articles, government records such as deeds and annual town reports, church records, oral histories, business directories, and census reports. These sources are supplemented by many secondary sources including magazine articles and books. The sources are listed in a separate section.

We hope that this volume will serve as a useful and informative resource for anyone interested in African American history and life in the Upper Housatonic Valley. And we hope that four various audiences will especially benefit. First, the general public, who for too long have had too little information about this visible but invisible minority in the region. Second, history tourists who want to explore the full history of the Berkshires. Third, teachers and students for whom this is meant as an historical and resource guide. And most especially, African Americans with ties to the Upper Housatonic Valley, whose rich and dynamic story deserves to be told.

The Upper Housatonic Valley African American Heritage Trail is a physical trail that interprets and visualizes the heritage themes that tell the story of African Americans in the Upper Housatonic Valley. The trail and the sites it showcases are vehicles for educational initiatives and for a program of heritage tourism—lecture series, publications, audio tours, a web site, signage, and other amenities.

Advisory Council

Co-Chairpersons

Rachel Fletcher, Trustee, Upper Housatonic Valley National Heritage Area

Frances Jones-Sneed, Professor of History, Massachusetts College of Liberal Arts

Council

Barbara Allen, Curator, Stockbridge Library Association Historical Collection

Barbara Bartle, Professor, Berkshire Community College

Ellen Broderick, Former Teacher and W. E. B. Du Bois Curriculum Director, Berkshire Country Day School

Brian Burke, President, Great Barrington Historical Society

Richard Courage, Professor of English, Westchester Community College–SUNY

Susan Denault, Reference Librarian and Archivist, Massachusetts College of Liberal Arts

Barbara Dowling, Historic Site Administrator, Western Region, The Trustees of Reservations

Esther Dozier, Pastor, Clinton A. M. E. Zion Church, Great Barrington

Bernard A. Drew, Local Historian, Great Barrington

David Graham Du Bois, Founding President and CEO, W.E.B. Du Bois Foundation, Inc., University of Massachusetts Professor of Journalism/Afro-American Studies, deceased

Heather Eagan, Historical Commission, City of Pittsfield

Will Garrison, Historic Resources Manager, Western Region, The Trustees of Reservations

Elaine S. Gunn, W. E. B. Du Bois Memorial Committee

Wray M. Gunn, President, Sheffield Historical Society

John James, Architect, Sheffield

Evelyn Jeffers, University of Massachusetts–Amherst, W. E. B. Du Bois Foundation

James S. King, Professor of African American Studies, Simon's Rock College

David Levinson, Anthropologist and President, Berkshire Publishing Group LLC

Homer Meade, National Evaluation Systems; Berkshire Country Day School

James Miller, Sheffield Historical Society

MaryNell Morgan, Professor, SUNY–Empire State College

Nancy Muller, Professor, Massachusetts College of Liberal Arts

Anne M. Munn, Intern, Massachusetts College of Liberal Arts

Ivan Newton, Historian, Second Congregational Church, Pittsfield

Jonathan Olly, National Heritage Museum, Lexington, Massachusetts

Robert Paynter, Professor of Anthropology, University of Massachusetts–Amherst

Emilie Piper, Local Historian, Berkshire Athenaeum

Thomas Shachtman, Trustee, Upper Housatonic Valley National Heritage Area

Betsy Sherman, President, Board of Trustees, Berkshire Historical Society

Linda M. Tyer, City Councilor–Ward 3, Pittsfield; President, Samuel Harrison Society

Randy Weinstein, Director, The Du Bois Center of American History, Great Barrington

Megan P. Whilden, Director, Office of Cultural Development, Pittsfield

Alex Willingham, Professor of Political Science, Williams College

Acknowledgments

The Upper Housatonic Valley National Heritage Trail includes the twenty-nine communities in western Massachusetts and northwest Connecticut that constitute the Upper Housatonic Valley National Heritage Area. We gratefully acknowledge the National Park Service; Heritage Partners, Inc.; Massachusetts Foundation for the Humanities; Berkshire Taconic Community Foundation; National Endowment for the Humanities; Great Barrington, Pittsfield, and Stockbridge Cultural Councils, local agencies supported by the Massachusetts Cultural Council; and local contributors to Upper Housatonic Valley National Heritage Area, Inc. for funding the project.

We want to acknowledge and thank the many people who have conducted the research and written the entries for this guide. The Advisory Council devoted several meetings to developing the list of people, places, events, and topics to be covered. Elaine Gunn and Wray Gunn deserve special thanks for pushing us beyond the lives of famous and influential people to include coverage of African American daily life in the region. The authors of the entries searched far and deep for information and then worked hard to fit our format and submit their entries on schedule. Barbara Allen, Daniel Allentuck, Katharine Bambery, Barbara Bartle, Ellen Broderick, June Cobb, Sue Denault, Ruth Dinerman, Bernard Drew, Judith Gaines, Will Garrison, Elaine Gunn, Homer "Skip" Meade, MaryNell Morgan, Ivan Newton, Emilie Piper, Robert Paynter, Tom Thel, Barbara S. Weeks, and Randy Weinstein deserve special thanks for each reading nearly all the entries and supplying us with helpful comments. Patricia Andreucci, William Bell, Kathryn Boughton, Constance N. Brooks, Katherine Chilcoat, Dana Cummings, Gige Darey, Willard Durant, Clinton Elliott, Ernest Galliford, Betty Gubert, Barbara Hanger, Michael Kirk, John Hanson Mitchell, Roberta Neizer, Jonathan Olly, Joan R. Olshansky, Norton Owen, Emilie Piper, Catherine Reynolds, Bernard F. Rodgers, David Rutstein, Donna Mussenden VanDerZee, Alex Willingham and Caroline Meyer Young provided special research, information and advice. Francesca Forrest, Sharon Wirt, Marcy Ross, and Mary Bagg did their usual stellar job of fact checking and copyediting. Erik Callahan, Anne Munn, Zachary Mino, Jenna Turner and Donald B. Victor took a number of the photographs, and Thomas Christensen and Joeseph DiStefano organized and processed them. Special assistance in obtaining photos was given by Joan Goodkind of Simon's Rock College, Danielle Kovacs of Special Collections and Archives, W. E. B. Du Bois Library, University of Massachusetts, Amherst, Gary Leveille of the Great Barrington Historical Society, James Miller of the Sheffield Historical Society, Norton Owen of Jacob's Pillow Dance Festival, Linda Pero and Ellen Swan Mazzer of the Norman Rockwell Museum, John Rockwell of the Norman Rockwell Family Agency, and Donna Mussenden VanDerZee.

We close on a melancholy note by mentioning and paying tribute to several individuals involved in Black heritage in the region who passed away during the months the time this book was written: Ruth D. Jones, Ossie Davis, David Graham Du Bois, and Eloise Brinson Woods.

**Rachel Fletcher, Frances Jones-Sneed,
and David Levinson**

Contributors

Barbara Allen, Stockbridge Library Association Historical Collection

Ann Elizabeth Barnes, Fellow, NEH Shaping Role of Place African American Biography Curriculum Project

Barbara Bartle, Berkshire Community College

Deb Calderara, Massachusetts College of Liberal Arts

Mary Jane Caliento, Dalton Historical Commission

Richard Courage, Westchester Community College–SUNY

Ellen Broderick, Pittsfield

Mae Brown, Housatonic

Susan Denault, Massachusetts College of Liberal Arts

Bernard A. Drew, Great Barrington

Heather Eagan, Historical Commission, City of Pittsfield

Rachel Fletcher, Upper Housatonic Valley National Heritage Area

Derek Gentile, *Berkshire Eagle*

Elaine S. Gunn, W.E. B. Du Bois Memorial Committee

Tim Herene, Massachusetts College of Liberal Arts

Frances Jones-Sneed, Massachusetts College of Liberal Arts

David Levinson, Berkshire Publishing Group LLC

MaryNell Morgan, SUNY–Empire State College

Dawn Morin, Massachusetts College of Liberal Arts

Anne Munn, Massachusetts College of Liberal Arts

Suzette Naylor, Massachusetts College of Liberal Arts

Jonathan Olly, National Heritage Museum, Lexington, Massachusetts

Norton Owen, Jacob's Pillow Dance Festival

Eve Perera, Massachusetts College of Liberal Arts

Sarah Piling, Massachusetts College of Liberal Arts

Gail Pinna, Dalton Historical Commission

Emilie Piper, Berkshire Athenaeum

Claudette Webster, Secondary Coordinator for the NEH Shaping Role of Place African American Biography Curriculum Project

Randy Weinstein, The Du Bois Center of American History

Alex Willingham, Williams College

Timeline of African American History in the Upper Housatonic Valley

This chronology lists key dates in African American history and life in the Upper Housatonic Valley region and neighboring towns. It also includes a highly selective listing of key dates in general African American history and regional history to provide historical context.

1619	A Dutch ship brings 20 African indentured servants to the English colony of Jamestown, Virginia.
1629	Massachusetts Bay Colony is established under the Massachusetts Bay Charter by the English.
1630–1730	Connecticut enacts special laws, known collectively as the slave code, to control slaves and restrict free Blacks.
1638	First record of enslaved Africans brought to Boston.
1692	The first European settlement in Berkshire County is established in Mount Washington by the Dutch, settlers of the colony of New Amsterdam.
1705	Massachusetts enacts a law banning interracial marriage.
1705	A land patent, "Westenhook," is granted the Dutch to extend their colony east to the Housatonic Valley.
1733	The Town of Sheffield, Massachusetts, is incorporated.
1739	The Town of Stockbridge, Massachusetts, and the townships of Canaan, Kent, and Sharon, Connecticut, are incorporated.
1740	The Township of Cornwall, Connecticut, is incorporated.
1741	The Township of Salisbury, Connecticut, is incorporated.
1746	Cuffee and Nana Negro of Stockbridge become the first free Blacks in the Berkshires.
1758	The first Black church in North America is founded in Mecklenburg, Virginia. The Township of Norfolk, Connecticut, is incorporated.
1761	The Town of Great Barrington and City of Pittsfield are incorporated in Massachusetts, and Berkshire County is formed.
1762	The Massachusetts towns of Tyringham and Sandisfield are incorporated.
1765	The Massachusetts towns of Becket, Lanesboro, Richmond, and Williamstown are incorporated.
1767	The *Connecticut Courant* in Hartford publishes its first runaway slave notice for a runaway from northwest Connecticut. The last is published in 1807.

1771	The Massachusetts towns of Peru and Windsor are incorporated.
1774	The Town of West Stockbridge, Massachusetts, is incorporated. Connecticut bans the importation of slaves into the colony.
1775	The Massachusetts towns of Alford, Egremont, Lenox, and New Marlborough are incorporated. Blacks begin enlisting in military companies to fight in the American Revolution. Enlistment by Blacks is then banned until 1777.
1777	Agrippa Hull of Stockbridge begins his service in the American Revolution. The Massachusetts towns of Lee and Mount Washington are incorporated.
1779	Lemuel Haynes receives training for the clergy in North Canaan.
1780	The Constitution of the Commonwealth of Massachusetts is ratified.
1780s	A Black neighborhood of Sharon, later known as Guinea, is settled.
1781	Elizabeth Freeman files "suit for liberty" in Great Barrington.
1783	Slavery is abolished in Massachusetts through a judicial interpretation of the state constitution.
1784	The Town of Dalton, Massachusetts, is incorporated. Connecticut passes a law that gradually abolishes slavery. The law grants freedom at age 25 to Black children born after 1 March 1784.
1785	Lucy Terry Prince fails in her attempt to have the trustees of Williams College admit her son as a student. New York state restricts but does not end slavery.
1786	The Township of Warren, Connecticut, is incorporated.
1786–1787	Shays' Rebellion in Massachusetts takes place among farmers angry about economic hardship.
1790	Berkshire County population, 30,291; nonwhite free persons, 323. Methodist preachers Freeborn Garretson and "Black Harry" Hosier tour towns in northwest Connecticut. The Connecticut Anti-Slavery Society is founded.
1793	Congress passes the first Fugitive Slave Act, making it a crime to harbor an escaped slave.
1800	Berkshire County population, 33,885; Black population, 494
c. 1800	The New Guinea neighborhood in Sheffield emerges as a Black neighborhood.
1804	The Town of Hinsdale, Massachusetts, is incorporated.
1805	The Town of Florida, Massachusetts, is incorporated.
1808	Congress enacts a law prohibiting the importation of slaves.

1810	Berkshire County population, 35,907; Black population, 653. The Town of Otis, Massachusetts, is incorporated.
1817	New York state grants freedom in 1827 to slaves born before 4 July 1799.
1820	Berkshire County population, 35,720; Black population, 759 (334 males, 425 females).
1825	The first collegiate antislavery society in the United States is founded at Williams College, in Williamstown.
1827	A committee is appointed in Pittsfield to consider establishing a separate school for Black children. The idea is rejected.
1830	Berkshire County population, 37,835; Black population, 991 (484 males, 507 females).
1831–1861	Using the Underground Railroad, about 75,000 slaves escape to the North and freedom.
1835	Slavery is fully abolished in New York state.
1837	The Litchfield, Connecticut, Anti-Slavery Society is founded.
1838	An Anti-Slavery Society convention led by Rev. Amasa Phelps of Boston is held in Lenox.
1840	Berkshire County population, 41,745; free Black population, 1,278 (654 males, 624 females).
1844	The Norfolk, Connecticut, Anti-Slavery Society is founded.
1846	The Second Congregational Church is founded in Pittsfield.
1848	Connecticut abolishes slavery.
1850	Berkshire County population, 41,745; Black population, 1,333 (671 males, 662 females). Samuel Harrison is ordained a preacher by the Congregational Church. He becomes minister of the Second Congregational Church of Pittsfield and later in 1863 the chaplain of the 54th Massachusetts Regiment.
1852	An African Methodist Episcopal Church opens in Lee. Harriet Beecher Stowe's *Uncle Tom's Cabin* is published.
1857	In the Dred Scott case the Supreme Court decides that Blacks are not citizens of the United States and that Congress has no power to restrict slavery in any federal territory.
1858	The Township of North Canaan, from Canaan, Connecticut, is incorporated.
1860	Berkshire County population, 55,111; free Black population, 1,210 (579 males, 631 females).
1861	The Civil War begins after Southern states secede from the Union. The secretary of the navy authorizes enlistment of slaves as Union sailors. Norfolk, Connecticut, Congregational minister Joseph Eldridge delivers a sermon demonstrating that the Bible does not condone slavery.

1863   President Abraham Lincoln's Emancipation Proclamation frees
   all slaves in the Confederacy.
The 54th Massachusetts Volunteer Infantry Regiment is formed, with men from
   Berkshire County enlisting under the command of Col. Robert Gould Shaw.
Milo J. Freeland of East Canaan becomes the first Black man to enlist and to serve
   his full term from the North in the 54th Regiment.
Sylvanus Grant cuts down the Pittsfield Elm.

1864   James Mars of Norfolk and Pittsfield publishes his *Life of James Mars,*
   a Slave Born and Sold in Connecticut.
Congress authorizes equal pay, uniforms, equipment, and health care
   for Black Union troops.

1865   Slavery ends in the United States with passage of the Thirteenth Amendment,
   which is ratified on 7 February by Massachusetts and on 4 May by Connecticut.
Frederick Douglass lectures in Pittsfield.
Frank Grant is born in Pittsfield. He later becomes one of the best players
   in organized baseball.

1868   The Fourteenth Amendment to the Constitution is ratified, guaranteeing equal
   protection under the law to all citizens. Citizenship to Blacks is also granted.
W. E. B. Du Bois is born in Great Barrington.

1870   Berkshire County population, 64,827; Black population, 1,322.

1878   The Town of North Adams, Massachusetts, is incorporated.

1880   Berkshire County population, 69,032; Black population, 1,315.

1880s   Jason Cooley and Manuel Mason open restaurants in Great Barrington.

1883   Blacks in Great Barrington form a literary society.

1885   A Black chapel is built in Sheffield.
Sharon, Connecticut, erects a monument honoring white and Black soldiers
   from town killed in the Civil War.

1886   James VanDerZee is born in Lenox. He becomes a leading photographer
   in the United States.

1887   The Clinton African Methodist Episcopal Zion Church is dedicated in Great Barrington.

1890   Berkshire County population, 69,032; Black population, 1,216 (617 males, 599 females).
Florence Edmonds is born in Pittsfield. She becomes the first Black public-health nurse
   in the city.

1892   A second Black church is opened in Lee.

1895   Booker T. Washington lectures in Stockbridge.

1896	In *Plessy v. Ferguson* the U.S. Supreme Court rules that segregated, or "separate but equal," public facilities for whites and Blacks are legal. May Edward Chinn is born in Great Barrington. She is one of the first Black women to become a medical doctor.
1897	Jason and Almira Cooley in Great Barrington rent rooms to visiting Blacks.
1899	Burghardt Gomer Du Bois, the son of W. E. B. and Nina Gomer Du Bois is buried in Mahaiwe Cemetery in Great Barrington.
1900	Berkshire County population, 95,667; Black population, 1,364 (681 males, 683 females).
1901	Thomas Nelson Baker becomes the second pastor of the Second Congregational Church in Pittsfield and serves until 1939.
1903	*The Souls of Black Folk* by W. E. B. Du Bois is published. Town officials in Sheffield seek to establish segregated schools. The Black community successfully resists.
1909	The National Association for the Advancement of Colored People (NAACP) is founded.
1910	Berkshire County population, 105,259; Black population, 1,149 (563 males, 586 females).
c. 1910	Warren Davis starts a land and lumber business in Great Barrington.
1910–1920s	The Great Migration of African Americans from the South to the North.
1914	Alfred K. Persip of Pittsfield is the first African American in the Berkshires to enlist during World War I.
1918	The Berkshire County Chapter of the NAACP is organized in Pittsfield.
1919	During the so-called Red Summer, scores of race riots across the country leave at least 100 people dead.
1920	Berkshire County population, 113,003; Black population, 978 (473 males, 505 females).
1920s	Edgar Willoughby opens the Sunset Inn in Great Barrington. The Rosseter Street area emerges as a Black neighborhood in Great Barrington.
1920–1930	Period of the Harlem Renaissance.
1925	Susie and Albert Brinson open a dry cleaner in Great Barrington.
1926	Eubie Blake's all-Black musical *Shuffle Along* is performed in Pittsfield.
1928	Friends give W. E. B. Du Bois the Burghardt family home in Great Barrington.
1930	Berkshire County population, 120,700; Black population, 1,088 (549 males, 539 females). W. E. B. Du Bois delivers his "Housatonic River" speech at the Annual Meeting of the Alumni of Searles High School.

Timeline of African American History in the Upper Housatonic Valley

1930s	Charles Allen of Stockbridge runs a guest house for Black visitors.
1932	John Garrett Penn is born in Pittsfield. In 1992 he is appointed chief judge of the U.S. District Court for Washington, DC.
1935	Margaret Hart of Williamstown becomes the first black graduate of North Adams Normal School. She goes on to become the first Black teacher in Pittsfield.
1940	Berkshire County population, 122,273; Black population, 1,060.
1941	The Second Congregational Church in Pittsfield moves from First Street to Columbus Avenue.
1941–1945	The role of African Americans in the military expands during World War II.
1943	David Gunn Sr. becomes the first Black coach of a white team in the county when he coaches the Lenox High School baseball team. Asadata Dafora, the first artist to perform African dance on the concert stage, appears in the inaugural season of the Ted Shawn Theatre at Jacob's Pillow in Becket.
1943	Hannah G. E. Hoose of Pittsfield is the first African American woman in the county to enlist during World War II.
1943–1944	Martha Crawford opens an employment agency, tearoom, and inn in Great Barrington.
1944	The Macedonia Baptist Church is founded in Great Barrington. A Moorish Science Temple is established in Great Barrington. It closes in 1949.
1949	The Lenox Merchants basketball team is founded in Lenox.
1950	Berkshire County population, 132,966; Black population, 1,302 (620 males, 682 females).
1950	Nina Gomer Du Bois, wife of W. E. B. Du Bois, is buried in Great Barrington. The Barbers open the Music Inn in Stockbridge, which attracts many African American jazz musicians. Elizabeth Morehead Caesar is the first Black to graduate from St. Luke's School of Nursing, Pittsfield.
1954	In *Brown v. Board of Education of Topeka*, Kansas, the Supreme Court rules unanimously against school segregation, overturning its 1896 decision in *Plessy v. Ferguson*.
1955–1956	The public Bus Boycott takes place in Montgomery, Alabama.
1958	Black women in Great Barrington and Pittsfield found the Monday Nite Club. Fanny Copper establishes what becomes the Price Memorial African Methodist Episcopal Zion Church in her home in Pittsfield.
1959	The Col. John Ashley House Inc. is formed in Sheffield to operate as a museum.
1960	Berkshire County population, 142,135; Black population, 1,422 (706 males, 716 females). The Berkshire County branch of the NAACP pickets Woolworth's in Pittsfield.
1961	The Rev. Martin Luther King Jr. lectures at Williams College.
1963	W. E. B. Du Bois dies in Accra, Ghana, on 27 August.

| 1963 | More than 200,000 people participate in the March on Washington, DC, on 28 August, including 68 Berkshire County residents. |
| | Another protest takes place against Woolworth's in Pittsfield. |

| 1964 | The Civil Rights Act is signed into law. |
| | Berkshire County residents participate in Freedom Summer in Alabama and Mississippi under leadership of the local chapter of the NAACP. |

| 1968 | The Rev. Martin Luther King Jr. is assassinated in Memphis, Tennessee. |

| 1969 | The W. E. B. Du Bois boyhood homesite is dedicated as the W. E. B. Du Bois Memorial Park. |
| | "Harlem on My Mind," with photographs by James VanDerZee, opens at the Metropolitan Museum of Modern Art. |

1970	Berkshire County population, 147,393; Black population, 1,691.
	Barbara Hanger is the first Black board president of Action for Opportunity, a federally funded antipoverty agency in Pittsfield.
	The Simon's Rock College Library establishes its W. E. B. Du Bois Collection in Black history and culture, which is expanded each year.
	Jacob's Pillow hosts the first professional appearances of the Dance Theatre of Harlem.

| 1971 | Dorothy Amos founds the Early Childhood Development Center in Pittsfield, later named the Dorothy Amos Community Preschool. |

| 1972 | The Trustees of Reservations acquires the Ashley House in Sheffield, with the Mum Bett story a key part of the interpretation. |

| 1973 | *All This Freedom Talk,* a play about Mum Bett, is written by Sheffield resident Arthur C. Chase. |

| 1974 | The Rev. Martin Luther King Sr. speaks at St. Mark's School in Pittsfield. His speech focuses on the main tenet of his son's work, peaceful protest. |

| 1975 | The Ashley House in Sheffield is placed on the National Register of Historic Places. |

| 1976 | The W. E. B. Du Bois Memorial Park in Great Barrington is granted National Historic Landmark Status, as the W. E. B. Du Bois Boyhood Homesite. |

| 1977 | Fanny Copper founds the Warren Brown Chapel A. M. E. Zion, in North Adams. |

| 1980 | Berkshire County population, 145,110; Black population, 2,000. |

| 1980 | A bronze plaque is placed at the W. E. B. Du Bois Memorial Park National Landmark on Route 23 in Great Barrington. |

| 1982 | Willard Durant and Rosemary Morehead Durant become co-directors of the Christian Center in Pittsfield. |

| 1983 | American Legion Post 68 in Pittsfield is named after Charles Persip, and Persip Park is dedicated to the Persip family. |

1983	An archaeological field school is conducted at the W. E. B. Du Bois Memorial Park National Landmark on Route 23 in Great Barrington. Schools are conducted again in 1984 and 2003.
1984	Stephanie D. Wilson graduates from Taconic High School in Pittsfield. She later becomes a NASA astronaut.
1985	Simon's Rock College establishes a W. E. B. Du Bois Scholarship program, designed to recruit and support minority students.
1987	The W. E. B. Du Bois Boyhood Homesite National Landmark on Route 23 in Great Barrington is donated to the Commonwealth of Massachusetts.
1988	A 22-cent James Weldon Johnson commemorative stamp is issued.
1989	The movie *Glory* depicts the exploits of the 54th Massachusetts Volunteer Infantry Regiment in the Civil War. It wins the Academy Award for best picture.
1990	Berkshire County population, 134,177; Black population, 2,454.
1992	A 29-cent W. E. B. Du Bois commemorative stamp is issued.
1994	Simon's Rock College, Great Barrington Savings Bank, and the Great Barrington Historical Society join to organize a series of events to honor and celebrate the life and legacy of W. E. B. Du Bois. The Great Barrington Historical Society places plaques at the W. E. B. Du Bois birth site and in Mahaiwe Cemetery.
1996	Milo Freeland's gravestone is replaced in Canaan, and he is honored with a parade. Simon's Rock College in Great Barrington begins its annual W. E. B. Du Bois lecture.
1997	The Berkshire County Historical Society initiates the "Invisible Community" Project to document the lives of African Americans in Berkshire County. The Project collects census records, photographs, and news clippings, and completes 30 oral histories.
1998	Civil rights leader Rev. Jesse Jackson is a Dowmel Lecturer in Great Barrington. A 32-cent W. E. B. Du Bois commemorative stamp is issued.
1999	Esther Dozier is appointed the first female pastor of the Clinton African Methodist Episcopal Zion Church in Great Barrington.
2000	Berkshire County population, 133,310; Black population, 2,666. Educator Marion Wright Edelman is a Dowmel Lecturer in Great Barrington. The Massachusetts Historical Commission determines that the Reverend Samuel Harrison House in Pittsfield is eligible for the National Registry.
2001	The first Du Bois celebration lecture is presented by the Clinton A. M. E. Zion Church, with the lecture delivered by David Graham Du Bois and a program by the students of the Jubilee School in Philadelphia.
2002	The W. E. B. Du Bois River Garden park in Great Barrington is dedicated.

2002 A scholarship is established in honor of Margaret Hart at Massachusetts College of Liberal Arts in North Adams.

Berkshire Country Day School establishes a yearlong K–12 curriculum focused on W. E. B. Du Bois and African American history and culture.

Radio host and politician Alan Keyes is a Dowmel Lecturer in Great Barrington.

2003 Dr. David Satcher, former U.S. surgeon general, is a Dowmel Lecturer in Great Barrington.

The W. E. B. Du Bois mural in the Taconic parking lot in Great Barrington —painted by the Railroad Street Youth Project—is dedicated.

2003- *The World Beyond the Hill: The Life and Times of W. E. B. Du Bois*, written by Mickey Friedman and directed by John Hadden (both of Great Barrington) is performed at the Berkshire Theatre Festival in Stockbridge.

2004 A movement emerges in Great Barrington and neighboring towns to name one of the new schools after W. E. B. Du Bois. The initiative fails.

The Samuel Harrison Society, Inc., is founded in Pittsfield.

2005 The library at Reid Middle School in Pittsfield is named in honor of Margaret Hart, the first Black teacher in Pittsfield.

Michael Kirk's film *A Trumpet at the Walls of Jericho: The Untold Story of Samuel Harrison* premieres in Pittsfield at a Samuel Harrison Society gala and airs on PBS.

Voters in Great Barrington approve a nonbinding resolution by an almost 2–1 margin to support placing signs at each end of town noting that Great Barrington is the birthplace of W. E. B. Du Bois.

The Ashley House in Sheffield creates a new, guided tour with the theme of freedom, and Mum Bett's story is a central element of this reinterpretation.

The first draft of *African American Heritage in the Upper Housatonic Valley*, a project of the Upper Housatonic Valley National Heritage Area (the basis for this book), is published.

2006 Signs noting that Great Barrington is the birthplace of W. E. B. Du Bois are placed on roads at the entrances to town.

The Du Bois Center of American History opens in Great Barrington.

Friends of the Du Bois Homesite is founded to develop the homesite on Route 23 in Great Barrington.

Nineteenth-century baseball player Frank Grant from Pittsfield is elected to the Baseball Hall of Fame.

The Samuel Harrison House is accepted for inclusion in the National Register of Historic Places on 22 March.

Stephanie Wilson goes into space on July 4 as a crew member on the Space Shuttle *Discovery*. At Wilson's request, James Weldon Johnson's "Lift Every Voice and Sing" is played as the wake-up call for the shuttle astronauts on July 5.

Sarah Piling, Frances Jones-Sneed, Bernard A. Drew, David Levinson, Rachel Fletcher, Barbara Hanger, Bernard Rogers, and Elaine S. Gunn

Business and Professional Life

Discrimination long confined Black people to unskilled and semiskilled work. Nonetheless, from the mid-1700s to the present, some men and women found ways to start their own businesses or, through education, to earn employment in the professions. As the entries below describe, some of these business ventures served the general community, while others were confined mainly to the Black community.

Black Entrepreneurs

Agrippa and Peggy Hull of Stockbridge, Massachusetts, were among the first Black entrepreneurs in the Berkshires. They were noted for their catering talents in the late Colonial era. "The pair combined talents; hers was the making of wedding cakes, gingerbread and root beer, and his the efficient management of elaborate social functions," *Berkshire Eagle* columnist Gerard Chapman wrote. Jason Cooley and Manuel Mason carried on the tradition, operating small restaurants in Great Barrington, Massachusetts, in the late nineteenth century and running food concessions at the Housatonic Agricultural Fair. George Jackson followed with a restaurant in the early twentieth century. Other restauranteurs ran establishments in Lee and Pittsfield later in the century. Gary M. and Maria C. Devore of Tyringham, owned the Morgan House in Lee from 1974 to 1979. Maria Devore was the remarried widow of the singer Nat King Cole and mother of Natalie Cole.

Prior to the 1850s when manufacturing began to replace farming as the dominant industry in the region, several Blacks owned substantial farms. These included the Hall and Hoose families in Lanesboro;

Four employees at an inn in Sheffield c. 1900; probably the Conway House (which was on the site where the Mobil station is now, Rt. 7 Sheffield). Photo courtesy of Sheffield Historical Society, Mark Dewey Research Center, Carrie Smith Lorraine photo.

the Seamertons and Schermerhorns in Lenox; the Joneses, Browns, and Davises of Pittsfield; the Way family of Otis; and the Cooleys, Hectors, and Loreans in Sheffield. Before 1850 and after in some towns, Blacks were tradespeople. Probably the most prosperous were the Lloyd brothers—Samuel, Augustus, and William—in Lanesboro and Cheshire, who made and fixed wagons and wagon wheels from the 1850s into the 1870s. In 1870 William's personal estate was valued at $4,100 and his factory at $7,400. Others worked as woodcutters, black-smiths, dressmakers, brush makers, shoemakers, and "hair dealers."

Franklin A. Brown ran a clothes-cleaning estab-lishment in Pittsfield in 1850. From the late 1800s into the 1930s, the Osterhout sisters ran a laundry and the Bristers a bakery from their homes in Lenox.

Clothes cleaning also was the business of Albert and Susie Brinson, who came to Great Barrington from Georgia and started a dry-cleaning business in the Caligari Block on Main Street in 1925. For some years the Brinsons were the only Black business-owners in Berkshire County. "I've been very proud of them," daughter Eloise Woods said. Woods remembered James Weldon Johnson and his wife Grace were good customers. In the 1940s and 1950s pressing was considered "skilled labor" for Black men, and several found such employment in local, white-owned dry-cleaning establishments. In Great Barrington, Rev. Le Chia of the Clinton A. M. E. Zion Church had a plan to open a summer-employment agency for Blacks in the early 1900s. The plan never materialized, but in the 1940s Martha Crawford opened a summer-employment agency, a bed and

The Fanny Egbert Home and Bakery in Lenox, c. 1901. The sign says: The Home Bakery. Mrs. F M Egbert and Sister. Bakers, Caterers. Photograph by James VanDerZee. Copyright Donna Mussenden VanDerZee.

breakfast, and a tearoom in extra space in her home on Elm Court. She also helped found the Macedonia Baptist Church in 1944. Warren Davis, also in Great Barrington, ran a lumber business and bought and sold land from about 1910 to the late 1950s. Davis owned, as well, a popular nightclub for Blacks on Route 23 in Columbia County.

Archie Caesar in Dalton and Alfred Persip in Pittsfield both had bustling landscaping businesses in the mid- to late twentieth century. The family trucking business begun by the Van Allens in Lenox was continued by David Gunn Sr. in the 1940s. In the twentieth century, Pittsfield had been home to the most Black-owned businesses, including a taxi service, tailor shop, garage, restaurants, a pool hall, and barbershop. Jim Williamson operated an appliance retail business in Pittsfield in the 1970s and 1980s, succeeded by his daughter, Jamie Williamson, who became the first African American city councilwoman in Pittsfield in the 1990s.

Bernard A. Drew

Warren H. Davis, Entrepreneur

Warren Davis (1884–1960) was a land speculator and lumber dealer and the acquaintance of several major figures of Berkshire regional and national history. Electrical inventor William Stanley recruited the North Carolina native to be a hostler at his Great Barrington estate, Brookside, in 1902. Two years later Stanley sponsored Davis to attend the Stockbridge School of Agriculture in Amherst. Davis soon established himself as a land speculator and lumberman. For much of his adult life, he lived at 11 Rosseter Street in Great Barrington. From about 1910 until his death, he operated out of an office at his home—often, his front porch. He bought and sold sizable tracts of forest in western Massachusetts and eastern New York state, and was a major supplier of lumber to local yards and to the railroad. Some 228 documents are recorded in three registries of deeds in Massachusetts and New York, from 1907 to the 1950s, under his own name and as agent for his mother, Nannie Davis. They are

solid testimony to his prolific business activity. In early years he bought land and sold it after removing timber. Eventually he simply secured timber rights, usually on mountainside properties.

In 1920 Davis acquired more than 5,000 acres of land on Beartown (now part of Beartown State Forest) in the northern section of town for $28,000. Within months he sold that land to the Commonwealth of Massachusetts, which soon established Beartown State Forest. The state paid $23,283. But Davis took no loss; he retained nine years' worth of timber rights on the land, and the harvest profits allowed him to purchase a former street trolley car barn and establish a sawmill in Sheffield.

Davis worked very comfortably in the white business community. He did business in three states, easily obtaining credit when needed. "Warren Davis was an awfully nice guy," said Loring Tacy, a retired Schodack, New York, lumberman, who said his grandfather's Tacy Lumber Corporation one time placed an

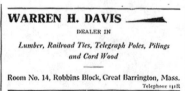

WARREN H. DAVIS
DEALER IN
Lumber, Railroad Ties, Telegraph Poles, Pilings and Cord Wood

Room No. 14, Robbins Block, Great Barrington, Mass.
Telephone 111R

Advertisement placed by Warren H. Davis of Great Barrington in the *Southern Berkshire Directory* in 1914.

"The great beams which span the auditorium were the work of Warren Davis, a 74-year old negro who chose the trees himself on Lebanon mountain, felled them, and hand hewed each beam from one huge fallen tree. He is one of the four or five men left living who can hand hew beams of this size." Ted Shawn, *How Beautiful Upon the Mountain*, 1943.

order that yielded Davis "$1,000 a week for pilings. They were used to build bridges."

Davis sometimes served as a real estate go-between for the Black community; he negotiated the transfer of the Burghardt property to W. E. B. Du Bois in 1928 and helped the civil rights activist secure local tradespeople to begin restoration of the old family homestead. In 1942 Davis's knowledge of local forests was critical to obtaining logs from Lebanon Mountain of sufficient length to span the new theater at Jacob's Pillow in Becket. Davis, according to the dance festival's guiding light, Ted Shawn, personally hand-hewed the beams.

Davis's reported penchant for gambling meant he was never enormously wealthy. The Great Depression took a significant toll on his finances, reducing his personal three-vehicle fleet, which included a Cadillac

Brougham in 1929, to only a ten-year-old Stewart truck in 1931. Davis and his housekeeper and book-keeper Maybelle Gunn (1885–1959) purchased a restaurant, the Harlem Inn, in the Craryville section of Copake, New York, and operated it from 1938 to the early 1950s. Live bands provided music on weekends. Davis and Gunn, who never married, were also guardians for Irene Chinn, a cousin of Dr. May Edward Chinn. Maybelle Gunn was a significant local figure in her own right, active in the Red Cross and the National Association for the Advancement of Colored People (NAACP). The Pittsfield office of the NAACP established an award in her name in 1960. Warren Davis died at the Gunn family homestead in Stockbridge in 1960, after a brief illness.

Bernard A. Drew and David Levinson

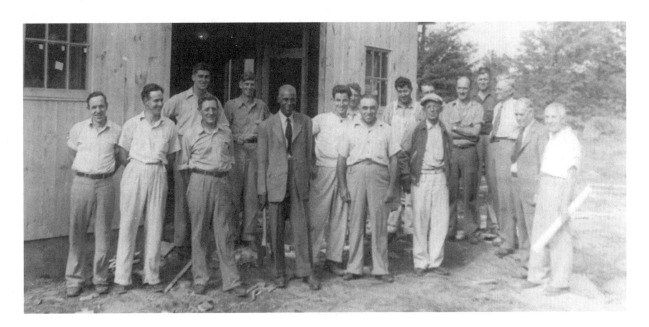

The men who built the Ted Shawn Theatre at Jacob's Pillow Dance Festival in 1942. Warren H. Davis is sixth from the left. Architect Joseph Franz is standing at far right. Photo courtesy of Jacob's Pillow Dance Festival Archives.

Food Purveyors at the Fair Grounds

For several years Jason Cooley and Manuel Mason were major purveyors of food at the annual agricultural fair in Great Barrington. Their food was praised several times by the *Berkshire Courier* (22 September 1882, 4; 30 September 1885, 4).

Mr. Jason Colley and Manuel Mason have erected a temporary home on the Fair Grounds, where visitors to next week's Cattle Show will find excellent provisions for supplying the wants of the inner man, and the inner man should be well looked after at cattle Show time. [1882]

Messrs. Cooley & Mason, will as in years heretofore, have their refreshment booth open during the Fair, and furnish eatables of the best to those desiring. Any one who has ever been to their establishment once will always go a second time. [1885]

Sylvanus Grant, Hewer of the Pittsfield Elm

Sylvanus Grant. Source: *Berkshire Eagle,* 18 October 1984.

Perhaps the Berkshire region's most famed tree was the towering elm that dominated the center of the oval known as Park Square in Pittsfield, Massachusetts. Three and a half centuries old, it was standing when militia rallied nearby to march to Bennington during the Revolutionary War. Elkanah Watson exhibited merino sheep in the country's first agricultural fair in the tree's shadow in 1808. The Marquis de Lafayette passed beneath its branches when he visited in 1825. Herman Melville alluded to it in *Moby Dick.* But by 1863 the lightning-scarred tree was in dangerous condition, and Pittsfield selectmen engaged a skilled woodsman to cut it down. That man was Sylvanus Grant (1844–1927), a Black man who still has descendants in the county. It was certainly a challenge for one man: the tree stood 128 feet tall with a 28-foot circumference. The Berkshire County Historical Society has in its collection a photograph of the tree, in a frame made from the tree's own wood.

Grant spent most of his life in Lenox. His parents were Ranselier and Maria Grant and his grandparents Jacob and Lena Grant, who had a home on Main Street in Lenox, probably located where O'Brien's Market stood in the twenty-first century. His cousin was baseball player Frank Grant, and Evelyn Haile in Great Barrington is a surviving granddaughter. He had three children with his first wife, Louisa Duncan of Lanesboro, although only his son Edward lived to adulthood. With his second wife, Anna Simmons, he had five daughters and one adopted daughter.

Bernard A. Drew

Men's Work: 1863–1946

Enlistment and draft registration records for the Civil War, World War I, and World War II provide much information about the civilian occupations of Black men in the Berkshires. It is important to keep in mind that this information is limited because it pertains only to younger men who chose to enlist during the Civil War or World War II. The information for World War I is a bit broader, since it is all men who registered for the draft, not just those who joined. Unfortunately, we do not have similar information for women or for men who were beyond the age of military service. The information we do have allows us to build occupational portraits for three points in time and to compare those portraits to document changes over time.

In 1863 when Berkshire men were enlisting in the 54th Infantry and 5th Calvary regiments, farmer and laborer each were the occupations of 38% of the men. Many of the men listed as laborers were farm laborers, meaning that at least 50 percent of Black men earned their living working on farms, either their own or farms owned by white farmers. This is not surprising, since farming was still a major industry in the region. There were a handful of tradesmen, including a mason, stonecutter, carpenter, and chair maker, and a few small-business owners, including four barbers and a butcher. The only professional listed was the Congregational minister, Rev. Samuel Harrison in Pittsfield.

In 1917–1918, laborer remained the most frequent occupation, but by this time only 25 percent of Black men—down from 38 percent in 1863—worked as laborers. Farming had now declined across the region, and only 6.5 percent of the men listed their occupation as farmer. After the Civil War, tourism became a major component of the regional economy, and by 1918 many Black men were engaged in the hospitality industry. Some 17 percent worked as waiters (twenty-eight men), cooks (fifteen men), kitchen helpers (three men), and caterer (one man). Hotels employed an additional 7 percent of men as bellmen and porters. A subgroup of these hotel and restaurant workers was a cluster of eleven men in Lenox, all born in Bermuda and who perhaps were recruited by hotels in the Berkshires. Industry provided some employment, though limited, for Black men. General Electric was probably the major employer of Black men, but across all industries only 10 percent of the men were employed as workers and foremen in factories, mills, and foundries and on the railroad. Service work provided more opportunity and employed 17 percent as drivers, teamsters, janitors, elevator operators, butlers, and several other occupations. Tradesmen were few in number and included gardeners, log cutters and rollers, a tailor, a carpenter, an iceman, and a mason. The only professionals were a dentist and perhaps a lawyer in Pittsfield.

Columbia Mill Workers in Lee, c. 1885. Two Black workers are in the front row on the left. Columbia Mill, on Mill Street a little north of downtown, was part of Smith's Paper Company, now Schweitzer-Mauduit Intl., Inc. Photo courtesy of Caroline Meyer Young, Lee Historical Commission, Lee Library Association Collection.

Black Male Occupations—Berkshire County

1863							
Farmer	47	Driver	24	Soda bottler	1	Gas/Oil man	2
Laborer	47	Farmer	18	Hostler	1	Blacksmith	2
Barber	4	Cook	15	Lawyer	1	Band leader	2
Waiter	4	Teamster	15	Locksmith	1	Surveyor	2
Teamster	3	Hotel/RR porter	12	Teamster	1	Laundry machine	
Blacksmith	2	Janitor	8	Iceman	1	operator	2
Seaman	2	Bellman	8	Caterer	1	Medical equipment	
Porter	2	Factory/Mill		Molder	1	technician	2
Cook	2	worker	8	Press operator	1	Railroad worker	1
Clergyman	1	Elevator operator	7	Cleaner	1	Geographer	1
Gardener	1	Railroad worker	6	Seamster	1	Warehouseman	1
Mason	1	Foundry worker	5	Dentist	1	Electroplater	1
Clerk	1	Foreman	5	Lumber dealer	1	Quarryman	1
Stonecutter	1	Gardener	5	Watchman	1	Pump operator	1
Boatman	1	Butler/Houseman	4	U.S. Mail worker	1	Welder	1
Hostler	1	Clerk	4	Mason	1	Bridge builder	1
Carpenter	1	Log cutter/roller	4	Brass maker	1	Blaster	1
Butcher	1	Machinist	4			Toolroom keeper	1
Chair maker	1	Kitchen helper	3	**1941–1945**		Switchboard	
		Auto cleaner	2	Driver	12	installer	1
		Carpenter	2	Mechanic	4	Laborer	1
1917–1918		Coaler	2	Clerk	3	Submarine cable	
Laborer	71	Tailor	1	Actor	3	station operator	1
Waiter	28	Lime Burner	1	Cook	3	Ship fitter	1

By 1941 the economic transformation from farming to industry was nearly complete. No Black man listed himself as a farmer, and only one as a laborer. Twenty-three percent were truck drivers or chauffeurs, several doubling as both. Most of the other men held semiskilled or skilled jobs as mechanics, surveyors, technicians, and machine operators. Service jobs and jobs in the hospitality industry had virtually disappeared, perhaps because of the effects of World War II.

David Levinson, based on data collected by Deb Calderara, Dawn Morin, and Susan Denault

An advertisement for George Jackson's restaurant in Great Barrington in the 1909–1911 *Southern Berkshire Directory.*

May Edward Chinn, Physician

May Edward Chinn (1896–1980) was the first Black woman from the Berkshires to become a medical doctor. With her family's support, both in Great Barrington, where she was born, and later on Long Island, she was able to twice attend college, first to study music (she was for a time piano accompanist to singer Paul Robeson), then medicine. In 1926 she became the first Black woman to graduate from what later became New York University, Bellevue Medical School. She researched cytological methods for detecting cancer with Dr. George Papanicolaou, the developer of the Pap smear test for detecting cervical cancer. Chinn eventually overcame discrimination to gain admitting privileges at Harlem Hospital. In 1944 she joined the Strang Cancer Clinic in New York City. Columbia University awarded her an honorary doctorate of science for her contributions to medicine in 1980. The home the Chinns owned at the foot of Church Street in Great Barrington was, by the twenty-first century, the site of a commercial building.

Bernard A. Drew

May Edward Chinn, in 1916 at age 20, possibly on a trip to Great Barrington. Photo courtesy of the George Davis Collection.

Florence Edmonds, Public-health Nurse

Florence Edmonds c. 1971.
Photo courtesy of
Samuel Harrison Society, Inc.

Florence Edmonds (1890–1983) was the first Black public-health nurse in Pittsfield, Massachusetts. Valedictorian of her high school class of 1908, she was turned down for nurse's training in Pittsfield. Undaunted, she applied and was accepted at Lincoln Hospital in New York City. From there she won a scholarship to Teachers College at Columbia University. Her first job after graduation was at the Henry Street Settlement, on Manhattan's Lower East Side.

Returning home to Pittsfield, Edmonds married and raised four children. During World War II she resumed her nursing, and from 1945 to 1956 she was a member of the Pittsfield Visiting Nurse Association. From 1956 to 1968 Edmonds taught nursing at Pittsfield General Hospital—the hospital, ironically, that had refused to let her do her training there. After retiring, she was active with the Red Cross bloodmobile and as the organist in the Second Congregational Church, where her grandfather, the Rev. Samuel Harrison, had been a minister.

Edmonds was named "Mother of the Year" in Pittsfield in 1962. She has earned a place in the history of Blacks in the Berkshires and will be remembered, thanks to the efforts of her daughter, Ruth Edmonds Hill, coordinator of the Black Women Oral History Project at the Schlesinger Library of Radcliffe College (renamed the Radcliffe Institute), who recorded Edmonds's life.

Barbara Bartle

Henry Jenkins Roberts, Physician

The Berkshire Medical Institute in Pittsfield, Massachusetts, was, by the standards of its time, a prestigious and venerable institution. During its tenure from 1822 to 1867, between 1,500 and 2,000 students passed through its doors. One of these was Henry Jenkins Roberts (c. 1821–1863) in the class of 1847. Three who followed him were James E. Brown (class of 1850), Randolph C. Cooper (class of 1857), and Samuel B. DeLyon (class of 1857). These young men all shared the mutual distinction of color and citizenship, being free Blacks from Monrovia, Liberia.

Henry Jenkins Roberts was born a free Black in Petersburg, West Virginia. After the death of his father in 1829, his mother made the decision to emigrate to Liberia with her children. Together they boarded the ship *Harriet* and set sail for their new land. Once there, contrary to the experiences of many Liberian immigrants, they prospered. Joseph Jenkins Roberts, Roberts's older brother, became the first nonwhite governor of Liberia in 1841 and, in 1847, when Roberts was in medical school in Pittsfield, Liberia's first president. Another brother, John Wright Jenkins, became the first Methodist bishop in Liberia.

Sponsored by the American Colonization Society, Roberts returned to the United States to attend the Berkshire Medical Institute. Upon graduation he returned to Monrovia, where he filled the post of chief physician for the American Colonization Society. While David Peck, who graduated from Rush Medical School in Chicago in 1847, is considered to be the first Black to graduate from medical school in America, he actually shares that honor with Roberts. However, there was a significant difference between the situations. Whereas Peck was free to practice medicine in the United States, Roberts's alma mater, the Berkshire Medical Institute, accepted Black students sponsored by the American Colonization Society (who would emigrate or return to Liberia), but would not accept Black students who planned to practice medicine in the United States.

Heather Eagan

John Garrett Penn, Federal Judge

Portrait of John Garrett Penn by African American artist Simmie Knox in 2003 which hangs in the U. S. District Court in Washington D.C. Photo courtesy of John Garrett and Ann Rollison Penn Collection.

John Garrett Penn (born 1932), chief judge of the United States District Court for the District of Columbia, was born in Pittsfield, Massachusetts, during the Great Depression, the son of John Penn of Reidsville, North Carolina, and Eugenie G. Heyliger Penn, who immigrated to the United States from Bermuda in the early 1920s. Penn's father was a carpenter and draftsman by trade but could not find any work in Pittsfield. "It was well known," Judge Penn writes, "that certain areas of the city and certain jobs were off limits [to blacks]." His father eventually worked as a machinist at a factory that made machinery for paper mills. Penn's father had a great influence on his son. Penn writes, "My father . . . placed strong emphasis on Black history since he felt that this rich background of our heritage was not adequately addressed in school, in national news, or elsewhere. I recall that my parents subscribed to such papers as the *Chicago Defender,* the *Pittsburgh Courier,* and the Baltimore *Afro-American* and that they clipped out articles on Black history and Black achievements and pasted them in a scrapbook. . . . They also followed the achievements of such people as Thurgood Marshall and William Hastie and other Black Americans who labored to improve our lifestyle. . . . All of the above had a tremendous influence in my life and caused me to want to achieve and not just accept the status quo."

Penn attended the Pittsfield public schools, graduating from Pittsfield High School in 1950. Although his high school teachers tried to steer Blacks in his class into vocational training, he went on to get an AB from the University of Massachusetts in 1954 and a law degree from Boston University in 1957. He also attended, from 1967 to 1968, the Woodrow Wilson School of International and Public Affairs at Princeton University, as a National Institute of Public Affairs Fellow. Later Penn attended the National Judicial College at the University of Nevada. He served in the U.S. Army, Judge Advocate General's Corps, from 1958 to 1961; and as a trial attorney, reviewer, and assistant chief of the general litigation section of the tax division of the U.S. Department of Justice from 1961 to 1970. In 1970 Pres. Richard Nixon appointed Penn to the Superior Court of Washington, D.C., and in 1979 Pres. Jimmy Carter appointed Penn to the federal bench, the venue being the U.S. District Court for the District of Columbia. He presided as its Chief Judge from 1992 to 1997.

Penn, known to be a slow, deliberate jurist, adjudicated some very high-profile cases, including the 1991 case regarding whether Richard Nixon was to be compensated for his presidential papers. Judge Penn said, "I decided to become a lawyer because I felt it was one way to engage in the struggle for equal rights for all Americans. I was also moved by the feats of Clarence Darrow, who seemed to me to be a fighter for lost causes, and by others who labored in the courtrooms to bring about equality for all Americans."

Frances Jones-Sneed

Comments by Justice Ruth Ginsberg, Justice of the United States Supreme Court, on John Garrett Penn

His judgments were earthbound; he riveted attention on how people, in fact, arranged their lives.

Judge Penn's opinions have the same human quality. He never treats judicial power casually; he is ever mindful of how that power affects human lives, not the least, the lives of society's outcasts. From his early days on the bench, he invited former defendants to write to him to let him know how they were faring in the community or in prison. He visited the places where people he sentenced served time to see firsthand how those institutions worked.

Source: Transcript of Portrait Presentation Ceremony, John Garrett Penn, U. S. District Judge. 15 December 2003, United States Courthouse, Washington, D. C.

Sources

Black Entrepreneurs

Chapman, Gerard. "Agrippa Hull: Stockbridge Immortal." *Berkshire Eagle*, 15 July 1980.

Drew, Bernard A. *Great Barrington: Great Town and Great History*. Great Barrington, MA: Great Barrington Historical Society, 1999.

Gunn, Elaine. Personal communication with the author, July 2004.

Gunn, Wray. Personal communication with the author, August 2004.

Sills, Eugenie. "The View from Dexter Street: Jamie Williamson Fights Back for Fair Housing." *Women's Times*, March 2004.

Turner, Steve. "Berkshire Blacks: The Struggle for Equality Began Two Centuries Ago." *Berkshire Eagle*, 28 Aug. 1976.

Warren Davis, Entrepreneur

"Beartown Land Sold to State." *Berkshire Courier*, 14 Oct. 1920.

"Mabel Gunn." *Berkshire Courier*, 23 April 1959.

Gunn, Wray, and Elaine Gunn. Personal communications with the authors, 2004 and 2005.

Shawn, Ted, *How Beautiful upon the Mountain: A History of Jacob's Pillow* (n.p.: c. 1943).

"Warren Davis." *Berkshire Courier*, 1 Dec. 1960.

Sylvanus Grant, Hewer of the Pittsfield Elm

Gunn, Elaine, et al. "African Americans in Lenox." Talk at the Lenox Community Center, 9 Feb. 1997. Unpublished manuscript.

Sass, Samuel. "Sylvanus Grant and the Pittsfield Elm." *Berkshire Eagle*, 18 Oct. 1984.

Men's Work: 1863–1946

Ancestry. Civil War Soldiers & Sailors System Database. http://www.itd.nps.gov/cwss/soldiers.htm (accessed 2 Nov. 2004).

Conte, Silvio O. Archives, Civil War Muster Rolls, Pittsfield, MA.

Dorman, Franklin A. *Twenty Families of Color in Massachusetts 1742–1998.* Boston: New England Historic Genealogical Society, 1998.

"Proud to Be 'First' Selected in Draft." *Springfield Republican*, 19 March 1942.

"Second Church to Honor Negro Servicemen." *Berkshire Evening Eagle*, 23 Jan. 1943.

May Edward Chinn, Physician

African American Registry. "An Early Pioneer in Medicine, May Chinn." http://www.aaregistry.com/african_american_history/819/An_early_pioneer_in_medicine_May_Chinn (accessed 2 Nov. 2004).

Florence Edmonds, Public Health Nurse

Berkshire Eagle, 5 April 1982.
Berkshire Eagle, 21 Dec. l983.

Henry Jenkins Roberts, Physician

Berkshire Medical Institute yearly catalogs. [Available in the Local History Room, Berkshire Athenaeum. Pittsfield, MA.]

Childs, Dr. H. H., to Oliver Wendell Holmes. Personal communication, 12 Dec. 1850. Martin Delany File, Countway Library, Harvard Medical School, Boston, MA.

Drickamer, Lee C., and Karen Drickamer. "Berkshire's Medical College." *Berkshire History* 1, no. 1: 1–5.

Duke University Medical Center Library. "Black History Month: A Medical Perspective." http://www.mclibrary.duke.edu/hot/blkhist.html (accessed 12 Nov. 2004).

Shick, Tom. "Ships' Records, Emigrants to Liberia, 1820–1843: An Alphabetical Listing." Liberian Studies Research Working Paper No. 2., Department of History, University of Wisconsin, 1971.

Smith, David Jr. The *Africa American Presidents: The Founding Fathers of Liberia, 1848-1904.* Atlanta: New African American History Press, 2004.

Tazewell, C. W., ed. *Virginia's Ninth President, Joseph Jenkins Roberts.* Virginia Beach, VA: W. S. Dawson Co., 1992.

John Garrett Penn, Federal Judge

DC Bar: For Lawyers. "Legends in the Law: A Conversation with Judge John Garrett Penn." [Originally pub. in *Bar Report*, August–September 1997] http://www.dcbar.org/for_lawyers/resources/legends_in_the_law/penn.cfm (accessed 9 Nov. 2004).

U.S. District Court, District of Columbia. "Senior Judge John Garrett Penn." http://www.dcd.uscourts.gov/penn-bio.html (accessed 9 Nov. 2004).

Just the Beginning Foundation. "Judge John Garrett Penn." http://www.jtbf.org/article_iii_judges/penn_j.htm (accessed 9 Nov. 2004).

Civil Rights and Social Activism

Although it is little talked about, some Black people were slaves in Northwest Connecticut into the 1800s and in the Berkshires into the late 1700s. The early activism of individuals such as Rev. Lemuel Haynes, James Mars, and Rev. James Eldridge in Connecticut, and Mum Bett and Rev. Samuel Harrison in Massachusetts, helped end slavery and give Blacks more rights. The activism of W. E. B. Du Bois and James Weldon Johnson in the early to mid-twentieth century is an important piece of the history of the Berkshires, the nation, and the world. Their work and ideas were influential far beyond the region. And later there were also others in the region, such as Ruth D. Jones, David Gunn Sr., and Rev. Willard Durant, who continued the battle for equality. These three and many others worked with the NAACP from the 1950s into the 1980s.

Slavery in Northwest Connecticut

In 1849 poet Fitz-Greene Halleck retired from his job in New York City as a trustee for the Astor Library and returned to his hometown of Guilford, Connecticut. There, in a house adjoining the village green, he continued writing until his death, in 1867. One of these final poems was an ode to his native land entitled "Connecticut." The first stanza reads in part:

'Tis a rough land of earth, and stone, and tree,
Where breathes no castled lord nor cabined slave;
Where thoughts, and tongues, and hands are bold and free,
And friends will find a welcome, and foes a grave;
And where none kneel, save when to Heaven they pray,
Nor even then, unless in their own way. (Steiner 1975, 9)

While a popular poem, it glossed over the state's history even as it celebrated it. In 1848, a year before Halleck's retirement, Connecticut finally outlawed slavery, freeing the final dozen or so people still held in bondage. In Connecticut's Upper Housatonic Valley, slavery existed until the 1830s, with the last slave, a man between fifty-five and ninety-nine years old, appearing in the 1830 census in the eight-member household of John Russell of Salisbury, a sixty-eight-year old farmer and war veteran. That Connecticut did not end slavery until 1848, sixty-five years after Massachusetts did so in 1783, is an important consideration for this volume. It meant that the Black experience in northwest Connecticut was different from that in western Massachusetts.

What in the twenty-first century comprises Litchfield County was in the early 1700s the colony's last frontier, a sparsely populated and heavily forested region. But within a few decades enough Euramerican settlers moved in to eventually incorporate nine townships: Kent (1739), Sharon (1739), Canaan (1739), Cornwall (1740), Salisbury (1741), Norfolk (1758), Colebrook (1779), Warren (land from Kent, 1786), and North Canaan (from Canaan, 1858).

Though comprising less than 3 percent of Connecticut's population during the colonial period, the increase in Blacks prompted special laws, known collectively as the slave code, to "control" them. Enacted primarily between 1690 and 1730, the laws forbade slaves from being ferried across rivers, traveling outside of town, being served alcoholic beverages in inns, and being outside after 9 p.m. without written permission of their master. Additionally they could not sell goods to whites or argue or fight with them. Free Blacks also suffered under these laws, as they had to carry proof of their freedom lest they be detained as runaway slaves, beaten, or both. And a 1702 law kept the numbers of freed slaves low by making owners financially responsible for former slaves' well-being should they ever become destitute. If a master failed to do so, a 1711 law shifted the burden to the town but also gave it the right to sue the former master to recoup expenses. Similar laws existed throughout the colonies.

A runaway slave ad for "a Negro Wench named ZIL" placed in the *Connecticut Courant and Weekly Intelligencer* on 9 March 1779. Photo courtesy of American Antiquarian Society.

By the eve of the Revolution, a quarter of all adult men owned slaves in Connecticut. While half of these men were farmers, traders, and merchants, the rest included half of all ministers, lawyers, and public officials, and a third of all doctors. Slaves performed essential jobs as domestic servants, laborers, and skilled workers, helping to run the home, farm, or business, especially in the households of professional men frequently away on business. Most slave owners had one or two slaves, but a larger number of white households also employed free Blacks, indentured whites, and Native Americans who lived and worked with the families.

Many whites defended the institution of slavery as not just financially beneficial, or as a sign of social status, but in their charge's best interests. Whites often viewed Blacks as children, incapable of supporting themselves, and benefiting from permanent employment, control, and Christianity. Some slaves were baptized, attended church, and received rudimentary education. Churches often segregated Black members in separate pews in a balcony or at the back of the room.

Though the form of slavery practiced in Connecticut was generally not as harsh as the large-scale plantation slavery of the South, it mattered little to those in bondage. The *Connecticut Courant* newspaper published nine advertisements for runaways from northwest Connecticut towns in the Upper Housatonic River Valley between 1767 and 1807.

In the years leading up to and immediately following the American Revolution, Connecticut reappraised its slavery policy. In October of 1774 it banned the importation of slaves into the colony. A decade later, in 1784, the state finally passed a gradual abolition bill. All slaves born after 1 March 1784 would be freed on their twenty-fifth birthday. Children born to slaves not yet twenty-five, however, became slaves until their twenty-fifth birthday. Additionally, the law did not apply to slaves born before March of 1784. They remained enslaved for

A runaway slave ad for "a NEGRO MAN, named DARBY" placed in the *Connecticut Courant and Weekly Intelligencer* on 30 July 1782. Photo courtesy of American Antiquarian Society.

17

life. In 1788 the state passed a slave trade prohibition act, imposing harsh fines on any Connecticut resident or vessel engaged in the slave trade or on individuals trying to kidnap free Blacks or Indians from the state. In 1797 the age for manumission was lowered to twenty-one, and the slave code was finally abolished.

The year 1790 marked the founding of the Connecticut Anti-Slavery Society. Mirroring organizations established in other states, it agitated for the destruction of slavery within the state and the nation. It was a slow fight. In 1792 Connecticut outlawed the sale of slaves outside of the state, but the final blow to the institution would not come for fifty-six years. The state's slave population had been swiftly dropping since 1790: 951 in 1800; 310 in 1810; 97 in 1820; 25 in 1830; and 17 in 1840. In the interim, regional and town antislavery societies started up, including those in Litchfield County in 1837 and Norfolk in 1844. Citizens also individually fought state and federal laws, helping slaves escape northward through a loose system of safe houses and conductors known as the Underground Railroad. Finally, with New York having outlawed slavery in 1827, and Rhode Island in 1843, Connecticut became the last state in the Northeast to ban slavery in 1848.

Jonathan Olly

Slavery in Connecticut

Some told me that they did not know that slavery was ever allowed in Connecticut, and some affirm that it never did exist in the State. What I have written of my own history, seems to satisfy the minds of those that read it, that the so called, favored state, the land of good morals and steady habits, was ever a slave state, and that slaves were driven through the streets tied or fastened together for market. This seems to surprise some that I meet, but it was true. I have it from reliable authority. Yes, this was done in Connecticut.

Source: Mars, James. *Life of James Mars, A Slave Born and Sold in Connecticut*. Hartford, CT: Case, Lockwood & Co., 1868.
http://docsouth.unc.edu/neh/mars/mars.html
(accessed 16 Dec. 2005).

James Mars, Community Leader and Activist

James Mars (c. 1790–1880) was born a slave in North Canaan, Connecticut. His father, Jupiter Mars, served in the American Revolution. In 1798 the family was given its freedom, but James and his brother were required to work as indentured farm laborers until they reached twenty-five years of age. Mars worked for a Norfolk, Connecticut, farmer until 1815 and then continued as an independent laborer until the 1830s, when he moved to Hartford. His life as an indentured laborer is described in his autobiography, *Life of James Mars, a Slave Born and Sold in Connecticut*, first published in 1864.

In Hartford, Mars soon emerged as a leader of the Black community. He was a founder and deacon of the Talcott Street Congregational Church and helped place the North African School at the church. He petitioned the General Assembly in 1842 for the right to vote, successfully filed suit to keep a slave named Nancy from being taken south by her owners, and fought for the rights of slaves and free Blacks.

Resisting slavery and calling attention to slavery in the North was a lifelong cause, and in the late 1840s he moved his family (now numbering eight children) to Pittsfield, Massachusetts. In his autobiography he explained the move:

One thing in my history I have not mentioned, which I think of importance. Although born and raised in Connecticut, yes, and lived in Connecticut more than three-fourths of my life, it has been my privilege to vote at five Presidential elections. Twice it was my privilege and pleasure to help elect the lamented and murdered Lincoln, and if my life is spared I intend to be where I can show that I have the principles of a man, and act like a man, and vote like a man, but not in my native State; I cannot do it there, I must remove to the old Bay State for the right to be a man. Connecticut, I love thy name, but not thy restrictions. I think the time is not far distant when the colored man will have his rights in Connecticut. (Mars 1868, 38)

Mars's wife and one son died in Pittsfield within four years, causing him much personal distress. His autobiography, which went through eight editions over the next five years, was heavily edited by his white abolitionist sponsors and reads more like an antislavery tract than an autobiography. In 1866 Mars was badly injured in an accident and

James Mars c. 1880 in an albumen print by T. M. V. Doughty. Photo courtesy of The Connecticut Historical Society, Hartford, Connecticut.

moved to New York City to be cared for by a Quaker family. He evidently lived the last years of his life in Norfolk, where he furnished material for the town history, published in 1900. Mars died in June 1880 in Ashley Falls. He is buried in Center Cemetery on Old Colony Road off Route 272 in Norfolk, next to his father and near other local Blacks, including the Freedom family and Alanson Freeman.

David Levinson

James Mars on Slavery

During those ten days I had a fair opportunity to see how strong a hold slavery had on the feelings of the people in Hartford. I was frowned upon; I was blamed; I was told that I had done wrong; the house where I lived would be pulled down; I should be mobbed; and all kinds of scarecrows were talked about, and this by men of wealth and standing. I kept on about my work, not much alarmed.

Source: Mars, James. *Life of James Mars, A Slave Born and Sold in Connecticut*. Hartford, CT: Case, Lockwood & Co., 1868. http://docsouth.unc.edu/neh/mars/mars.html (accessed 16 Dec. 2005).

Slavery in the Berkshires

There were slaves in the southern Berkshires as early as the 1740s. The Massachusetts Tax Valuation List of 1771 carries the names of a dozen Sheffield families with at least one "servant for life" in the household. Jn'o Fellows had two; John Ashley and his son had eight between them. There were nineteen slaves all told in Sheffield, seven in Stockbridge, three in Egremont. There were slaves farther north as well. Early newspaper advertisements of runaway slaves were inserted in the *Hartford Courant* by Pittsfield masters. In his *History of Pittsfield*, Smith reports that in 1772 Mr. Elisha Jones advertised two runaway mulatto slaves in the *Courant*. Colonel Williams of Pittsfield held several slaves. In 1761 he purchased, for £50, "a negro girl named Pendar" (Smith, 1869).

Local histories indicate that some slaves fled to the Berkshires from New York and Connecticut, since these states abolished slavery much later than Massachusetts. Vermont was the first New England state to abolish slavery, while Connecticut was the last. In northern Berkshire County around 1802, "a colored woman, who had fled from slavery in the State of New York, came to North Adams, closely pursued by some kidnappers from the town of Hoosick" (*History of Berkshire County* 1885, 472). Captain Jeremiah Colegrove managed to hide the fugitive successfully from the bounty hunters.

Catharine M. Sedgwick of Stockbridge painted a benign picture of slavery in western New England, in stark contrast to that of the deep South: "The slaves in Massachusetts were treated with almost parental kindness. They were incorporated into the family, and each puritan household being a sort of religious structure, the relative duties of master and servant were clearly defined. No doubt the severest and

A photograph of "Negro Girl Called Pendar" of Pittsfield, taken when she was probably in her nineties. Photo by Buell & Seaver, Photographers. Courtesy of The Berkshire County Historical Society Collections.

longest task fell to the slave, but in the household of the farmer or artisan, the master and the mistress shared it, and when it was finished, the white and the black, like the feudal chief and his household servant, sat down to the same table, and shared the same viands" (Sedgwick 1853).

Nonetheless, slavery was slavery, and there were strict and even cruel masters and mistresses. As the historian Lorenzo J. Greene (1969) observed, "The brutal punishment to which the plantation Negroes were subjected was very infrequent in New England". Slaves were whipped, however, and James Mars provides a firsthand account of being enslaved in North Canaan, Connecticut, in his autobiography published in 1864.

There were relatively few slaves in interior New England because of the terrain and economy. "A large percentage of the rural population was engaged in subsistence farming," observed the historian Ronald Takaki (1993), "growing food crops mainly for their own needs. Living in the interior regions, many of these farmers found that the transportation of surplus crops to the market was too expensive." Thus slaves in large numbers were impractical, and those who were here were generally household and farm workers. Slavery ended in Massachusetts in 1783.

A number of Berkshire residents preached against slavery. The Rev. Samuel Hopkins (1721–1803), the first settled minister in Great Barrington,

Bill of sale for "Girl Called Pendar," Westfield, 7 November 1761. Photo courtesy of The Berkshire County Historical Society Collections.

denounced slavery before the American Revolution. At the time he served a pulpit in Newport, Rhode Island. His "A Dialogue Concerning the Slavery of the Africans . . ." was published in 1776.

Jonathan Edwards Jr. (1745–1801), who grew up in Northampton and Stockbridge and served as minister in New Haven, Connecticut, wrote the sermon "The Injustice and Impolity of the Slave Trade and the Slavery of Africans" in 1791, and it was published and then republished often. Edwards was the son of Jonathan Edwards (1703–1758), the "Stockbridge Missionary," who served as minister in Stockbridge from 1751 to 1757. The elder Edwards owned slaves, including one woman known as Venus purchased in 1731.

Another Stockbridge notable, Theodore Sedgwick II (1780–1839), delivered a lecture titled "The Practicability of the Abolition of Slavery" at the Lyceum in Stockbridge in 1831, and it was published later that year. His sister, Catharine M. Sedgwick (1789–1867), published her account of slavery in New England in *Bentley's Miscellany* in 1853.

Harriet Beecher Stowe (1811–1896), who was born in Litchfield, Connecticut, wrote the landmark antislavery novel *Uncle Tom's Cabin* (1851), which energized its readers in the abolitionist cause. Stowe's daughter married a minister in Stockbridge, and so the famous writer was a familiar face in town, as well as in Lenox, where her brother Henry Ward Beecher (1813–1887) had a home, Blossom Hill. An activist preacher and abolitionist, Beecher wrote the 1863 antislavery essay "Freedom and War." Blossom Hill, later called Beecher Hill, later became part of Cranwell Resort.

Bernard A. Drew

Slavery during the American Revolution

The following is an account from a "private letter from New England, Nov 15 1777 to Oct 10 1778" by a Hessian (German) officer who was captured at the Battle of Saratoga and was being marched to Boston.

The second thing which attracted my attention was the negroes. From this place [Kinderhook] to Springfield few farmhouses are met that do not have one negro family living near by in an out-house. Negroes, in common with other cattle, are very prolific here. The young are well fed, especially at the calf age. Take it all in all, slavery is not so bad. The negro is looked upon in the light of a servant to the farmer, the negress doing all the heavy housework, while the pickaninnies wait upon their young white masters.

The negro is sometimes sent to war instead of his youthful owner; and for this reason there is scarcely a regiment in which you shall not find some well-built and hardy fellows. Many families of free negroes are also met with here who reside in good houses, are in comfortable circumstances, and live as well as their white neighbors. It is an amusing sight to see a young negress—her woolly hair gathered up in a knot behind, a sun-bonnet perched upon her head, and encircled by a wrap—ambling along, with a negro slave shuffling in her wake.

Source: Stone, William L., trans. *Letters of Brunswick and Hessian Officers during the American Revolution.* Albany, NY: Joel Munsell's Sons, Publishers, 1891, 142–143.

Cuffee and Nana Negro, Pioneer Blacks in Berkshire County

Cuffee Negro (died 1763) and Nana Negro are the earliest documented free Blacks in Berkshire County. Dutch fur trader and land speculator Elias Van Schaack of Stockbridge, Massachusetts, signed a deed in 1746 attesting to their manumission "in consideration for the past faithful Service and good Behaviour" (Springfield Registry, 1746). Cuffee became something of a real estate speculator himself, sometimes in partnership with Samuel Brown Jr., and purchased significant tracts of land—100 acres in western Stockbridge from Wounenauwohhoot, a Mohican, in 1761 for £10 and a like-sized parcel west of Monument Mountain from Johoiakim Van Valkenburgh, a Dutchman, in 1758 for £12. Some of his land dealings got Cuffee in hot water with colonial authorities. He advanced £40 to Jonas Etawecomb, a Stockbridge Indian jailed in Albany, New York, for debt, for example, in exchange for 8 acres of land. Cuffee and Nana Negro lived in the vicinity of Mohawk Lake.

Bernard A. Drew and Emilie Piper

Mum Bett (Elizabeth Freeman), Antislavery Pioneer

Mum Bett (c. 1744–1829) was born in Claverack, New York. From the age of six months, she was a slave in the Sheffield, Massachusetts, home of Col. John Ashley and his wife Hannah. In 1735 Ashley and his new bride, Hannah Hogeboom, moved into their new house at the western edge of the Massachusetts Colony. Over the next sixty-five years, the Ashleys' house became the center of Sheffield's social, economic, and political life. Hannah Ashley had a violent temper, and Bett one day took a blow from a hot oven shovel intended for Bett's younger sister. Having heard wording of the new Massachusetts Constitution discussed in the Ashley household, Bett sought out the lawyer Theodore Sedgwick, who then lived in Sheffield. His grandson Henry Dwight Sedgwick related that his grandfather "had always intense antislavery convictions." "Sir," said Bett, "I heard that paper read yesterday, that says, 'All men are born equal and that every man has a right to freedom.' I am not a dumb critter; won't the law give me my freedom?" (Sedgwick, 1853).

Bett was not the first slave to seek legal recourse in Massachusetts, but her suit for liberty was the first to prevail. She left the Ashley household, and Sedgwick initiated legal action. In August 1781 the case was heard at the Inferior Court of Common Pleas in Great Barrington. The formal case was brought by "Brom a Negro Man and Bett a Negro Woman." (Since women were yet to have standing before the courts, Brom, an enslaved man in the Ashley household, was listed first in the complaint.)

Sedgwick, a future Massachusetts Supreme Court justice, enlisted the distinguished Connecticut attorney Tapping Reeve to argue that no previous law established the validity of slavery in Massachusetts, and that even if it did, it was canceled by the new state constitution. The jury found the

"Any time, any time while I was a slave, if one minute's freedom had been offered to me, and I had been told I must die at the end of that minute, I would have taken it—just to stand one minute on God's airth a free women—I would."
Mum Bett, quoted by Catherine Marie Sedgwick in "Slavery in New England," 1853.

Portrait of "Mumbet," watercolor on ivory by Susan Anne Livingston Ridley Sedgwick, 1811. Copyright, Massachusetts Historical Society, Boston, MA.

strong judgment, a quick and firm decision, an iron resolution, an incorruptible integrity, an integrity that never for a moment parlayed with temptation, a truth that never varied from the straight line."

Freeman retired from the Sedgwick family in 1808, when Judge Sedgwick married for the third time. She by then owned a small dwelling south of town, with a view of Monument Mountain. By her will, we know she had one daughter who survived to adulthood and even a great-grandchild in her lifetime.

Freeman is buried in the famed circular "Sedgwick Pie" in Stockbridge Cemetery. "She was born a slave and remained a slave for nearly thirty years," reads her epitaph, written by Charles Sedgwick. "She could neither read nor write; yet in her own sphere she had no superior nor equal. She neither wasted time nor property. She never violated a truth, nor failed to perform a duty. In every situation of domestic trial, she was the most efficient helper and the tenderest friend. Good mother, farewell."

Bernard A. Drew and Emilie Piper

plaintiffs "are not and were not at the time of the purchase of the original writ the legal Negro servants of him the said John Ashley during their life" (Massachusetts, Inferior Court of Common Pleas, 1781). Now free, Mum Bett took the name Elizabeth Freeman and went to work for the Sedgwick family, first in Sheffield, and then in Stockbridge, when the family relocated there in 1785. During Shays' Rebellion she protected the Sedgwick silverware and hid their horse from rowdy Shaysites.

Elizabeth Freeman was adored by Catharine M. Sedgwick, who wrote in her journal in 1829, "Mumbet ('Mother') my nurse (my faithful friend) she who first received me into her arms . . . Her talents were not small nor limited: a clear mind,

Underground Railroad

The Underground Railroad has a special place in our historical memory. It is one of the finest examples of the struggle against oppression. Although the Underground Railroad was certainly a reality, however, much of the material relating to it is in the realm of folklore.

Taking its name from the new industrial invention of the day—the locomotive—it was never an actual railroad of steel and steam. There are several stories about the origin of the term. One is an abolitionist paper's cartoon, with the caption "Liberty Line," showing happy fugitives in a railroad car going to Canada from the United States, and the image stuck. Another is that it took its name from an incident involving Tice Davids, a slave who escaped from Kentucky by swimming across the Ohio River. He vanished on reaching shore, and his owner told others he must have escaped on an underground road.

The Underground Railroad was actually a network of paths through woods, fields, and river crossings through which fugitives escaped to free states and Canada, most often on foot. Transportation could also include canoes, steamboats, and wagons. It was most active from the 1840s through the 1860s, but probably began earlier. Houses and churches where fugitives could hide were called stations; and the homeowners, station agents. The individuals who guided the fugitives (many were free Blacks) were the con-

The Todd House on the north side of old County Road in the "Jones Crossing" area of Lanesboro. Now gone, it is believed to have been an Underground Railroad station. Photo by Edward P. Knurow, Local History Department, Berkshire Athenaeum, Knurow Collection, Vol. 1, 137.

ductors, while vigilance committees arranged food and shelter, and stockholders contributed money, food, and clothing.

Most fugitives made their way to the North alone and, when they arrived, were aided by abolitionists, free Blacks, and women's antislavery societies. Important to the history of the Underground Railroad was the Fugitive Slave Act of 1850, part of the Compromise of 1850. Extremely stringent, it denied a fugitive's right to trial by jury. Under the law, cases were handled by special commissioners, and the commissions were paid $5 if the fugitive was released or $10 if he or she was returned to an owner. In addition, more federal officials were assigned to enforcing the law. Because legally freed slaves were sometimes seized and returned to slavery, the new law was a disaster for Blacks in the North, whether slave or free. An estimated twenty thousand moved to Canada. Passage of the Fugitive Slave Act made abolitionists resolve to put an end to slavery, and the Underground Railroad became more active, reaching its peak between 1850 and 1860.

At the time of this writing, the most popular view of the Underground Railroad is that of the revisionist historians. This represents the African American point of view, which challenges traditional histories and the overemphasis on Quaker involvement and on white abolitionists who wrote profusely on the subject. In their writings, the fugitive slaves appear passive, almost invisible, although this was not the case. Most Black fugitives made their way alone to the North, occasionally helped by the exceptional white.

In Massachusetts, Boston and Springfield were the principal centers, but there were also limited stops in the western part of the state. In Berkshire County several splinter routes led to a number of

Conway House, Bow Wow Road, Sheffield, in 2005. It is believed to have been an Underground Railroad station. Photo by Rachel Fletcher.

safe houses, or stations. One route led to Jacob's Pillow. Fugitives were brought up from Connecticut in hay wagons, housed in the barn (which later became the Pillow store), and then moved on to Williamstown, Massachusetts, on the way to Canada.

Another route went from Winsted, Connecticut, through Norfolk and Canaan, Connecticut, and then followed the Housatonic River north to Stockbridge and Pittsfield, Massachusetts, and on north to Vermont. Safe houses were about 10 miles apart. One was the home of the Norfolk Congregational Church deacon, Amos Pettibone, a strong abolitionist. According to recollections in the Crissey (1900, 295–99) town history, "Dea. Pettibone used to take the passengers on to the next 'station' in New Malboro. I remember his stopping one morning at my home to have us children see a young runaway slave whom he had kept over night, and was then on his way to the next 'station.' He showed the scars on his ankles where he had worn irons." And there were other reported stations in Norfolk in the 1850s, owing to the town having a strong abolitionist minority of residents. In the Connecticut township of Warren, town minister Harley Goodwin was reportedly involved in the railroad, and a house in town once known as the Star Tavern was also reportedly a station. In New Marlboro, Massachusetts, the Margaret Etzel home on Beech Plain Road was a station for those who crossed the state line. It had a walk-in closet and hidden trapdoor. Another house on Beech Plain Road had a hidden room. A parsonage in Sandisfield (at this writing, a private home) had two large columns supporting the porch, one being hollow and having had a ladder to a secret hiding place.

A third route ran from south of Albany, New York, east into Massachusetts. One safe house was on the Loring farm near the junction of Route 71 and Seekonk Cross Road, with hidden rooms in the attic and basement. Other safe houses in South County were the Conway house on Bow Wow Road in Sheffield, the Russell house (later to become the Community Health Program) on Castle Street in Great Barrington, and a house on Pine Street in Stockbridge. In Lee the Judge Branning house on Franklin Street was a station.

In the central Berkshires, there were safe houses in Pittsfield and Lanesboro. It is likely that slaves were transported from Sand Lake, New York, in wagons used to pick up loads of sand in Lanesboro for the Fox family glass factory. A marker on the outer edge of the Berkshire Mall marks the location of a since-demolished house that was a station that received many people. In Pittsfield the Dr. John Milton Brewster house was a station. There was also a line from Lebanon Mountain, New York, through Pittsfield, Dalton, and Worthington in Massachusetts.

In north Berkshire County, it is possible that fugitive slaves from Troy, New York, traveled along a coach route to Williamstown, where they worked as laundresses and carpenters. In Adams, Job Anthony's shop was a station, and Cheshire Harbor sheltered people, not boats. In Peru, Massachusetts, a cave sheltered people on their way to Canada.

The study of the Underground Railroad in the Upper Housatonic Valley was in its early stages in the early twenty-first century. As part of an ongoing project to document the presence of Blacks in the Berkshires, researchers started to collect and document oral histories regarding potential sites in the county. Much of the research has focused on

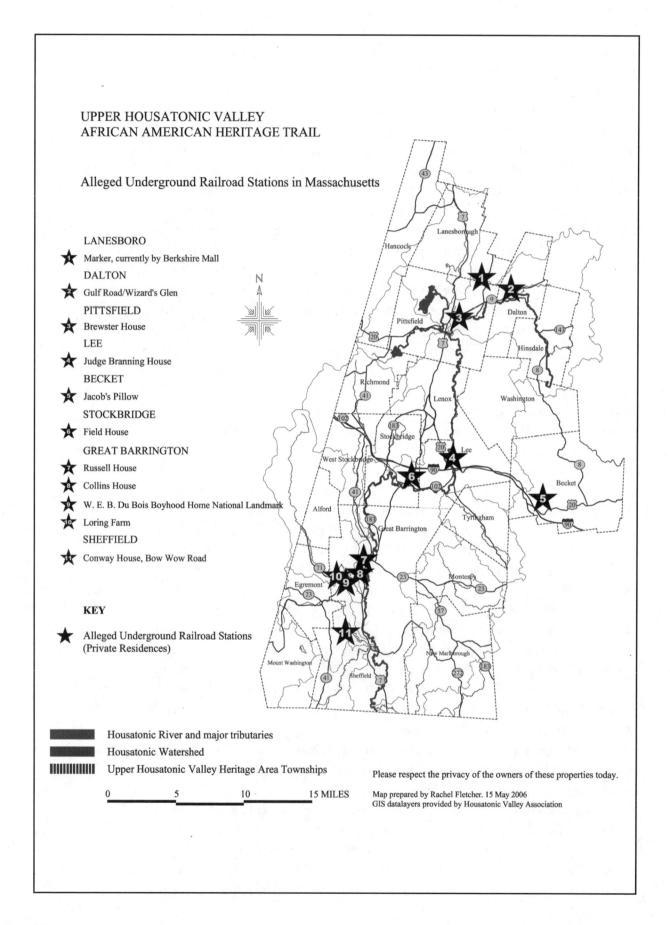

UPPER HOUSATONIC VALLEY
AFRICAN AMERICAN HERITAGE TRAIL

Alleged Underground Railroad Stations in Massachusetts

LANESBORO
Marker, currently by Berkshire Mall
DALTON
Gulf Road/Wizard's Glen
PITTSFIELD
Brewster House
LEE
Judge Branning House
BECKET
Jacob's Pillow
STOCKBRIDGE
Field House
GREAT BARRINGTON
Russell House
Collins House
W. E. B. Du Bois Boyhood Home National Landmark
Loring Farm
SHEFFIELD
Conway House, Bow Wow Road

KEY

Alleged Underground Railroad Stations
(Private Residences)

Housatonic River and major tributaries
Housatonic Watershed
Upper Housatonic Valley Heritage Area Townships

0   5   10   15 MILES

Please respect the privacy of the owners of these properties today.

Map prepared by Rachel Fletcher. 15 May 2006
GIS datalayers provided by Housatonic Valley Association

verifying claimed Underground Railroad sites. Often it has been difficult to document these sites because they may have been hidden rooms or chambers that have been altered, the houses may have been demolished, or sites may have consisted only of barns, caves, and secret passageways.

Secondary sources indicate several prominent citizens acted on three different levels, as agents, operators, or conductors and financiers of the Underground Railroad movement in the region:

South County

- Bradley, Jared, Col.; East Lee (fugitive slaves hid in his house on Bradley St.)
- Freeman, Frank, Dr.; Lee (clergyman who sheltered many fugitives on Prospect St.)
- Higby, Rev.; Sandisfield
- Milton, John, Dr.; Lenox
- Stanley, George W.; Great Barrington
- Whiting, E.; Great Barrington

Central County

- Brewster, John Milton, M.D.; Pittsfield (he was a strong abolitionist and often assisted slaves to the next station on the Underground Railroad at Dr. Sabin's in Williamstown)
- Brown, John; Pittsfield (abolitionist and a cousin of John Brown who was killed at Harper's Ferry)
- Carter, Stephen; Becket (his house was a station)
- Crane, Zenas Marshall; Dalton
- Griffin, Isaac; Pittsfield (his home was the local meeting place for the antislavery party and a safe hiding place for fugitive slaves)
- Hall, Lyman W.; Lanesboro
- Walker, William M.; Pittsfield
- Wood, Oliver Louis; Pittsfield (an ardent abolitionist)

North County

- Babbitt, Andrew J.; Savoy
- Cummings, Alonzo; Cheshire (the "boy engineer")
- Dawes, Henry L.; North Adams
- Frissell, Augustus C.; Peru (leading abolitionist in town, intimate friend of William Lloyd Garrison)
- Kirkpatrick, Robert; Adams
- Phillips, Henry P.; North Adams
- Sabin, Henry L., Dr.; Williamstown

Oral tradition has played a role in describing and preserving information about sites that were stations on the Underground Railroad. Since historical records with respect to the movement of fugitive slaves are sparse or nonexistent because of its secretive nature, documenting these sites has been difficult. Historians, then, have had to rely on oral histories to tell the stories of the fugitives' flight to freedom. Frequently it is has been difficult to substantiate and accurately document the places on the Underground Railroad because some sites have had a different function and use by the parties involved.

The National Park Service was, as of this writing, spearheading an ongoing project to document sites on the Underground Railroad in the eastern and midwestern states (see http://www.cr.nps.gov/history/online_books/ugrr/exuggr1.htm). Comparatively speaking, in relation to other sections of the country, little work has been done in western Massachusetts, especially in Berkshire County. Over the past several years, however, there has been an increased awareness and desire to document sites and the people associated with the Underground Railroad in Berkshire County. Continued research might show that Berkshire County was an integral part of the Underground Railroad system through which many Blacks established themselves across the county.

Barbara Bartle, Elaine S. Gunn, Eve Perera, and Sue Denault

William Edward Burghardt Du Bois, Scholar and Activist

A leader in the early civil rights movement, W. E. B. Du Bois (1868–1963) was born in Great Barrington, Massachusetts, the only child of Alfred Du Bois and Mary Burghardt. Du Bois, led a life of achievements. He was the first Black person to receive a PhD from Harvard University, helped establish the National Association for the Advancement of Colored People (NAACP), edited the NAACP magazine, *The Crisis,* and wrote *The Souls of Black Folk,* his seminal work on race and Black life and culture. He also transformed the fields of sociology, politics, and history, and became an international figure by helping spearhead the Pan-African conferences. Although his turn to Communism in the later years of his life was controversial, he is probably the most internationally respected and significant person from Berkshire County to date.

He is the founder of the modern civil rights movement. His early organizational work with the ground-breaking Niagara Movement in 1905 to 1908 led to the founding of the NAACP. His untiring work with the NAACP is a testament to his commitment to public service to promote civil rights and full citizenship for African Americans. It was through the editorship of the *The Crisis* that he forged one the leading sources of information about what was happening in the United States and what the NAACP was doing to achieve its goals.

W. E. B. Du Bois's mother's family, the Burghardts, was one of the founding families of Great Barrington, moving from the Dutch territory of New York in the eighteenth century. At the time of Du Bois's birth, there were about fifty Blacks in the town of Great Barrington, and most of them could claim that their ancestors were among the pioneer Black residents to the area.

According to family legend, Mary Burghardt's family did not approve of her husband and his

W. E. B. Du Bois in 1907. Photo courtesy of Special Collections and Archives, W. E. B. Du Bois Library, University of Massachusetts, Amherst. Photo from Ruth D. Jones Collection, W. E. B. Du Bois Memorial Committee.

Mary Sylvina Burghardt Du Bois with her infant son, "Willie." Photo courtesy of Special Collections and Archives, W. E. B. Du Bois Library, University of Massachusetts, Amherst.

"light" complexion. Alfred Du Bois finally abandoned his wife and son less than a year after Du Bois was born, and his mother moved in with her parents. Du Bois's grandfather, Othello, died when Du Bois was age five. After Othello's death the family became financially strained, and they moved around a great deal. In 1875 Du Bois's grandmother died, shortly after which his mother suffered a stroke that left her partially paralyzed. Mary's brother and sister helped them out for a while, and young Du Bois himself undertook little jobs here and there after school. Some townspeople also were helpful to the family.

Du Bois's mother was one of the major forces in his life. None of the Burghardts had gone further than elementary school, but his mother knew the value of an education and wanted the best for her son. She wanted, in his words, him to find "a place for himself beyond the Berkshires."

During his elementary school years, Du Bois noticed little or no racism. "There was no real discrimination on the account of color," he wrote. All of that changed, however, one spring day in 1878: "I remember well when the shadows swept across me. I was a little thing, away up in the hills of New England. . . . In a wee wooden schoolhouse, something put it into the boys' and girls' heads to buy gorgeous

The Great Barrington High School class of 1884. W. E. B. Du Bois stands at left. Principal Frank Hosmer is seated, center. Photo courtesy of Special Collections and Archives, W. E. B. Du Bois Library, University of Massachusetts, Amherst.

visiting-cards—ten cents a package—and exchange. The exchange was merry till one girl, a tall newcomer, refused my card—refused it peremptorily, with a glance. Then it dawned upon me with a certain suddenness that I was different from the others; or like, mayhap, in heart and life and longing, but shut out from their world by a vast veil" (Du Bois 1968). Instead of destroying him, the incident filled Du Bois with an even greater desire to succeed. He excelled at Great Barrington High School, from which he graduated in 1884, coediting the school newspaper and writing for the *New York Globe*, a Black newspaper. In March 1885 his mother died. Through the efforts of his principal Frank Hosmer and the Congregational Church pastor in Great Barrington, Du Bois was able to attend Fisk University, in Nashville, Tennessee. And thus began his journey from the Berkshires. After Fisk he gained admission to Harvard and became the first Black person to earn a PhD there. He went on to become one of the most effective scholars, leaders, and educators of his time.

Du Bois maintained a deep affection for and contact with his hometown of Great Barrington throughout his life. He corresponded with relatives and others, made sure that his growing list of achievements was reported in the *Berkshire Courier*, and returned to visit and lecture several times. After the Burghardt property was given to him in 1928, he made plans, which were only partially carried out, to renovate the farmhouse and use it as a meeting center and part-time residence. His children were born in Great Barrington, his daughter attended grade school there, and his first wife, son, and daughter are buried in Mahaiwe Cemetery. Du Bois's lengthy description of his life in Great Barrington in his 1968 autobiography remains the finest description of the town as it existed in the late 1800s.

Frances Jones-Sneed

Mary White Ovington in Alford

For many years, whenever she herself [Mary White Ovington], or a fellow worker was getting too stressed, they went to her home in Alford, to Riverbank, for a rest in the Berkshires. James Weldon Johnson liked his visits so much that he bought a home in Great Barrington too. He is the one who wrote "Lift Every Voice and Sing." She also brought the African American women students, whose education she sponsored at Smith, to come for a break to Riverbank. By the way, local historian Bernie Drew notes that all these interracial activities in Alford did not seem to bother her neighbors, but she was well accepted, and for a time became president of the Alford Garden Club.

Source: Duhon, Rev. Kathy. Sermon delivered at Unitarian Universalist Meeting of South Berkshire, 7 March 2004.

James Weldon Johnson, Essayist and Activist

James Weldon Johnson (1871–1938), who appeared on a U.S. commemorative postage stamp in 1988, won international acclaim as a novelist, poet, songwriter, journalist, playwright, diplomat, and champion of human rights. Born and educated in Florida, as well as in Georgia, he founded the first high school in Florida for African Americans, established a newspaper, studied law, and became the first Black to pass the Florida Bar exam. He collaborated with his musically gifted brother, John Rosamond Johnson, on "Lift Every Voice and Sing" (1900), which is regarded as the African American national anthem.

After moving to New York City in 1902, Johnson composed more than two hundred popular songs (many used in Broadway productions) and became active in politics, writing two songs for Theodore Roosevelt's presidential campaign. In 1906 Roosevelt appointed him U.S. consul to Venezuela. Three years later Johnson was promoted to U.S. consul to Nicaragua. In 1910 he married longtime friend Grace Nail (1885–1976), whose brother John, a Harlem real estate entrepreneur, later acquired a summer home in Great Barrington.

In 1912 Johnson anonymously published *The Autobiography of an Ex-Colored Man*, the earliest Black-authored, first-person fictional narrative. Resigning his consular position in 1913 because of party politics and racial prejudice, he was hired as a contributing editor of the *New York Age*, the nation's most influential Black newspaper. Johnson, joining the NAACP in 1915, soon became the organization's field secretary. In 1917 he published *Fifty Years and Other Poems*, perhaps the Harlem Renaissance's earliest prosodic call to arms. During that same year he and W. E. B. Du Bois led more than twelve thousand marchers in New York City to protest lynching; both men also supported the American entry into World War I. In 1920 Johnson became the NAACP's first African American secretary, a position from which he resigned ten years later (while being appointed vice president and board member) in order to accept a professorial position at Fisk University.

James Weldon Johnson's writing shed at his summer home in Great Barrington, c. 1999. Photo by Erik Callahan.

33

W. E. B. Du Bois and James Weldon Johnson (both in second row) in an NAACP sponsored demonstration against lynching and mob violence against Blacks in New York City in 1917. Photo courtesy of Special Collections and Archives, W. E. B. Du Bois Library, University of Massachusetts, Amherst.

Exhausted and needing respite from work, Johnson was introduced to the Berkshires in the early 1920s by Mary White Ovington, a founder of the NAACP, who had a summer cottage in Alford. In 1926 Johnson recalled in *Along This Way*, "I bought a little place in Great Barrington. I rode one day by an overgrown place where a little red barn was all that stood out amongst the weeds; the house on the place had burned down. A bright little river ran under a bridge and circled round behind the barn. On inquiry, I learned that there were five acres in the tract, and I said, 'This is just the place for me.'"

Johnson remodeled the barn to make a dwelling. "The way to learn to write," Johnson once explained to a *Berkshire Courier* reporter, "is to write. Everything that goes out from here [he indicated his little studio workshop, hidden in the pines on the bank of the Seekonk brook] is written three times. By the time the last draft is out of the typewriter, the chances are that I've said about what I intended to" (*Berkshire Courier* 1937).

The same year that he purchased his Great Barrington home, Johnson wrote *God's Trombones: Seven Negro Sermons in Verse*. Arguably his greatest creation, the collection of verse was inspired by vague childhood memories of sermons preached in Florida. He took "the prime stuff" and, through art-governed expression, made it into poetry. The first two poems were composed in New York between Thanksgiving and the Christmas holidays, 1926; the last five were written at his studio workshop and at the Mason Library in Great Barrington. Portions of *Black Manhattan* (1930), which Du Bois had assessed "the best contribution ever made to the history of American Negro art"; the celebrated *Along This Way* (1933); *Negro Americans, What Now?* (1934), perhaps the clearest published statement about the philosophy and aims of the NAACP; and his last published work, *Saint Peter Relates an Incident: Selected Poems* (1935), also may have been written in Great Barrington, where

Lift Every Voice and Sing
by James Weldon Johnson

Lift every voice and sing

Till earth and heaven ring,

Ring with the harmonies of Liberty;

Let our rejoicing rise

High as the listening skies,

Let it resound loud as the rolling sea.

Sing a song full of the faith that the
    dark past has taught us,

Sing a song full of the hope that the
    present has brought us,

Facing the rising sun of our new day begun

Let us march on till victory is won."

Source: Academy of American Poets.
http://www.poets.org/viewmedia.php/prmM
ID/15588 (accessed 18 April 2006).

Johnson spent considerable time (usually between June and October) until his death.

Johnson died in an automobile accident in Maine in 1938. Langston Hughes and Du Bois were among the two thousand people who attended the funeral in Harlem. The *Berkshire Courier*, quoting a New York newspaper, unhesitatingly judged Johnson a "man of great personal dignity, [who] fought over the long years for the just recognition of the black race" (*Berkshire Courier* 1938).

After his death, Johnson's widow, Grace Nail Johnson, continued to visit Great Barrington for many years.

Randy F. Weinstein and Bernard A. Drew

National Association for the Advancement of Colored People (NAACP)

Berkshire County had an active chapter of the NAACP, the national organization that was founded to promote civil rights for African Americans. W. E. B. Du Bois (1868–1963), who hailed from Great Barrington, helped found the organization in 1909. A keen observer of Great Barrington town politics when he was a teenager, Du Bois knew the story of Elizabeth Freeman (c. 1744–1829), a slave woman who had successfully sued for her freedom. In addition to Du Bois, two women with ties to the Berkshires were involved in founding the NAACP. One was New York human rights advocate Mary White Ovington (1865–1951), who later had a summer cottage in Alford. White, one of the first supporters of the organization,

became executive secretary in 1910 and then worked in various roles and served on the board for thirty-eight years. The other was union leader and author Helen Marot (1865–1940), who contributed to such publications as *The Masses* and *The Dial*. From 1905 through 1925 she spent her summers in Becket, where she owned a 100-acre farm adjacent to the property that would later become Jacob's Pillow.

The Berkshire County chapter of the NAACP was organized in 1918, functioned until the mid-1920s, and was reactivated in 1945. The local offices were located at 467 North Street in Pittsfield. The height of activity for the organization came in the 1960s and 1970s. Actions taken by the organization in those years included picketing the Woolworth's

Telegram from Jack Greenberg, Director Counsel, confirming legal representation of the W. E. B. Du Bois Memorial Committee by attorneys of the NAACP Legal Defense and Educational Fund October 17, 1969. Photo courtesy of Ruth D. Jones Collection, W. E. B. Du Bois Memorial Committee.

THIS IS TO OFFICIALLY CONFIRM REPRESENTATION OF THE W.E.B. DU BOIS MEMORIAL COMMITTEE BY ATTORNEYS OF THE NAACP LEGAL DEFENSE AND EDUCATIONAL FUND, INC., IN THE EVENT THAT THE TOWN OF GREAT BARRINGTON PRESSES CHARGES THAT THE DUBBIS MEMORIAL PARK CONSTITUTES A VIOLATION OF THE LOCAL ZONING ORDINANCES. THE LDF HAS BEEN ASSURED BY GREAT BARRINGTON OFFICIALS THAT THE DEDICATION CEREMONIES WILL GO FORWARD TOMORROW UNIMPEDED. THEY HAVE ASSURED US THAT LOCAL LAW OFFICIALS WILL RENDER PROTECTION AGAINST ANY POSSIBLE OUTSIDE INTERFERENCE. MEANWHILE, WE HAVE ASSIGNED ASSISTANT-COUNSEL JONATHAN SHAPIRO TO ASSUME SPECIFIC RESPONSIBILITY IN THIS MATTER. IT IS FITTING THAT LDF ATTORNEYS PROVIDE THIS REPRESENTATION BECAUSE IT WAS DR. DUBOIS' FORESIGHT THAT DETERMINED THAT THE STRUGGLE FOR BLACK EQUALITY IN AMERICA DURING THE 20TH CENTURY SHOULD FOLLOW THE LEGAL, LEGISLATIVE AND EDUCATIONAL APPROACHES. SINCE THE LDF, NOW A SEPARATE ORGANIZATION, IS AN OUTGROWTH OF THE NAACP WE WILL STRIVE TO DO EVERYTHING WITHIN OUR PROFESSIONAL CAPACITY TO RENDER THE MOST EFFECTIVE LEGAL REPRESENTATION POSSIBLE.

JACK GREENBERG DIRECTOR COUNSEL NAACP LEGAL DEFENSE AND EDUCA FUND INC.

on North Street, participating in the 1963 March on Washington, sending residents to register voters in Alabama and Mississippi during the Freedom Summer of 1964, creating opportunities for affordable housing in Pittsfield, setting up a community library, supporting the election of the first Black school board member, organizing annual Black festivals, and sponsoring nationally prominent speakers.

Monitoring equal opportunity in the county, the local chapter of the NAACP was a promoter of Black cultural activities and a clearinghouse for many other organizations. The chapter enlisted the assistance of the organization's national legal defense team in 1969 when a group in Great Barrington could not obtain permission from town leaders to have a memorial ceremony for W. E. B. Du Bois at his boyhood home site. Meetings in southern Berkshire County were regularly held in Great Barrington, and the First Congregational Church in Stockbridge was the locale of activity in that community. Although the chapter was active through the 1980s, it later languished as new organizations arose and as many of its active members died or left the area.

Local presidents have included Magdalene Adams, Lafayette Walker, Willard H. Durant, Floyd Walker, Frank Walker, Eula Aiken, and B. C. Robillard, who had the distinction of being the first white to head the local chapter in 1966. Active in South Berkshire County were David Gunn Sr. and Sinclara Gunn of Stockbridge, and Elaine Gunn, Ruth D. Jones, and Mabel Gunn of Great Barrington.

Frances Jones-Sneed

The Fight For Freedom has undertaken to raise the necessary funds.

We appeal to your to contribute what you can toward this fund and toward a united America, where citizens of all races can have equal opportunity for life, liberty and the pursuit of happiness.

Make checks payable to the Berkshire County Branch of the National Association For the Advancement of Colored People. Enclosed is an addressed envelope for your convenience.

Respectfully,

Myrtle M. Rollison

Myrtle M. Rollison, Chairman
Fight For Freedom Committee

Part of a fund raising letter sent out by the Berkshire branch of the NAACP in the 1960s. Photo courtesy of Clinton A. M. E. Zion Church, Great Barrington.

W. E. B. Du Bois Memorial Committee

The lumber dealer and land speculator Warren Davis first introduced Walter Wilson to the Burghardt home on the Egremont Plain in Great Barrington, Massachusetts. This was the farmstead where the maternal family of W. E. B. Du Bois lived from the 1820s, if not before, and Du Bois himself lived for a time as a young boy in the early 1870s. Du Bois cherished the wrought-iron tongs that stood by the fireplace when he was a child. "Long years I have carried them tenderly over all the earth," he wrote in 1928, when friends presented him with the property as a sixtieth-birthday gift. He hoped "to see them resting again in fire worship . . . when the old fireplace rises again" (Du Bois 1928). Du Bois made plans to remodel the home and live there part of the year. But the house was never again made habitable, and in 1954 he sold the property.

Walter Wilson, a white Southerner who had moved to East Chatham, New York, was a lifelong member of the NAACP, a former Southern secretary of the American Civil Liberties Union, and a land developer. Twenty-five years or so after his meeting with Davis, he discovered the Burghardt house for sale, the house by that time in ruins. With Edmund W. Gordon, a renowned scholar of psychology and education and former national research director for Project Head Start, he purchased the property in 1967, assembling a five-acre, U-shaped parcel, hoping one day to establish a memorial for Du Bois in his own town. In 1968 Wilson and Gordon cofounded the Du Bois Memorial Foundation, which received the property in 1969. The foundation's committee of incorporators included David Gunn, Frederick Lord, and Ruth D. Jones, a cataloger at Simon's Rock College,

Artist's Conception of the House of the Black Burghardts. Prepared for the W. E. B. Du Bois Memorial Committee in 1969. Photo courtesy of Ruth D. Jones Collection, W. E. B. Du Bois Memorial Committee.

"The problem of the Twentieth Century is the problem of the color-line."
W. E. B. Du Bois, *The Souls of Black Folk*, 1903.

who served as secretary and treasurer. Among more than two hundred founding sponsors were Horace Mann Bond, Edward W. Brooke, Aaron Copland, Ossie Davis, Ruby Dee, Martin Luther King Jr., Sidney Poitier, and Norman Rockwell.

In 1968 the assassination of Dr. King spurred the committee to create a memorial in earnest. When the committee presented its plans for a park in 1969, the Great Barrington selectmen and local citizens threatened to stop the effort with numerous legal and political challenges. Editorial comments in the *Berkshire Courier* (recanted in 1979), neighboring property owners, and members of the American Legion and Veterans of Foreign Wars criticized Du Bois for joining the Communist Party at age ninety-three and alleged, incorrectly, that he had renounced his U.S. citizenship. The FBI later said that it had taken part in stirring up local opposition, although *Berkshire Eagle* writer Stephen Fay concluded that it was largely homegrown.

The NAACP lent the committee the services of legal defense counsel Jack Greenberg. Although the legality of using the property for a park remained in question, the right to free assembly prevailed, and on 18 October 1969 Du Bois's boyhood home was dedicated as the W. E. B. Du Bois Memorial Park. Civil rights activist and future Georgia legislator Julian Bond gave the keynote address, and Ossie Davis presided as master of ceremonies.

The dedication took place amid newspaper attacks and reported threats of violence and disruption, both from "local ultrapatriots" and "black militant groups" (*Berkshire Eagle* 1969). Medical personnel and ambulances were on hand, as were local police equipped with riot gear shipped from Hartford, Connecticut. A state police single-engine aircraft made passes overhead, and a unit of the National Guard stood by. But Great Barrington resident Elaine Gunn recalled: "It was a beautiful day, a lovely day; people sat around on bales of hay. The afternoon came off without a hitch, then everyone left quietly" (Gunn 2004). A reported eight hundred people came from as far away as Boston and New York City. In 1970 Du Bois's widow, Shirley Graham Du Bois, visited the site for a ceremony that included Gordon, Wilson, *Freedomways* editor Esther Jackson, and others.

A ten-ton granite boulder had been trucked to the property, intended to hold a bronze memorial plaque, which was never fabricated. For many years, owing to fear of vandalism and retribution, nothing was installed in the park, although the committee continued to maintain the site. Wilson, working with the Afro-American Bicentennial Corporation, obtained national historic landmark status for the park, which it received from the U.S. Department of the Interior in 1976. Three years later, on 20 October 1979, a dedication ceremony at Tanglewood, organized by Homer Meade of Stockbridge, was attended by returning keynote speaker Julian Bond; Xie Qime, from the embassy of the People's Republic of China; Alexander Quaison-Sackey, permanent representative to the

United Nations from Ghana; Walter Wilson; Ruth D. Jones; Randolph Bromery; David Graham Du Bois; Pete Seeger; Michael Thelwell; and William Strickland, among others. On 12 July 1980 the committee reconvened to place a new bronze plaque at the site, designating its national landmark status and replacing the wooden sign placed there previously.

The property was donated in 1987 to the Commonwealth of Massachusetts, with the University of Massachusetts, Amherst, as its custodian. Since the 1980s it has been the subject of intensive archaeological research under the leadership of archaeologist Robert Paynter. There have been three on-site field schools at the property (1983, 1984, and 2003).

The Du Bois Memorial Committee continues to advocate for a memorial at the site, which in early 2006 remains unkempt, overgrown, and mostly ignored, marked only by a rusted sign nearly invisible to passersby. In 2006 the Committee joined forces with the Great Barrington Land Conservancy, the Great Barrington Historical Society, Clinton A. M. E. Zion Church of Great Barrington, and the Upper Housatonic Valley African American Heritage Trail. It is the hope of these Friends of the Du Bois Homesite to assist the University of Massachusetts in the creation of a fitting memorial.

Rachel Fletcher

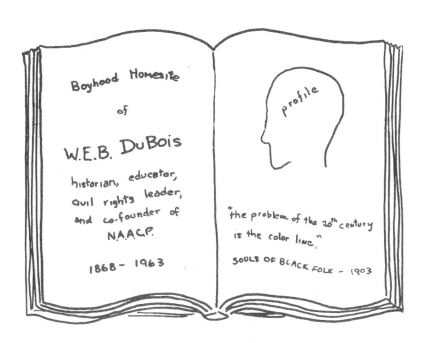

Sketch of plaque, which was to be placed on a boulder at the Du Bois Memorial Park dedication in 1969. Photo courtesy of Ruth D. Jones Collection, W. E. B. Du Bois Memorial Committee.

W. E. B. Du Bois Boyhood Homesite Photo Essay

W. E. B. Du Bois, Nina Gomer Du Bois and James Weldon Johnson (right) at the Burghardt home on Route 23, in Great Barrington on 23 February 1928, on the occasion of Du Bois's sixtieth birthday. Photo courtesy of Special Collections and Archives, W. E. B. Du Bois Library, University of Massachusetts, Amherst. Photo from Ruth D. Jones Collection, W. E. B. Du Bois Memorial Committee.

W. E. B. Du Bois and Shirley Graham Du Bois examine the Burghardt home site, in disrepair, in the early 1950s. Photo courtesy of Special Collections and Archives, W. E. B. Du Bois Library, University of Massachusetts, Amherst.

Du Bois Memorial Committee Co-Chairman Walter Wilson at the W. E. B. Du Bois Memorial Park Dedication, Great Barrington, 18 October 1969. Photo from, W. E. B. Du Bois Memorial Park, National Historic Landmark Dedication Program (20 October 1979).

Du Bois Memorial Committee Co-Chairman Edmund Gordon at the W. E. B. Du Bois Memorial Park Dedication, Great Barrington, 18 October 1969.

Ossie Davis at the W. E. B. Du Bois Memorial Park Dedication, Great Barrington, 18 October 1969. Photo from, W. E. B. Du Bois Memorial Park, National Historic Landmark Dedication Program (20 October 1979).

Ruth Jones (far right), Frederick Lord (third from right), William Gibson, and Dr. Margaret Brenman-Gibson (fourth and fifth from right) at the W. E. B. Du Bois Memorial Park Dedication, Great Barrington, 18 October 1969. Photo from, W. E. B. Du Bois Memorial Park, National Historic Landmark Dedication Program (20 October 1979).

Right: Julian Bond at the W. E. B. Du Bois Memorial Park Dedication, Great Barrington, 18 October 1969. Photo from, W. E. B. Du Bois Memorial Park, National Historic Landmark Dedication Program (20 October 1979).

On-stage guests at Tanglewood in Lenox on 20 October 1979 at the W. E. B. Du Bois Memorial Park National Historic Landmark Dedication. From left: Walter Wilson (standing at podium); The Counselor Mr. Xie Qime, Embassy of the People's Republic of China (second seated person, front row from left); His Excellency Dr. Quaison-Sackey, Ambassador to the United States from Ghana (third seated person, front row from left); Julian Bond (fourth seated person, front row from left); Ruth D. Jones (fifth seated person, front row from left); Randolph Bromery (seventh seated person, front row from left); David Graham Du Bois (second seated person, front row from right); Pete Seeger (front row, far right); and William Strickland (third seated person, back row from right) (Above) State Rep. Dennis Duffin, third from left. Photo by Donald B. Victor.

On-stage guests Ruth D. Jones (center) and Walter Wilson (right) at Tanglewood in Lenox on 20 October 1979 at the W. E. B. Du Bois Memorial Park National Historic Landmark Dedication. Photo by Donald B. Victor.

Program cover for the W. E. B. Du Bois Memorial Park, Great Barrington National Historic Landmark Dedication, October 20, 1979, Tanglewood Concert Theatre, Lenox.

Volunteers cleaning up the W. E. B. Du Bois Boyhood homesite in 1976. Photo by Donald B. Victor.

The W. E. B. Du Bois Memorial Committee places a bronze National Landmark plaque at the Boyhood Homesite on 12 July 1980. In the front are Walter Wilson and Ruth D. Jones. Standing behind Ruth Jones are David Gunn, Sr. (left) and William Gibson (right). Photo by Donald B. Victor.

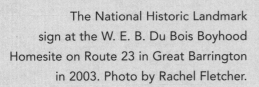

The National Historic Landmark sign at the W. E. B. Du Bois Boyhood Homesite on Route 23 in Great Barrington in 2003. Photo by Rachel Fletcher.

Archaeology students from the University of Massachusetts at Amherst working at the W. E. B. Du Bois Homesite on Route 23 in Great Barrington July 1983. Field school director Professor Robert Paynter is at lower right in checkered shirt. Photo by Donald B. Victor.

Archaeology students from the University of Massachusetts at Amherst working on the house pits at the W. E. B. Du Bois Homesite on Route 23 in Great Barrington in July 2003. Photo by Rachel Fletcher.

Frederick Lord, Elaine Gunn, Wray Gunn, Homer Meade and Cora Portnoff (left to right) in Great Barrington in 2006, viewing film footage, for the first time, of the 1969 W. E. B. Du Bois Memorial dedication. Photo by Rachel Fletcher.

Ruth D. Jones,
Preserver of the Legacy of W. E. B. Du Bois

Ruth D. Jones (1931–2005) was born on 7 January 1931 in Brooklyn, New York. She came to Great Barrington with her family, including her older sister Helen and younger brother Jesse, in 1946, when their father, the Rev. Raleigh Dove, was appointed pastor of the Clinton A. M. E. Zion Church. (Her parents moved back to Brooklyn in 1951, when her father's tenure at the Clinton Church ended.) Jones graduated from Searles High School in 1949 and later that year on 3 September was married by her father to David Jones, a presser at Kaplan Cleaners on Railroad Street. The couple had four children—David Jr., Duane, James, and Jonathan. David Sr. died in 1984.

Ruth Jones had a rich and varied life as a wife, mother, library cataloger for over twenty years, worker for the NAACP, and resident of New York, Massachusetts, California, Tennessee, and Colorado. She is significant in Berkshire and national African American history as the individual who worked the longest and hardest to make known and preserve the legacy of W. E. B. Du Bois in his hometown. Walter Wilson, the force behind the W. E. B. Du Bois Homesite Memorial Park on Route 23, summarized her achievements:

> The collection of the materials which are included herein [1979 Du Bois Memorial Park dedication program] has in large part been the task of Ruth D. Jones, incorporator of the Committee and the present treasurer. It has been a task that has demanded many, many hours when this incorporator was away from the responsibilities as librarian at Simon's Rock of Bard College or away from raising a family or away from her successful work in raising funds for the Martin Luther King scholarship fund or away from creating a "Du Bois Collection" in the Simon's Rock Library. She worked many hours compiling this record, preserving the story of Dr. Du Bois in Great Barrington and the slow creation of the Du Bois Memorial Park. I feel confident that her work will find a place in American archives preserving a part of the essential liberal-radical-democratic tradition. (Wilson 1979)

Elaine Gunn recalled that she and Jones became aware of the civil rights movement in the 1950s and were fully involved later in the decade. They made phone calls to encourage people to vote; attended NAACP meetings in Great Barrington, Stockbridge, and Pittsfield; and solicited memberships. In 1965 Jones became involved in the Berkshire Community Action Council and Head Start. In 1966 she was appointed cataloger at Simon's Rock College Library and two years later became involved with Walter Wilson in working to create a memorial to W. E. B. Du Bois. Elaine Gunn remarked that "Walter needed a person to record this information, to contact people, to keep notes. That's where Ruth came in. She became the Secretary and Treasurer. Ruth kept track of all articles and correspondence. She set up meetings. She became Walter's right arm" (Gunn 2005).

Julian Bond and Ruth D. Jones, on stage at Tanglewood in Lenox on 20 October 1979 at the W. E. B. Du Bois Memorial Park National Historic Landmark Dedication. Photo by Donald B. Victor.

Jones also worked with Gunn and other Black women to set up a Martin Luther King Jr. Scholarship Committee in 1968, which awarded two or three scholarships a year to both Black and white Berkshire high school students into the 1980s. At Simon's Rock Jones continued to preserve Du Bois's legacy by creating and expanding the Du Bois Collection in the 1970s and 1980s with the support of college librarian Comstock Small. Linda Small, the wife of Comstock Small, remembers her at Simon's Rock: "That wonderful outgoing personality drew everyone in. Ruth wanted to know about everyone. She was the face of the Simon's Rock library. She loved the kids, had personal relationships with all of them. She was just right there whatever task was to be done. She was there to do it" (Small and Small 2005).

In June 1984, after a lengthy illness, David Jones passed away. The next year Ruth concluded twenty years of service at Simon's Rock and moved to Los Angeles to work as a cataloger at the University of California, Los Angeles, library. Retiring in 1992, she moved in 1993 to Chattanooga, Tennessee, where her brother lived, and then to Colorado Springs, Colorado, in 2001 to be with her ailing sister. Ruth D. Jones died of cancer on 2 May 2005.

Elaine S. Gunn and Rachel Fletcher

David Graham Du Bois, Scholar and Activist

David Graham Du Bois (1925–2005) could not recall when he had first visited Great Barrington. But he knew its role in shaping W. E. B. Du Bois's Yankee optimism and puritanism and stubbornness.

Often in the Berkshires during his later years, he dedicated the Du Bois River Garden and Park, which is part of Great Barrington's River Walk. He spoke at Simon's Rock College, at Taconic High School, at the Clinton A. M. E. Zion Church. David attended the W. E. B. Du Bois play, commissioned by the Berkshire Country Day School, at the Berkshire Theatre Festival, and he admired the Du Bois mural on the wall of Carr Hardware in Great Barrington. Along with following the discussion of naming one of the new Berkshire Hills schools for W. E. B. Du Bois, he was an adviser to the Upper Housatonic Valley African American Heritage Trail project and this book.

Educated at Hunter College and New York University, David was a journalist in Cairo in the 1960s, during a time of decolonization and political change. He later edited the Black Panther weekly newspaper in California; the organization had by then shifted from a revolutionary to a political agenda. In addition, he taught journalism and African American studies at the University of Massachusetts at Amherst.

David was fully W. E. B. Du Bois's son in spirit, if not blood. His mother, Shirley Graham, was long divorced from her first husband, Shadrack McCants, when she married W. E. B. Du Bois in 1951. David came to know W. E. B. in fits and spurts, but recognized the old man was disappointed that a son had died in childhood. "I experienced some of this with him. It was part of the reason I asked if he would allow me to become his son. . . . I took his name when I was 27." Raised by grandparents, David knew no father. His only brother, Robert, had died in 1944.

After his mother's death, David became Du Bois's literary executor and established the Du Bois Foundation. He worked tirelessly to remind people of the continued international significance of W. E. B. Du Bois.

Bernard A. Drew

David Graham Du Bois, with Evelyn Jeffers, on the occasion of the dedication of the W. E. B. Du Bois River Garden on 28 September 2002. Photo by Monica Fadding.

Activist Orators

Eloquent and engaging speakers for Black rights in the nineteenth and twentieth centuries appeared before receptive Berkshire County audiences. When the abolitionist Frederick Douglass (1817–1895) spoke at West's Hall in Pittsfield in December 1865 (30¢ for admission), an advertisement suggested that the speaker "approaches nearer to the eloquence of Daniel Webster than any other man in this country." About his well-attended talk, "Assassination and Its Lessons," the *Berkshire Evening Eagle* said, "The speaker took extremely radical ground in handling national affairs and looked at things from his peculiar stand point." One might dismiss this speech as merely one of hundreds Douglass gave, but for a sour incident beforehand. Several "negro haters," as the newspaper termed them, guests at the American House, objected to Douglass eating in the dining room. The proprietor arranged to serve the meal in Douglass's room. "This proposition did not suit the colored gentleman and he paid his bill and left, and took up his abode at the United States Hotel," the *Eagle* said.

Booker T. Washington (1856–1915) made at least three oratorical visits to Berkshire County. "A large congregation greeted Mr. Boaker [sic] T. Washington, at the Congregational church [in Stockbridge] last Sunday morning," *The Berkshire Courier* reported in July 1895, "and were very much interested by the excellent account he gave of the Tuscegee [sic] Normal and Industrial Institute in Alabama. A liberal collection was taken at the close of the service for the benefit of the institute the speaker represented."

Two months after this talk in Stockbridge, Washington delivered his seminal speech at the 1895 Cotton States and International Exposition in Atlanta, Georgia. Called the "Atlanta Compromise,"

Frederick Douglass and the Governor

Riding from Boston to Albany, a few years ago, I found myself in a large car, well filled with passengers. The seat next to me was about the only vacant one. At every stopping place we took in new passengers, all of whom, on reaching the seat next to me, cast a disdainful glance upon it, and passed to another car, leaving me in the full enjoyment of a whole form. For a time, I did not know but that my riding there was prejudicial to the interest of the railroad company. A circumstance occurred, however, which gave me an elevated position at once. Among the passengers on this train was [Massachusetts] Gov. George N. Briggs. I was not acquainted with him, and had no idea that I was known to him. Known to him, however, I was, for upon observing me, the governor left his place, and making his way toward me, respectfully asked the privilege of a seat by my side; and upon introducing himself, we entered into a conversation very pleasant and instructive to me. The despised seat now became honored. His excellency had removed all the prejudice against sitting by the side of a negro; and upon his leaving it, as he did, on reaching Pittsfield, there were at least one dozen applicants for the place. The governor had, without changing my skin a single shade, made the place respectable which before was despicable.

Douglass, Frederick. *My Bondage and My Freedom. Part II—Life as a Freeman.* New York: Miller, Orton & Mulligan,1855. http://docsouth.unc.edu/neh/douglass55/doug.lass55html (accessed 3 Jan. 2006).

his disquisition began, "One-third of the population of the South is of the Negro race. No enterprise seeking the material, civil, or moral welfare of this section can disregard this element of our population and reach the highest success" (Washington 1895). Washington assured his audience of Southern businesspeople that men and women of his race would be content to live "by the productions of our hands." One of the reasons for his coming to speak was to tap the same pool of donors that supported his mentor Samuel Chapman Armstrong, founder of Hampton Normal and Agricultural Institute in Alabama. Armstrong, great-nephew of Reuben Chapman of Stockbridge, was married to Emmeline Dean Walker of the same town.

When Washington again came to Stockbridge, in 1904, having spoken before Great Barrington's library association during his stay, he was a famous man and not only addressed Stockbridge's leading social organization, the Laurel Hill Association, but was also a guest at the home of Alexander Sedgwick. At a lunch in Washington's honor, he ate with "Baron Bussche, first secretary of the German Legation, John E. Parsons of Lenox, James D. Hague, Dr. W. Gillman Thomson, Bishop McVicker [of Rhode Island] and Dr. [Rev. Arthur] Lawrence," the weekly newspaper (*The Berkshire Courier*) reported in September 1904. A Great Barrington resident, Dale Culleton, owns a copy of Washington's book *The Future of the American Negro*, from the library of his great-great-grandfather, the above-mentioned John E. Parsons. With it is a letter, signed by Washington, thanking Parsons for his support of Tuskegee. Washington was a polished fundraiser.

In the Laurel Hill grove behind Plain School in Stockbridge in 1904, Washington surely was pleased that the audience included "quite a liberal sprinkling of colored people." He expressed exasperation at the disparity in education for whites and Blacks, making a jab worthy of W. E. B. Du Bois's sharp tongue: "This has got to be changed. No doubt

many white boys are stupid, but I do not believe that it is necessary to spend ten times as much on their education."

Washington's acceptance of vocational servitude was of course at odds with the views of Great Barrington native Du Bois (1868–1963) by this same time. An impatient Du Bois had challenged Washington in his 1903 *The Souls of Black Folk*, in an impassioned chapter in which he attacked Washington's gradualism and accommodation. The agreements and disagreements of Du Bois and Washington deserve far better attention than this publication allows. But as Elaine S. Gunn of Great Barrington, a former teacher and a NAACP member, has suggested, "We needed both Booker Washington and Du Bois. One was pragmatic and the other intellectual." Du Bois had spoken in Great Barrington in the 1890s and early 1900s, but more often on sociological than race-relations topics. As he took on a national role in civil rights, he took his message to much larger and vital venues.

A civil rights giant of a later generation, the Rev. Martin Luther King Jr. (1928–1968) explained his philosophy of nonviolence and civil disobedience to an audience at Williams College in 1961: "Resistance without violence, hatred of segregation without hatred of the segregationist, a desire to rouse the conscience of the opponent rather than to humiliate him" (*Berkshire Eagle* 1961).

The Pittsfield office of the NAACP brought several important civil rights leaders to the region in the 1960s and 1970s, including Roy Wilkins and the Rev. Martin Luther King Sr. The Rev. Stephen Gill Spottswood, bishop of the A. M. E. Zion Church and head of the national NAACP from 1961 to 1974, spoke at the Second Congregational and Price Memorial churches in Pittsfield and the Clinton A. M. E. Zion Church in Great Barrington and lectured in Torrington, Connecticut, during his tenure.

Bernard A. Drew

Sources

Slavery in Northwest Connecticut

Connecticut Courant and the Weekly Advertiser, no. 98, 10 Nov. 1766, 1.

Connecticut Courant and the Weekly Advertiser, no. 121, 20 April 1767, 3.

Connecticut Courant and Weekly Hartford Intelligencer, no. 489, 3 May 1774, 3.

Connecticut Courant and Weekly Hartford Intelligencer, no. 493, 7 June, 1774, 3.

Connecticut Courant and Weekly Intelligencer, no. 736, 2 March 1779, 2.

Connecticut Courant and Weekly Intelligencer, no. 912, 16 July 1782, 1.

Connecticut Courant and Weekly Intelligencer, no. 1021, 17 Aug. 1784, 3

Connecticut Courant, vol. XXX, no. 1588, 29 June 1795, 3.

Connecticut Courant, vol. XXXIII, no. 1738, 14 May 1798, 3.

Connecticut Courant, vol. XLIII, no. 2226, 23 Sept. 1807, 2.

History of Litchfield County, Connecticut, with Illustrations and Biographical Sketches of Its Prominent Men and Pioneers. Philadelphia, PA: J. W. Lewis & Co., 1881.

Melish, Joanne Pope. *Disowning Slavery: Gradual Emancipation and "Race" in New England, 1780–1860.* Ithaca, NY: Cornell University Press, 1998.

Steiner, Bernard Christian. *History of Guilford and Madison, Connecticut.* Guilford, CT: Guilford Free Library, 1975.

Van Dusen, Albert E.. *Connecticut.* New York: Random House, 1961.

Van Dusen, Albert E. *Puritans against the Wilderness: Connecticut History to 1763.* Chester, CT: Pequot Press, 1975.

Weld, Ralph Foster. *Slavery in Connecticut.* New Haven, CT: Tercentenary Commission, 1935.

White, David O. "Blacks in Connecticut." http://www.ctheritage.org/encyclopedia/topical-surveys/blacks.htm (accessed 16 March 2006).

United States Bureau of the Census. *Heads of Families at the First Census of the United States Taken in the Year 1790: Connecticut.* Washington, DC: Government Printing Office, 1908.

United States Census Office. *Return of the Whole Number of Persons within the Several Districts of the United States: Second census/U.S. Census Office.* Second census, 1800. New York: Arno Press, 1976.

United States Census Office. *Aggregate Amount of Each Description of Persons within the United States of America and the Territories in the Year 1810/U.S. Census Office.* Third census, 1810. New York: Arno Press, 1976.

United States Census Office. *Census for 1820/U.S. Census Office.* Fourth census, 1820. New York: Arno Press, 1976.

United States Bureau of the Census. *Fifth Census; or, Enumeration of the Inhabitants of the United States. 1830. To Which is refixed, a Schedule of the Whole Number of Persons within the Several Districts of the United States, Taken According to the Acts of 1790, 1800, 1810, 1820.* Pub. by Authority of an Act of Congress. Fifth census, 1830. Washington, D.C.: D. Green, 1832.

United States Census Office. *The Seventh Census of the United States: 1850.* Seventh census. 1850. Washington, D.C.: R. Armstrong 1853.

United States Census Office. *Population of the United States in 1860; compiled from the original returns of the eighth census, under the direction of the Secretary of the Interior.* Eighth census, 1860. Washington, D.C.: Government Printing Office, 1864.

James Mars, Community Leader and Activist

Mars, James. *Life of James Mars, a Slave Born and Sold in Connecticut.* 6th ed. Hartford, CT: Case, Lockwood & Co., 1868.

Ripley, C. Peter, ed. *The Black Abolitionist Papers.* Chapel Hill: University of North Carolina Press, 1985–1992.

"Slavery in New England." *The Berkshire Courier*, 9 June 1880.

White, David O. *Connecticut's Black Soldiers, 1775–1783.* Chester, CT: Pequot Press, 1973.

White, David O. "Hartford's African Free Schools, 1830–1868." *CHSB* 39: 47–51.

Slavery in the Berkshires

Ferm, Robert L. *Jonathan Edwards the Younger: A Colonial Pastor.* William B. Eerdmans, 1976.

Greene, Lorenzo Johnston. *The Negro in Colonial New England.* New York: Atheneum, 1969.

History of Berkshire County, Massachusetts, with Biographical Sketches of Its Prominent Men. Vol. 1. New York: J. B. Beers & Co., 1885.

Mars, James. *Life of James Mars, A Slave Born and Sold in Connecticut.* 6th ed. Hartford, CT: Case, Lockwood & Co., 1868.

Pruitt, Bettye Hobbs. *The Massachusetts Tax Valuation List of 1771*. Boston: G. K. Hall, 1978.

Sedgwick, Miss [Catharine M.]. "Slavery in New England." *Bentley's Miscellany* 34 (1853): 421.

Sedgwick, Theodore, III. T*he Practicability of the Abolition of Slavery: A Lecture Delivered at the Lyceum in Stockbridge, Massachusetts, February 1831*. New York: J. Seymour, 1831.

Smith, J. E. A. *History of Pittsfield, Berkshire County, Massachusetts from the Year 1734 to the Year 1860*. Boston: Lee and Shepard, 1869.

Smith, John E., et al., eds. *A Jonathan Edwards Reader*. New Haven, CT: Yale University Press, 1995.

Takaki, Ronald. *A Different Mirror: A History of Multicultural America*. Boston: Little, Brown, 1993.

Cuffee and Nana Negro, Pioneer Blacks in Berkshire County

Berkshire Middle District Registry of Deeds. Book 2, 328. Pittsfield, MA.

Massachusetts Archives Collection. Vol. 33, 277–288. [Available at the Massachusetts Archives, State Archives Building, Boston.]

Springfield Registry of Deeds. Book Q, 431, for "Cuffee My Negro Man Servant and Nanna My Negro Woman Servant." Springfield, MA.

Springfield Registry of Deeds. Book S, 475. Springfield, MA.

Mum Bett (Elizabeth Freeman), Antislavery Pioneer

Brom & Bett v. J. Ashley Esq. Court Records, Berkshire County Courthouse, Great Barrington, Massachusetts, Inferior Court of Common Pleas. Vol. 4A, no. 1, 28

May 1781, 55. [Microfilm available at the Berkshire Athenaeum, Pittsfield, MA.]

Kelley, Mary, ed. *The Power of Her Sympathy: The Autobiography and Journal of Catharine Maria Sedgwick*. Boston: Massachusetts Historical Society, 1993.

Sedgwick, Miss [Catharine M.]. "Slavery in New England." *Bentley's Miscellany* 34 (1853): 421.

Sedgwick, H[enry]. D. "The Sedgwicks in Berkshire." In *Collections of the Berkshire Historical and Scientific Society*. Vol. 3, no. 97. Pittsfield, MA: Pittsfield Sun, 1899.

Sedgwick, Theodore, II. *The Practicability of the Abolition of Slavery: A Lecture Delivered at the Lyceum in Stockbridge, Massachusetts, February 1831*. New York: J. Seymour, 1831.

Zilversmit, Arthur. "Quok Walker, Mumbet, and the Abolition of Slavery in Massachusetts." *William and Mary Quarterly* 25, no. 4 (October 1968): 622.

Underground Railroad

Archer, Cathaline, et al. *A Bicentennial History of Becket, Berkshire County, Mass. Incorporated June 21, 1765*. Pittsfield, MA: n.p., 1965.

Bial, Raymond. *The Underground Railroad*. Boston: Houghton Mifflin, 1995.

Biographical Review, Containing Life Sketches of Leading Citizens of Berkshire County, Mass. Boston: Biographical Review Publishing Co., 1899.

Bua, Elena. "Berkshire Monument Marks Underground Railway Depot." *Sunday Republican*, 15 Oct. 1989.

Consolati, Florence. *See All the People or Life in Lee*. Lee, MA: Studley Press, 1978.

Crissey, Theron Wilmot, ed. *History of Norfolk, Litchfield County, Connecticut*. Everett, MA: n.p., 1900.

Curtiss, Lucy Sackett. *The Congregational Church, Warren, Connecticut, 1756–1956*. n.p.: c. 1956.

Gara, Larry. *The Liberty Line: The Legend of the Underground Railroad*. Lexington: University of Kentucky Press, 1996.

History of Berkshire County, Massachusetts, with Biographical Sketches of Its Prominent Men. Vol. 1. New York: J. B. Beers & Co., 1885.

Hoffman Anne. *Sandisfield: A Biography of a Town*. Sandisfield, MA: n.p., 1998.

"Invisible Wings." Jacob's Pillow Dance Festival, 25–29, Aug. 1998, Becket, MA.

Phillips, William H. *Berkshire Hills: A Historic Monthly*. Vol. 1, no. 5 (1 Jan. 1901). Pittsfield, MA.

Siebert, William H. "The Underground Railroad in Massachusetts." *Proceedings of the American Antiquarian Society* 45 (1935): 27.

Smith, J. E. A. *History of Pittsfield, Berkshire County, Massachusetts from the Year 1734 to the Year 1860*. Boston: Lee and Shepard, 1869.

Strother, Horatio T. T*he Underground Railroad in Connecticut*. Middletown, CT: Wesleyan University Press, 1962.

"Underground Railways in Berkshire County; and Remembrances of Interesting Local Blacks." *The Berkshire Sampler*, 23 May 1976, 15–16.

William Edward Burghardt Du Bois, Scholar and Activist

Andrews, William L., ed. *Critical Essays on W. E .B. Du Bois.* Boston: G. K. Hall, 1985.

Berry, Mary Frances. *Black Resistance, White Law: A History of Constitutional Racism in America.* New York: Penguin Press, 1994.

Broderick, Francis L. *W. E. B. Du Bois, Negro Leader in a Time of Crisis.* Stanford, CA: Stanford University Press, 1959.

Byerman, Keith E. *Seizing the Word: History, Art, and Self in the Work of W. E. B. Du Bois.* Athens: University of Georgia Press, 1994.

Clarke, John Henrik, et al. *Black Titan: W. E. B. Du Bois; An Anthology by the Editors of* Freedomways. Boston: Beacon Press, 1970.

DeMarco, Joseph P. *The Social Thought of W .E. B. Du Bois.* Lanham, MD: University Press of America, 1983.

Du Bois, Shirley Graham. *His Day Is Marching On: A Memoir of W. E. B. Du Bois.* Philadelphia: Lippincott, 1971.

Du Bois, W. E. B. *An ABC of Color.* New York: International Publishers, 1963.

Du Bois, W. E. B. *The Autobiography of W. E. B. Du Bois: A Soliloquy on Viewing My Life from the Last Decade of Its First Century.* New York: International Publishers, 1968.

Du Bois, W. E. B. *The Correspondence of W. E. B. Du Bois.* Ed. by Herbert Aptheker. 3 vols. Amherst: University of Massachusetts Press, 1973–1978.

Du Bois, W. E. B. *Dusk of Dawn: An Essay toward an Autobiography of a Race Concept.* New York: Harcourt, Brace and Co., 1940.

Du Bois, W. E. B. *The Souls of Black Folk.* New York: Vintage Books, 1990. [First pub. in 1903.]

Foner, Philip S. *W. E. B. Du Bois Speaks: Speeches and Addresses.* 2 vols. New York: Pathfinder Press, 1988.

Harris, Thomas E. *Analysis of the Clash over the Issues between Booker T. Washington and W. E. B. Du Bois.* New York: Garland, 1993.

Hawkins, Hugh, ed. *Booker T. Washington and His Critics: Black Leadership in Crisis.* Lexington, MA: Heath, 1974.

Horne, Gerald. *Black and Red: W. E. B. Du Bois and the Afro-American Response to the Cold War, 1944–1963.* Albany: State University of New York Press, 1985.

Ingersoll, W. T. *The Reminiscences of William Edward Burghardt Du Bois.* Glen Rock, NJ: Microfilming Corporation of America, 1972.

Kostelanetz, Richard. *Politics in the African-American Novel: James Weldon Johnson, W. E. B. Du Bois, Richard Wright and Ralph Ellison.* New York: Greenwood Press, 1991.

Lester, Julius, ed. *The Seventh Son: The Thought and Writings of W. E. B. Du Bois.* New York: Random House, 1971.

Lewis, David Levering. *W. E. B. Du Bois: Biography of a Race, 1868–1919.* New York: Henry Holt, 1993.

Logan, Rayford W. *W. E. B. Du Bois: A Profile.* New York: Hill and Wang, 1971.

Lusane, Clarence. *Race in the Global Era: African Americans at the Millennium.* Boston: South End Press, 1997.

Marable, Manning. *W. E. B. Du Bois: Black Radical Democrat.* Boston: Twayne, 1986.

Marable, Manning and Leith Mullings, eds., *Let Nobody Turn Us Around: Voices of Resistance, Reform, and Renewal: An African-American Anthology.* Lanham, MD: Rowan and Littlefield, 2000.

McDonnell, Robert W. *The Papers of W. E. B. Du Bois (1877–1963) 1979: A Guide.* Sanford, NC: Microfilming Corporation of America, 1981.

Moore, Jack B. *W. E. B. Du Bois.* Boston: Twayne Publishers, 1981.

Pilgrim, David, ed. *W. E. B. Du Bois in Memoriam: A Centennial Celebration of His Collegiate Education: Fisk University 1888, Harvard University, 1890.* Bristol, IN: Wyndham Hall Press, 1990.

Ramparsad, Arnold. *The Art and Imagination of W. E. B. Du Bois.* Cambridge, MA: Harvard University Press, 1982.

Sterne, Emma. *His Was the Voice: The Life of W. E. B. Du Bois.* Foreword by Ronald Severson. New York: Crowell-Collier Press, 1971.

Zamir, Shamoon. *Dark Voices: W. E. B. Du Bois and American Thought, 1888–1903.* Chicago: University of Chicago Press, 1995.

James Weldon Johnson, Essayist and Activist

"An Afternoon with a Literateur." *Berkshire Courier,* 9 Sept. 1937, 1, 7.

"Dr. Johnson Killed in Crossing Crash." *Berkshire Courier,* 30 June 1938, 1, 8.

"Johnson Honored." *Berkshire Courier,* 24 Sept. 1942.

Johnson, James Weldon. *Along This Way: The Autobiography of James Weldon Johnson.* New York: Viking Press, 1933.

Levy, Eugene. "James Weldon Johnson." *American National Biography*. Vol. 13. Ed. by John A. Garraty and Mark C. Carnes. New York: Oxford University Press, 1999.

Spingarn, Arthur. "An Appreciation of James Weldon Johnson." In *James Weldon Johnson*. Nashville: Fisk University, 1939.

Weinstein, Randy. *Against the Tide: Commentaries on a Collection of African Americana, 1711–1987*. New York: Glenn Horowitz, 1996.

Wilson, Sondra, ed. *The Selected Writings of James Weldon Johnson*. Vol. 1. New York: Oxford University Press, 1995.

National Association for the Advancement of Colored People (NAACP)

"Area NAACP To Picket Woolworth's." *Berkshire Eagle*, 18 June 1963.

"B. C. Robillard Elected Head of NAACP Branch." *Berkshire Eagle*, 12 April 1966.

"Berkshire NAACP to Join Southern Summer Project." *Berkshire Eagle*, 17 April 1965.

"City Elects 1st Negro in School Board Contest." *Berkshire Eagle*, 8 Nov. 1967.

"50 Picket Pittsfield Woolworth's." *Berkshire Eagle*, 21 June 1963.

"NAACP Area Field Secretary Coming to Outline Plans." *Berkshire Eagle*, 7 May 1965.

"NAACP Pickets Woolworth in Mild Demonstration Here." *Berkshire Eagle*, 28 March 1960.

"Negro Riots Not Expected Here by Area NAACP Head." *Berkshire Eagle*, 29 July 1967.

Katz, Judy. "Blacks Boycotted Berkshire Community Action Council Election." *Berkshire Eagle*, 9 Feb. 1979.

Katz, Judy. "Blacks in the City Pull Together." *Berkshire Eagle*, 18 June 1979.

King, Nick. "NAACP Establishing Library of Black History and Literature." *Berkshire Eagle*, 28 Dec. 1972.

O'Conner, Gerald. "Black Pittsfield: Notes of Hope, Notes of Despair." *Berkshire Eagle*, 21 May 1984.

Scheer, Peter. "Thousand Attend Black Festival," *Berkshire Eagle*, 22 July 1974.

White, Mark. "The March Remembered." *Berkshire Sampler*, 28 Aug. 1983.

W. E. B. Du Bois Memorial Committee

"Abutter Attempts Blockage." *Berkshire Courier*, 16 Oct. 1969.

Bell, William E. "Controversial Du Bois Park Scene of a Quiet Dedication." *Berkshire Eagle*, 20 Oct. 1969.

Bell, William E. "Du Bois State Memorial Proposed, Would Be in Great Barrington." *Berkshire Eagle*, 12 Feb. 1968.

"DuBois Group Works for Shrine," *Berkshire Courier*, 12 March 1970.

"Du Bois Rites Occasioned Strong Security Measures." *Berkshire Eagle*, 25 Oct. 1969.

Du Bois, W. E. B. *The Autobiography of W. E. B. Du Bois: A Soliloquy on Viewing My Life from the Last Decade of Its First Century*. New York: International Publishers, 1968.

Du Bois, W. E. B. "The House of the Black Burghardts." *The Crisis* 35, no. 4 (1928): 133–34.

Du Bois, W. E. B. *The Papers of W. E. B. Du Bois (1877–1963) 1979*, Series 19, Motion Pictures and Tapes, Years 1958–1979. W. E. B. Du Bois Memorial Library, University of Massachusetts, Amherst.

"Du Bois Widow Visits Site of Husband's Home." *Berkshire Courier*, 22 Oct. 1970.

Fay, Stephen. "FBI Takes Credit for Opposition to Du Bois Barrington Memorial." *Berkshire Eagle*, 30 Nov. 1977.

Fay, Stephen. "Prophetic Snoops." Op-ed piece, *Berkshire Eagle*, 3 Dec. 1977.

Francis, George. "Changing Attitudes." Editorial, *Berkshire Courier*, 18 Oct. 1979.

Francis, George. "Keeping Cool." Editorial, *Berkshire Courier*, 16 Oct. 1969.

Greenberg, Jack. Western Union telegram, 17 Sept. 1969.

Gunn, Elaine. Personal communication with the author, 16 Oct. 2004.

Keen, Mike Forrest. *Stalking the Sociological Imagination: J. Edgar Hoover's FBI Surveillance of American Sociology*. Westport, CT: Greenwood Press, 1999.

Meade, Homer. Address, New England Conference/National Council of Black Studies, Smith College, Northampton, MA, 7 April 1979.

"Memorial Backers Determined to Go Ahead with Dedication." *Berkshire Courier*, 16 Oct. 1969.

Moon, Henry Lee, "W. E. B. Du Bois Memorial Park." *The Crisis*, December 1969.

Murphy, Jeremiah V. "Park Dedicated to Du Bois Despite Outcry." *Boston Globe*, 19 Oct. 1969.

"NAACP Assigns Lawyer to Du Bois Case," *Berkshire Eagle*, 18 Oct. 1969.

National Register of Historic Places. "William E. B. Du Bois Boyhood Homesite." Nomination form, 30 Oct. 1975.

Paynter, Robert, et al. "Archaeological Report on the 2003 University of Massachusetts Amherst Summer Field School in Archaeology Work at the W. E. B. Du Bois Boyhood Homesite." Department of Anthropology, University of Massachusetts, Amherst, 2004. In preparation.

Robinson, Douglas. "Berkshires Park Named for Du Bois." *New York Times*, 19 Oct. 1969.

Robinson, Douglas. "Du Bois Hometown in the Berkshires Angered by Plans for Memorial Park." *New York Times*, 16 May 1969.

"Selectmen Allow Du Bois Rites; Park's Legality Still in Debate." *Berkshire Eagle*, 17 Oct. 1969.

W. E. B. Du Bois Memorial Committee. "News from the W. E. B. Du Bois Committee." Press release, Great Barrington, MA, 13 Oct. 1969.

W. E. B. Du Bois Memorial Park dedication program, 18 Oct. 1969).

W. E. B. Du Bois Memorial Park: National Historic Landmark dedication program (20 Oct. 1979).

W. E. B. Du Bois Memorial Park plaque-raising ceremony program, 12 July 1980.

Ruth D. Jones, Preserver of the Legacy of W. E. B. Du Bois

Gunn, Elaine. Interview with Rachel Fletcher, 2 Sept. 2005.

Jones, James. Correspondence with Elaine Gunn, October 2005.

Small, Linda, and Comstock Small. Interview with Rachel Fletcher, 7 Sept. 2005.

Wilson, Walter. "Foreward" to the National Historic Landmark dedication program, W. E. B. Du Bois Memorial Park, Great Barrington, MA, 20 Oct. 1979.

David Graham Du Bois, Scholar and Activist

Angelo, Holly. "Defender of Civil Rights David Du Bois, 79, Dies." *Springfield Union*, 4 Feb. 2005.

Du Bois, David Graham. Interviews with Bernard Drew, 2002–2004.

Activist Orators

Berkshire Courier, 18 July 1895.

Berkshire Courier, 8 Sept. 1904.

Berkshire Eagle, 17 April 1961.

Berkshire Evening Eagle, 14 Jan. 1866.

Drew, Bernard A. "Hobnobbing with B. T. Washington." *Berkshire Eagle*, 11 Feb. 2006.

Drew, Bernard A. "Was Frederick Douglass Snubbed?" *Berkshire Eagle*, 21 Feb. 2004.

Washington, Booker T. "Booker T. Washington Delivers the 1985 Atlanta Compromise Speech." www://history matters.gmu.edu/d/39.

Education

Achieving full educational equality has been a long struggle for Blacks in the region. From the time of Lemuel Haynes in Northwest Connecticut in the 1700s, and especially since the time of W. E. B. Du Bois in the 1870s, education has been the means by which some Black youth found their place in society. It has also provided, since the 1940s, employment for a few Black professionals and has been the arena in which several individuals have made major contributions to life in the Berkshires.

Struggles and Achievements

For Blacks in Berkshire County, as in the rest of the nation, the field of education has seen both great struggle and great achievement. In this region each step of the way has been a struggle—for Black children to attend schools and be considered college material, for Black teachers to get hired, and for Black history and culture to enter the curriculum. In sports, too, there were discrimination and restrictions on participation by Black youths and coaches. Lack of opportunity in public education was compensated for in part by education provided in church Sunday schools. In 1884 the Clinton A. M. E. Zion Society in Great Barrington began a Sunday school, which taught reading, public speaking, and other skills. And W. E. B. Du Bois acknowledged that his Sunday school attendance at the Congregational Church in Great Barrington supplemented what he learned in public school. Census records show that after Black children began to attend grammar school regularly after the Civil War, literacy in the Black community increased quickly. It seems likely that, as elsewhere, once children learned to read, they taught their parents at home to do the same.

An early example of discrimination is the case of Lucy Terry Prince, whose 1746 poem "Bars Fight" is widely credited as the first known work of literature by an African American. Although the documentary record is not definitive, Prince is reputed to have argued before the trustees of Williams College for admission of one of her sons in the 1790s. Despite the reported eloquence of her three-hour speech, which included extensive scriptural citations, Prince's suit was unsuccessful.

A more clearly documented event than that of Prince's appeal was an 1834 debate sponsored by Williams's Philotechnian Literary Society, which concluded that "people of colour" should be denied admission to "the colleges of New England." The debate may have been related to the graduation in 1823 of a Black student from Middlebury College

The school on Sheffield Plain which burned down in 1903 during a controversy about making it a segregated (all-Black) institution. Photo courtesy of Sheffield Historical Society, Mark Dewey Research Center.

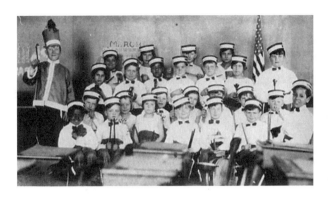

The Sheffield grade school band, c. 1930. Photo from Coenen, Christopher. *Sheffield 1773–1983; A Pictorial Recollection.* Sheffield: Sheffield 250th Anniversary Committee, 1983.

in Vermont. In any case, Williams did not award a degree to a Black person until Gauis Charles Bolin graduated in 1889. Today a dissertation fellowship for minority students honors Bolin's memory at Williams. Among the hundreds of talented African American students who have followed in Bolin's footsteps were Harrison Morgan Brown, the first Black doctor to graduate from Williams; George Montgomery Chadwell of Lee, the first Black Berkshire resident to graduate; and three pioneering scholars—historian Rayford Logan, poet and literary critic Sterling Brown, and W. Allison Davis, a distinguished professor of educational psychology.

Although Black children attended nonsegregated public schools in the county, segregation was sometimes an issue. In 1827 Pittsfield authorities rejected a proposal that would have established segregated schools in the city, primarily because there were not enough Black children to fill a separate school. Discrimination was also the policy at Pittsfield's Berkshire Medical Institute (BMI) in the 1840s and 1850s. The school did educate Henry Jenkins Roberts and other free Blacks from Liberia, who would be returning to Africa, but refused to accept Black applicants who wanted to practice medicine in the United States. In another "separate but equal" controversy, the Sheffield school committee decided in 1903 to educate Black and white children in separate schools, with a Black teacher for the Black students. The Black community objected and fought the proposal with help from Boston attorney Clarence Morgan, deemed an "outside agitator" by

the local press. The controversy was "resolved" when the Black school building, located where the American Legion building stands as of this writing, burned down one night. A school to serve the Black Sheffield "New Guinea" neighborhood was built and remained in service for several years.

In 1884 W. E. B. Du Bois broke the color line in South County when he became the first Black to graduate from Great Barrington High School and went on to become the first Black to earn a PhD from Harvard University. It was not until the 1930s, however, that other Blacks attended Berkshire County high schools on a regular basis. A significant number went on to college. A few returned to work in the Berkshires, often as teachers or nurses, but most chose to settle elsewhere.

Perhaps the first Black teacher in the region was Cora Fowler, a young woman in Sheffield who was hired to teach in the segregated all-Black school in 1903. But she never had a chance to teach, since the segregated school never opened. Florence Edmonds, the first Black public-health nurse in Pittsfield, was valedictorian of the Pittsfield High School class of 1908. While she was turned down for nurse's training at Pittsfield General Hospital, she was accepted at Lincoln Hospital in New York City. She eventually returned to Pittsfield, and, from 1956 to 1968, taught at the very hospital that had refused her for nursing training a half-century earlier. Great Barrington–born May Edward Chinn, daughter of an escaped slave, was the first Black woman to graduate from the Bellevue Hospital Medical College in

1930 and the first Black female intern at Harlem Hospital. She became a well-known physician and advocate for decent health care in Harlem. Her life is the basis of the biographical novel *Angel of Harlem* (2004) by Kuwana Haulsey.

In 1935 Williamstown-native Margaret Hart became the first Black person to graduate from North Adams Normal School (which later became the Massachusetts College of Liberal Arts [MCLA]). Three years later she received a master's degree from Teachers College, Columbia University. Hart's family had previously supported the higher education of Blacks by providing housing for Black students, who were not allowed to live on the Williams College campus in the 1920s and earlier. Hart became the first Black teacher in the Pittsfield school system. She also received an honorary doctor of pedagogy from MCLA in 1996, and in 2002 the college created a scholarship in her name. Dorothy Reid Amos, a graduate of Pittsfield High School who earned her BA at Central Ohio State College and her MA at North Adams State (later MCLA), became the first Black guidance counselor in the Pittsfield schools. In 1971 she founded the Early Childhood Development Center in Pittsfield, later renamed the Dorothy Amos Community Preschool.

Marchers carrying the Martin Luther King Jr. Scholarship Committee banner in a parade in Great Barrington in 1976. Photo by Donald B. Victor.

In the 1950s and 1960s, more Blacks entered the teaching ranks, including Martha Pierce, Earl Bean, George Taylor, and Homer "Skip" Meade at Monument Mountain High School and Elaine Gunn at Bryant Elementary in Great Barrington; Mae Brown at Lenox Memorial High School; Isaac Crawford at McCann Tech in North Adams; and Eleanor Persip, Rhoda Caesar, and Nancy Hall in Pittsfield. Skip Meade introduced a course in Black studies at Monument Mountain in the 1970s, at the urging of some students.

As part of the civil rights movement, Black women became more involved in supporting education for Black youth. In Pittsfield in the 1950s and 1960s, young married women worked through the Golden Leaves social club to help their peers stay focused on their educations and sponsored dances to raise scholarship money. The club drew members from Pittsfield and Great Barrington, including Elaine Gunn, Ruth D. Jones, Ruth Crawford Evans, and Barbara Walker Gunn. More recently, the Women of Color Giving Circle has honored each year and given stipends to graduating seniors from county high schools. In Great Barrington the Martin Luther King Jr. Scholarship Committee formed spontaneously following his assassination. Founding members included Evelyn Haile, Ruth D. Jones, Elaine Gunn, Nola Lawrence, and Mattie Bowens. It provided college scholarships to both Black and white high school graduates. The organization held a large well-attended fund-raising and awards banquet each year into the 1980s. In Great Barrington in the 1950s and 1960s, the Progressive Club provided college assistance as well.

In July 2006, the Pittsfield schools received some national attention when NASA astronaut Stephanie Wilson went into space on the Space Shuttle Discovery. Mrs. Wilson grew up in Pittsfield and her parents—Eugene and Barbara Wilson—still live there. She took mementos from the three Pittsfield schools she attended—Stearns, Crosby, and Taconic (graduated 1984)—with her. She told a reporter for the *Berkshire Eagle* (19 June 2006) that the teachers and staff at Taconic helped her achieve her goals: "They were very encouraging. They really told me that there weren't any limits, that I could do whatever I want, that I could study whatever I wanted to in school."

Support for Black education came sometimes from surprising sources. In 1872 Mary Goodman of Pittsfield, who worked all her life as a domestic in New Haven, Connecticut, left her modest estate to endow a theological scholarship "to educate men of her own color in Yale College for the Gospel ministry." In October 1900 the Great Barrington and Lenox schools sponsored and held an art exhibit. Bryant School (Great Barrington) used its Julia Bryant Room to display various works of art, prints, and so on. In the 1900–1901 School Committee Report to the town of Great Barrington, expenditures for the exhibit were reported as $122.99 and receipts as $145.05. Listed in the expenditures column was "Booker T. Washington,* 21.25." The asterisk indicated "including a gift to the Tuskegee Normal and Industrial Institute of Alabama which, with the approval of the teachers, was made in their name—Houdon's bust of Washington and bracket."

Richard Courage, David Levinson, and Elaine S. Gunn

Lucy Terry Prince, Author

Lucy Terry Prince (c. 1724–1821) is widely credited as the author of the earliest known literary work by an African American. This reputation rests on a single poem recording details of the last Indian raid on Deerfield, Massachusetts. Prince's ballad, "Bars Fight," was probably meant to be sung and may have been composed orally. Some have linked her poem and her role more generally as storyteller and spokesperson for fellow Blacks with the African tradition of the griot.

Prince was said to have been kidnapped in Africa at an early age and transported to Rhode Island, which dominated the colonial American slave trade. Soon after, her master, Ebenezer Wells, brought her to Deerfield, where she was baptized in 1735, during the religious revival known as the Great Awakening.

The Deerfield raid took place on 25 August 1746, a few days after the capture of Fort Massachusetts (North Adams) by a party of Frenchmen and Indians. After that surrender, sixty Abenakis hurried along the "Indian Path," near today's Mohawk Trail, and down the Deerfield Valley in search of more captives.

"Bars Fight" is the only surviving contemporaneous account of the attack, which occurred in a section south of the village known as "the Bars" (or meadows). Although Prince was enslaved at the time, her poem shows genuine sympathy for the white men and women who were killed that day, perhaps reflecting her status as a household servant and co-religionist with the colonists. The ballad was preserved in local memory until recorded in Josiah Holland's 1855 *History of Western Massachusetts*.

Lucy Terry remained a slave until an industrious free Black named Abijah (or Obijah) Prince married her in 1756. Their union produced six children, and two of the sons, Caesar and Festus, served in the War of Independence. Festus enlisted in the Continental Army at Stockbridge in 1779.

The Prince family was among the earliest settlers of Guilford, Vermont, and in 1785 became embroiled in a land dispute with a politically powerful white neighbor. Lucy Terry Prince, by then considered a "prodigy in conversation," addressed a petition to the authorities for redress. The governor, lieutenant governor, and six state councilors heard her presentation of the case and ruled in favor of the Princes.

Tradition links Prince with Williams College, specifically with an attempt to win admission of one of her sons, probably Festus. According to one account, "He was rejected on account of his race; the indignant mother argued the case in a '3-hour speech' before the Trustees, quoting abundantly text after text from the scriptures in support of her claim for his reception" (Proper 1997). Based on careful scrutiny of available written records, librarian and Deerfield historian David Proper concludes: "There is probably some truth behind this anecdote, although it defies documentation despite its plausibility."

Prince was sufficiently well known and respected in the area that, upon her death in 1821, a long obituary was published in newspapers in Greenfield, Massachusetts, and Bennington, Vermont, and a funeral oration was delivered by Rev. Lemuel Haynes, considered the most important Black man in America before Frederick Douglass's rise to prominence.

Richard Courage

Dorothy Amos, Educator

Born in Pittsfield, Massachusetts, Dorothy Reid Amos (1929–1974) was the youngest daughter of seven siblings. Her parents, Eula Blanks Reid and Edward Reid, left Winston Salem, North Carolina, to settle, in 1926, in Pittsfield, where a paternal uncle who worked for the railroad had stopped often. Dorothy grew up in a strong religious family and was a serious student from an early age, according to her older sister Rev. Fannie Reid Cooper. The family attended the Second Congregational Church, and Dorothy and her siblings were influenced by the teachings of Rev. Dr. Thomas Nelson Baker, the second minister at the church. Reverend Cooper said: "Dr. Baker made

An undated photo of Dorothy Amos. Photo courtesy of Reverend Willard Durant Collection.

sure that all of the children that came to his church were able to go to college. The older black people who came from the south made sure that their children got an education." Dorothy Amos was a product of such people.

Continuing her studies after graduation from Pittsfield High School, Amos received her BA from Central Ohio State College and her MA degree from North Adams State. She married John Amos— who ran a trucking business and was an amateur boxer—of North Adams. Dorothy became the first black guidance counselor in the Pittsfield school system. In 1970 she was named to the Massachusetts Advisory Committee to the U.S Commission on Civil Rights. In 1971 she founded the Early Childhood Development Center with her sister Rev. Fannie Cooper in Pittsfield. It was the first public day-care facility for low-income mothers in Pittsfield. An effective community leader, innovator, and educator, she died prematurely at forty-five. The child development center she founded now bears her name—the Dorothy Amos Community Preschool—and Pittsfield West Side Park, where she grew up, was renamed in her honor.

Frances Jones-Sneed

Eugene Brooks, Educator

Eugene ("Gene") LeRoy Brooks (1930–2001) was a much-admired educator in two states. An army veteran and graduate of State Teachers College at New Paltz, New York, he earned his master's degree from Teachers College at Columbia. He taught at Lincoln School in New Rochelle, New York, where he founded an adult evening school. Brooks then became principal of Webutuck Central School District's elementary school in Amenia, New York. After a brief "retirement," he served as assistant principal of Housatonic Valley Regional High School (HVRHS) in Falls Village, Connecticut, from 1985 until 1995. He was an active community member in Millerton, New York, where he lived, and with his wife, DeLora (DeShields), had two daughters.

Brooks, who had a booming voice and a fondness for Latin quotes, is remembered in three communities: the Eugene Brooks Middle School is named for him in Amenia; a garden and courtyard are dedicated to his memory at HVRHS; and the Harlem Valley Rail Trail's Eugene Brooks Rail Trail Station shelter bears his name in Millerton.

Bernard A. Drew

Margaret Alexander Hart, Educator

Margaret Alexander Hart as a teenager in her basketball uniform. Photo courtesy of Massachusetts College of Liberal Arts, Freel Library, Local History Archives.

Born on Hall Street in Williamstown, Massachusetts, Margaret Alexander Hart (1911–2004) was the only daughter of five children born to Henry Hart Sr. and Kate Curry Alexander. Margaret Hart's maternal grandmother, Margaret Curry Alexander, moved to Williamstown from North Carolina in the 1880s with Hart's mother. Her father migrated to upstate New York from North Carolina to work as a waiter in 1905. Later he came to Williamstown to find better employment and met Margaret's mother. The Harts were among the first Black entrepreneurs in Williamstown when Henry Hart started his own trucking business.

After graduating from Williamstown High School in 1930, Margaret Hart became the first Black graduate of the North Adams Normal School (later the Massachusetts College of Liberal Arts, or MCLA) in 1935. She completed her master's degree at Columbia Teachers College and then pursued a teaching career in Virginia, Indiana. Hart returned to her native Berkshires in the 1940s, where she was the first Black teacher in the Pittsfield public school system. Beginning her career in Pittsfield at Hubbard School, she also taught at the former Mercer School and retired in 1976 from North Junior High (later Reid Middle School), where she taught social studies as well as arts and crafts. Hart was always interested in the lives of the young people she met; she was able to engage students in conversations that bridged the gap between generations, speaking frankly in contemporary language. A consummate educator, she received an honorary doctorate for her work in education from MCLA in 1996, and in 2002 the college named a scholarship in her honor.

Because of her experience with discrimination, Hart became a member of the NAACP in Berkshire County. She ran its education division, creating quizzes for Black History Week.

An interviewer said of Hart, "She was one who always followed her dreams, persevered and never quit" (Hart 2000). Her high school yearbook notes that she was voted the Class Optimist and Best Natured. The quote below her name reads, "Oh, who will walk a mile with me along life's merry way?"—which illustrates how Hart came to live her life. She once said that her proudest moment was perhaps when she received an appointment at Hampton Institute (a historically Black college in Virginia, founded in 1870), because she felt the position allowed her to give back to her race. Hart was very proud of being an African American.

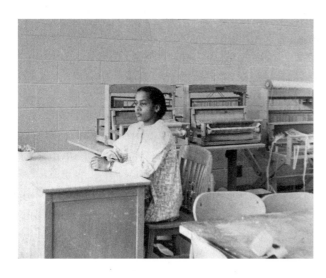

An undated photo of Margaret Alexander Hart teaching at her desk. Photo courtesy of Massachusetts College of Liberal Arts, Freel Library, Local History Archives.

When asked if she ever regretted returning to Williamstown in the 1940s when her father fell ill, Hart smiled her famous smile and replied simply, "No." As a student wrote in a tribute to her, "My sister stepped hard into the light. . . . She had dreams for you and me. So take the torch, and pass it on. . . . What rewards be yours is left up to you. The path she laid momentous beyond compare. My sister stepped hard into the light, barely stopping to gasp air."

Frances Jones-Sneed

David Lester Gunn Sr, Coach and Community Leader

David Lester Gunn Sr. (1899–1986) was born in Stockbridge, Massachusetts, on 12 November 1899 to Martin Sylvester Gunn and Sada Van Allen Gunn. While very young, he and his seven siblings migrated with their parents to the Berkshires from the state of New York.

David Gunn grew up and went to school in Stockbridge and then attended Hampton Institute and Benedict College, two historically African American schools in Virginia and South Carolina. After graduation he worked as a principal, coach, and athletic director in schools in Georgia, South Carolina, and North Carolina. He met Sinclara Hicks at Hampton Institute, and they were later married in Hillsdale, New York. The couple had three sons, David Lester Gunn Jr., St. Clair Reed Gunn, and Wray Martin Gunn.

In 1942 David Gunn returned to the Berkshires to help his sister Maude and her husband run their trucking business, Van Allen's Trucking, in Lenox. He coached basketball and baseball teams in 1943, 1945, and 1955 in the area, including at Lenox High School, Lenox School, Cornwall Academy, Windsor Mountain, and the Stockbridge School. At Cornwall Academy and Windsor Mountain, he was also athletic director. Gunn was probably the first Black coach hired at a public school in the county. He was certainly the first to be elected to the Hall of Fame at Lenox High School, as a coach, in 1985.

A community leader, Gunn also served as chairman of the deacons at the Congregational Church in Stockbridge and moderator of Berkshire South Congregational churches. Gunn and his siblings had grown up in the Congregational Church in

Stockbridge, although his sons and wife attended Clinton A. M. E. Zion Church in Great Barrington. In 1960 he was elected to the town Board of Health in Stockbridge and served several years as the health inspector, certainly a first in Stockbridge.

Gunn was active as well in a number of organizations, including the Stockbridge Lion's Club and St. John's Masonic Lodge #10 in Pittsfield, and was past chaplain of Prince Hall Masonic Temple. Both of these organizations were founded by African Americans and were connected to a large network of similar organizations. In addition, Gunn was a lifetime member and chairman of the Berkshire County branch of the NAACP. In fact, by traveling throughout the county to recruit people for the organization, he was instrumental in starting the Berkshire branch.

Frances Jones-Sneed

David Lester Gunn Sr. poses in the Stockbridge Library with a portrait of his ancestor Agrippa Hull. Photo courtesy of Stockbridge Library Historical Collection, Gary Leveille, and the *Berkshire Eagle*.

Teaching Black History and Culture

Since the 1970s there have been several different efforts to teach Black history and culture in the region's schools and colleges. It has not always been that way, and until after the civil rights movement of the 1950s and 1960s, Black history and culture was widely ignored. What was taught to Black children of their cultural heritage was done mostly in private—in homes by parents and grandparents and in church Sunday schools.

A pioneer in the teaching of Black history and culture has been Dr. Homer B. "Skip" Meade of Stockbridge. At the urging of several students who won approval from the Berkshire Hills Regional School Committee, he initiated a Black studies course at Monument Mountain Regional High School in 1971. Dr. Meade also taught at Simon's Rock College. In the spring of 2002 Berkshire Country Day School in Stockbridge launched a yearlong, school-wide study of the life and works of W. E. B. Du Bois. A member of the school's board of trustees, Meade brought awareness of the immense proportions of Du Bois's work to the school, as well as the significance of the centennial anniversary of the publishing of his most renowned work, *The Souls of Black Folk*. Students in every level were involved in a study of some aspect of Du Bois's life and contributions. Some students also explored writers of the Harlem Renaissance and the role of the artist in African American political life. The year culminated with an original play, *The World Beyond the Hill: The Life and Times of W. E. B. Du Bois*, written by Mickey Friedman and directed by John Hadden (both of Great Barrington) and performed at the Berkshire Theater Festival in Stockbridge. Chuck Cooper, Tony-winning actor from New York City, played Du Bois.

In 2001 the students of the Jubilee School of Philadelphia presented a program based on their yearlong study of W. E. B. Du Bois and his life in Great Barrington. The event was sponsored by the Clinton A. M. E. Zion Church, and Du Bois's stepson, David Graham Du Bois of the University of

The A.M.E Zion Mite Society

Churches provided education for Black children not available in public or private schools. Here, W. E. B. Du Bois, in one of his columns for the *New York Globe* (1884, 163) describes a performance of the African Methodist Episcopal Zion Mite Society in Great Barrington.

"Although the weather was at first threatening, it finally cleared off, so that at 3 P. M. the children began to gather at the residence of Mrs. L. Gardner, resplendent in holiday costumes. The afternoon was pleasantly passed until about six o'clock , when a beautiful repast was served to the young masters and misses. In the evening the parents began to arrive, and were treated to a literary and musical program which would have done justice to older heads. The opening was full chorus by the whole society. Then followed recitations by Miss Inez Gardner, Miss Bertha Wooster and Miss Jeanne Sumea, which was finely delivered. The solos and duets rendered by the Misses Bertha and Florence Wooster, Sumea, and Gardner, were very enjoyable. Master George Jackson also delivered an interesting declamation. Miss Lulu Jackson, who was the organist of the evening, played "Webster's Funeral March," "Lily Waltz" and several other pieces."

Ruth D. Jones at the Simon's Rock College Alumni Library in 2002. Photo courtesy of Joan Goodkind, Simon's Rock College Alumni Library.

Massachusetts at Amherst, was the guest speaker. This presentation was among the first to reflect back to the town what the town had so far failed to do to recognize Du Bois and his legacy. The Jubilee students also partnered with Undermountain Elementary School students in Sheffield and shared a yearlong distance-study experience together.

The three area colleges, as of this writing, have also been involved in teaching Black history and culture. Simon's Rock College in Great Barrington has, for many years, designated full-need scholarships for students of color. In the early 1970s the college library established a Du Bois Collection in African American history and culture, and with support from the Spingold Foundation, it hosts an annual Du Bois lecture. In 2006 Simon's Rock students were among those who went to Ghana on a study tour. Williams College offers an African-American Studies and Africana Diaspora Program, which cuts across the curriculum. The program is augmented by endowed special lectures, the Bolin and

Homer Meade in Great
Barrington in 2006, viewing
film footage of the 1969 W. E. B.
Du Bois Memorial dedication.
Photo by Rachel Fletcher.

Sterling Brown visiting professorships, the Allison Davis lecture series, and active theater, dance, and music ensembles. Williams faculty members hold winter study sessions in Africa, the Caribbean, or South America. At Berkshire Community College, Prof. Barbara Bartle teaches a course on the Harlem Renaissance.

Massachusetts College of Liberal Arts offers a Local History Program, and several students have gathered information on local Black history, including census and land records and oral histories. The college is also one of the sponsors, along with the Upper Housatonic Valley African American Heritage Trail, of "The Shaping Role of Place in African American Biography," a K–12 curriculum development project funded by the National Endowment for the Humanities (NEH) and given special designation as an NEH "We the People" project. The goal of this project initiative is to "encourage and strengthen the teaching, study, and understanding of American history and culture through the support of projects that explore significant events and themes in our nation's history and culture and that advance knowledge of the principles that define America." The project joins teachers from schools in Berkshire County, Massachusetts, with an interdisciplinary team of consulting scholars and local history researchers to explore intersections of the local landscape with nationally decisive moments. Using primary sources, historical narratives, and biographical accounts of these figures, participants generate curriculum units and materials to meet the challenges of new curriculum frameworks. The first institute was held in the summer of 2005, and a national conference was scheduled for September 2006. The University of Massachusetts at Amherst also has been active in the region. It has run three summer archaeological field schools at the Du Bois Homesite in Great Barrington under the direction of Prof. Robert Paynter. And several faculty members, including Profs. Paynter, David Graham Du Bois, and William Strickland, have lectured in Great Barrington.

David Levinson, Rachel Fletcher, Elaine S. Gunn,
Frances Jones-Sneed, and Ellen Broderick

Sources

Struggles and Achievements

Baskette, Dayna, et al. "Black Williams: A Written History." *Winter Study* (Jan. 2003).

Berkshire Eagle, 10 July 1969.

Berkshire Eagle, 5 April 1982.

Berkshire Eagle, Obituary, 21 Dec. l983.

Berkshire Eagle, Obituary, 23 Feb. 2004.

Berkshire Medical Institute. Yearly catalogs. [Available in the Local History Room, Berkshire Athenaeum. Pittsfield, MA.]

Childs, Dr. H. H. to Oliver Wendell Holmes. Letter, 12 Dec. 1850. Martin Delany File, Countway Library, Harvard Medical School, Boston, MA.

"City Elects 1st Negro in School Board Contest." *Berkshire Eagle*, 8 Nov. 1967.

Coenen, Christopher. *Sheffield 1773–1983; A Pictorial Recollection.* Sheffield, MA: Sheffield 250th Anniversary Committee, 1983.

Dombrowski, Tony. "The Final Frontier." *Berkshire Eagle*, 19 June 2006, A1, A5.

Gates, Henry Louis, and Nellie Y. McKay, eds. *Norton Anthology of African American Literature.* New York: W. W. Norton & Co., 2004.

Gunn, Elaine. Personal communication with David Levinson, 4 Nov. 2004.

Madisyn Consulting Services. "May Edward Chinn: Doctor of Science." http://www.hometoharlem.com/ harlem/hthcult.nsf/notables/ mayedwardchinn (accessed 11 Nov. 2004.

Proper, David R. *Lucy Terry Prince— Singer of History.* Deerfield, MA: Pocumtuck Valley Memorial Association and Historic Deerfield, Inc., 1992.

RandomHouse.com. "Online Catalog: Angel of Harlem: A Novel." http://www.randomhouse.com/ catalog/display.pperl?0375508708 (accessed 11 Nov. 2004).

"Simon's Rock Honors Du Bois." *Berkshire Eagle*, 24 Feb. 1973.

Smith, Jean. "Recognition and Reward." *Berkshire Eagle*, 20 May 2006.

Turner, Steve. "Berkshire Blacks: The Struggle for Equality Began Two Centuries Ago." *Berkshire Eagle*, 28 Aug. 1976.

Yale University. "Honoring a Local Nineteenth Century African-American Philanthropist." News release, 20 Oct. 1999. http://www. yale.edu/opa/newsr/99-10-20-03. all.html (accessed 11 Nov. 2004).

Lucy Terry Prince, Author

Gates, Henry Louis, and Nellie McKay, eds. *Norton Anthology of African American Literature.* New York: Norton, 2004.

Proper, David. *Lucy Terry Prince— Singer of History.* Deerfield, MA: Pocumtuck Valley Memorial Association and Historic Deerfield, Inc., 1997.

Southern, Eileen. *The Music of Black Americans: A History.* New York: Norton, 1971.

Dorothy Amos, Educator

Berkshire Eagle, 10 July 1969. Rev. Fannie Reid Cooper. Interview with Frances Jones-Sneed, August 2005.

Eugene Brooks, Educator

Epstein, Ruth, and Joy Barbieri. "Educator Brooks Much Beloved." *Lakeville Journal,* 12 April 2001.

"Eugene LeRoy Brooks." *Millerton News,* 12 April 2001.

Margaret Alexander Hart, Educator

Hart, Margaret A. Interview by Frances Jones-Sneed, 5 Dec. 2002, Williamstown, MA. [Located in the Local History Collection of the Eugene Freel Library at the Massachusetts College of Liberal Arts, North Adams, MA.]

Hart, Margaret A. Interview by Kassie Modzleski, 14 March 2000, Williamstown, MA. [Located in the Local History Collection of the Eugene Freel Library at the Massachusetts College of Liberal Arts, North Adams, MA.]

Hart, Margaret A. Interview by Michelle Pean and Earlisha Stanley, 15 March 2001, Williamstown, MA. [Located in the Local History Collection of the Eugene Freel Library at the Massachusetts College of Liberal Arts, North Adams, MA.]

"Margaret Hart." *Berkshire Eagle,* 21 May 1996.

"MCLA Honors First African American Graduate—Margaret Hart." *The Advocate,* 14 Feb. 2001.

David Lester Gunn, Sr., Coach and Community Leader

Obituary of David L. Gunn Sr., 27 March 1986, First Congregational Church, Stockbridge, MA.

Wray Gunn. Interview with Frances Jones-Sneed, April 2005, Stockbridge, MA.

Teaching Black History and Culture

Rodgers, Bernard F. "Letter to the Editor." *Berkshire Eagle,* 8 Sept. 2003.

Military Service

From the American Revolution to the Vietnam War, and into the war in Iraq, Black men (and sometimes women) from Berkshire County have willingly served in the military. This record of usually voluntary service is especially remarkable when one considers that only since the Vietnam War have African Americans enjoyed access to full civil rights and served in integrated units. The entries that follow trace some of this history of service and sacrifice.

American Revolution

During the War for Independence, which began in the spring of 1775, slaves and free Black men and women played a significant role in fighting for freedom for both the country and themselves, taking advantage of whatever opportunities were available to them. Military companies throughout the colony quickly formed or expanded—some with Black men in their ranks—and responded to events in Massachusetts and elsewhere. Black soldiers had been a part of military forces in America since at least the early 1700s. Though included during war, they were barred from the ranks during peacetime.

Beginning in 1775, thousands of Blacks ran away from owners; some hid and joined the American forces; some accepted the British invitation to help fight slave owners; others petitioned for their freedom in the courts on the grounds that it was their natural right. George Washington quickly ended Black service in the Continental Army, but this exclusionary policy was reversed in 1777 after Lord Dunmore, the British governor of Virginia, declared all Blacks free who were willing and able to bear arms in the British Army. Both the British Army and the Continental Army regiments and militia companies throughout the colonies were having difficulty filling ranks. In response, the Continental Army accepted both slave and free Blacks, promising slaves that they would receive their freedom at the end of their enlistment. Provisions were made for the government to pay compensation to owners for all slaves freed in this way. The owners were to receive $1,000, while the freed slave would receive $50 at the end of enlistment.

Each town had enlistment quotas to fill and was fined if they did not produce enough men. It was legal for people to hire substitutes, including free Blacks and slaves with their owners' permission. A 1777 law allowed slave owners to free their slaves without any future financial responsibility for them.

Some slaves were freed before enlisting, others after their service, while some had no agreement. They joined for freedom, patriotism, money, out of service to a master, or to escape from one.

Eight African Americans from the northwest Connecticut upper Housatonic Valley are known to have served during the Revolution: Thomas Sackett (1778), Jack Freedom (1781), Samuel Green (1776), and (Samuel?) Heth (?–1776) from Cornwall; Call Freeman (1777–1783) from Kent; Jupiter Mars from Norfolk; Negor from Sharon; and William James (1777–1780) from Warren. They served collectively for nearly the entire war.

Many Black men from western Massachusetts also fought in the Revolutionary War. Negroes Brister and Cyrus took up arms from Cheshire (then called New Providence), as did York Kilborn (or Kilburn), Negro Morton, and John Adams from Great Barrington. Negro Cato, William Johnson, Monday Manley, and Primus Putnam went from Lanesboro; Negro Peter, from Lee. Pittsfield sent quite a few: Jabez Abro, Anthony Clever (or Cleaver), Prince Hall, Jeffrey Hazard, Negro Titus, and Ezegial Comer. Thomas Brown was reported in the state record, without his residence, as a "Negro" servant to a Colonel Brown, serving as a waiter to the chaplain. Ishmael Richards went from Richmond, as did Thomas Smith and John Van Huff. Frank Dunkin (or Duncan) went from West Stockbridge. Stockbridge appears to have had the most: Samuel Adderthorn, Negro Guy, Humphrey Hubbard, James Storm, William Erving, Festus Prince, Caesar Freeman, Agrippa Hull, Negro Humphrey, Cato Mumford (also given as Mumfrey or Muffy), Titus Pomp, and Prince Wanton.

Barbara Bartle, Emilie Piper, Bernard A. Drew, and Jonathan Olly

Agrippa Hull, American Revolution Veteran and Caterer

I n his day Agrippa Hull (1759–1848) was the best-known Black person in Berkshire County. Born free in Northampton, he came to Stockbridge as a youth of six. Stockbridge was an unusual community at the time, being home not only to English and Dutch settlers and free and enslaved Blacks but also to a tribe of Native Americans (today known as the Stockbridge-Munsee Band of the Mohican Nation).

In 1777 Hull joined Maj. Gen. John Patterson's regiment; he then became an orderly to the Polish general Thaddeus Kosciusko, who served the American cause during the Revolutionary War. "Grippy" one day dressed himself in the absent general's resplendent uniform and performed for orderlies of the other officers, only to be caught in the act by the general and disciplined.

After the war Hull returned to Stockbridge and became a butler in the house of the lawyer Theodore Sedgwick, often accompanying Sedgwick as he fulfilled his duties in both the House of Representatives and Senate, which at that time met in New York. When the Marquis de Lafayette came to New York years after the war, Hull traveled there to renew his acquaintance with him. The historian Francis Parkman interviewed Hull during a visit to Stockbridge in 1844.

"Grippy is one of the few who will be immortal in our village annals," novelist Catharine M. Sedgwick declared, adding, "He had a fund of humor and mother wit, and was a sort of Sancho Panza in the village, always trimming other men's follies with a keen perception and the biting wit of wisdom" (Sedgwick 1871). Hull owned a home south of Stockbridge village, on Goodrich Street,

Portrait of Agrippa Hull, painted from an 1840s daguerreotype. Photo courtesy of Stockbridge Library Historical Collection.

now gone. His visage survives in a daguerreotype made by Anson Clark of West Stockbridge in about 1844. The photograph provided the basis for an oil portrait that shows an almost regal figure. Both images are in the Stockbridge Library collection.

Bernard A. Drew and Emilie Piper

"Grippy [Agrippa Hull] is one of the few who will be immortal in our village annals. He had a fund of humor and mother wit, and was a sort of Sancho Panza in the village, always trimming other men's follies with a keen perception and the biting wit of wisdom." Catharine M. Sedgwick

Civil War:
The 54th Massachusetts
Volunteer Infantry Regiment

The 54th Massachusetts Volunteer Infantry Regiment was the first official all-Black regiment from Massachusetts to serve in the United States armed forces. When war first broke out between the states, white northern officials considered the idea of forming an all-Black regiment. But the regiment was not created as part of the pursuit of equality; rather, it was born of the need in early 1863 for a new crop of fighting infantry to replenish a dwindling supply. The unit gained national fame in 1989 via the Academy Award–winning film *Glory*, depicting its exploits and starring Denzel Washington, Morgan Freeman, and Matthew Broderick.

There was no question of whether the men would enlist; these men, who had suffered mistreatment and disrespect, were nonetheless all too willing to fight to defend the Union. They wanted desperately to prove that they too were true citizens of the United States. But it did not prove to be easy. If war is hell, then what can be said for those

Veterans of the G. A. R. of Sheffield assembled in the early 1900s. Edward Augustus Croslear of the 54th Massachusetts is third from the right. Taken in front of the Town Hall with others from the 49th Massachusetts Regiment. Photo courtesy of Sheffield Historical Society, Mark Dewey Research Center.

whose existence had been hell before they faced war? Still, the men of the 54th Regiment pressed on. When it came time to receive their first wages for their greatly needed services, they discovered that their pay was a mere $7 instead of $10, $3 less than that of a white soldier. They declined these insulting wages, waiting until protests forced the government to give them full pay as well as back pay.

The commissioned officers were white. An exception to this rule was Edward Emerson from Pittsfield, who was commissioned a second lieutenant on 3 June 1863 as a seventeen-year-old student. He was promoted to first lieutenant on 19 July 1863. Wounded at Honey Hill, South Carolina, on 30 November 1864, he continued his service with the 54th until 14 July 1865, going on to serve as a captain with the 34th Massachusetts Infantry.

The 54th Regiment did not see any action until July 1863, when it made an assault on Fort Wagner, in South Carolina's Charleston harbor. Though nearly one-half of the regiment was killed, wounded, or taken prisoner, the failed assault proved that Black men would fight as bravely for their country as white men. Colonel Robert Gould Shaw, the white regiment commander, a member of a prominent Boston abolitionist family, died with his men in the attack. Shaw's widow, Anna Kneeland Haggerty of New York and Lenox, is buried in the cemetery of the Church on the Hill in Lenox. They had spent their honeymoon at her father's Lenox "cottage," Ventfort Hall.

In all, eighty-seven Black and white men from Berkshire County have been documented as serving in the 54th Massachusetts. The list follows on page 74.

Frances Jones-Sneed and David Levinson

Medallion of the Niagara Movement 1905 (precursor to the NAACP), depicting the monument dedicated to Col. Robert Gould Shaw and the soldiers of the 54th Massachusetts Regiment —the first Black unit in the north to serve in the Civil War. Based on sculpture by August Saint-Gaudens and the monument in the Boston Common, dedicated on 31 May 1897. Photo courtesy of Special Collections and Archives, W. E. B. Du Bois Library, University of Massachusetts, Amherst.

Berkshire County Volunteers in the 54th Massachusetts Regiment

Name	Age	Occupation	Enlistment/muster date
Becket			
Anthony L. King	21	gentleman	8/24/1864
Chester			
Justin M. Duncan	19	laborer	3/30/1863
Dalton			
Edward Hoose	21	farmer	12/04/1863
Great Barrington			
John R. Ferris	27	laborer	11/28/1863
Ralph B. Gardner	23	laborer	3/30/1863
Franklin Gover	19	farmer	3/30/1863
Abraham A. Jackson	24	farmer	7/15/1863
Francis J. Jackson	18	laborer	3/30/1863
James H. Jackson	18	waiter	3/30/1863
Levi H. Jackson	29	waiter	3/30/1863
William A. Stevens	19	farmer	3/30/1863
Jacob H. Thomas	26	farmer	3/30/1863
Charles P. Thompson	21	farmer	3/30/1863
David H. Van Allen	33	laborer	12/08/1863
Edward H. Williams	34	laborer	11/30/1863
Hinsdale			
Lorenzo S. Duncan	21	farmer	12/15/1863
Thompson Freeman	36	farmer	12/15/1863
Frank Hamilton	40	farmer	12/14/1863
Frank Hamilton II	22	farmer	12/15/1863
Charles W. Potter	28	barber	7/15/1863
Lanesboro			
Henry E. Jones	19	farmer	11/30/1863
William Parret	n.a.	n.a.	7/14/1863
Lee			
Henry F. Burghardt	22	mason	3/30/1863
George M. Pell	30	farmer	7/15/1863
James E. Sharts	24	farmer	3/30/1863
William H. Sharts	23	laborer	3/30/1863
Aaron Spencer	20	farmer	3/30/1863
Lenox			
David Addison	18	farmer	9/02/1864
Jacob Adams	39	laborer	3/20/1863
Henry J. Carter	29	stonecutter	4/23/1863
John Hall	34	sailor	3/30/1863

Thomas Jackson	21	unknown	3/30/1863
George G. Peters	19	farmer	3/30/1863
Edward Porter	44	farmer	9/19/1864
Peter H. Pruyn	26	boatman	3/30/1863
Charles Van Allen	29	farmer	3/30/1863
Henry Van Alstine	23	farmer	3/30/1863
John E. Vosburght	24	blacksmith	3/30/1863
George E. Waterman	27	farmer	3/30/1863
Samuel Weaver	30	farmer	3/30/1863
Monterey			
Charles Jackson	18	laborer	12/17/1863
Jeremiah Nokes	28	laborer	12/15/1863
Charles Swan	33	laborer	12/17/1863
Henry Swan	45	laborer	12/18/1863
William Wells	30	laborer	11/30/1863
Peru			
Joseph Kelson	22	laborer	12/17/1863
Pittsfield			
Levi Bird	37	blacksmith	4/23/1863
Orrin Duncan	30	seaman	8/17/1863
Edward B. Emerson	17	student	7/10/1863
Merrick Fletcher	43	farmer	3/30/1863
Moses Foster	19	farmer	12/21/1863
Eli Franklin	32	laborer	3/30/1863
Alexander Gaines	20	porter	12/14/1863
George W. Green	18	laborer	12/17/1863
Henry Hamilton	24	farmer	12/15/1863
Paul Hamilton	19	farmer	12/21/1863
Samuel Harrison	44	clergy	11/12/1863
Samuel D. Jackson	32	farmer	12/14/1863
Samuel Jones	19	laborer	12/17/1863
William Peters	27	porter	7/14/1863
Charles A. Potter	18	laborer	4/23/1863
George A. Ringgold	20	barber	3/30/1863
John Van Blake	21	laborer	3/30/1863
George A. Wilson	23	laborer	7/14/1863
Henry Wilson	19	laborer	12/17/1863
Sheffield			
David Addison	25	laborer	3/30/1863
Edward A. Croslear	26	laborer	12/07/1863
Milo J. Freeland	22	laborer	3/30/1863
John C. Harris	20	farmer	12/12/1863

George Jarvis	18	laborer	12/09/1863
Nathaniel H. Johnson	24	carpenter	3/30/1863
Norman Johnson	22	farmer	7/15/1863
William Jones	45	laborer	12/08/1863
Edward Moore	36	laborer	3/30/1863
Henry J. Tucker	34	butcher	3/30/1863
Ira Waterman	19	farmer	12/12/1863
South Adams			
Jeremiah L. W. Bradley	34	farmer	12/08/1863
Stockbridge			
John I. Clow	37	laborer	12/08/1863
Charles H. Piper	23	farmer	7/15/1863
Charles T. Way	21	laborer	5/13/1863
John Q. Williams	21	farmer	12/08/1863
Velorous W. Williams	43	laborer	12/15/1863
Tyringham			
William T. Taylor	18	farmer	12/18/1863
Amos Williams	25	farmer	7/15/1863

Milo J. Freeland, First to Fulfill His Term with the 54th Massachusetts Regiment

According to his gravestone in Hillside Cemetery, East Canaan, Connecticut, Milo Freeland was "the first Colored Man to enlist from the North in the rebellion of 1861." Recent research indicates that he was the second to enlist, but the first to fulfill his term. Freeland reported for military duty with the all-Black 54th Massachusetts Volunteer Infantry Regiment in February 1863, a month after Abraham Lincoln issued the Emancipation Proclamation. As a private,

Photographs of five soldiers of the 54th Massachusetts Regiment. Milo Freeland is in the center. Photo courtesy of Florida State Archives Collection.

76

he saw intense action in July 1863 at impregnable Fort Wagner in South Carolina. After his discharge Freeland farmed, off Boardman Street in Sheffield, Massachusetts. He later went to work for Lyman Dunning in East Canaan, and died there in 1883 of pneumonia, leaving behind a pregnant wife and five children. Freeland's deteriorated grave marker was replaced with a replica, dedicated with a parade and ceremony in 1996. The cemetery is off Route 44; his grave is at the upper, east end of the cemetery.

Bernard A. Drew

Edward Augustus Croslear, Civil War Veteran and Farmer

A native of New York state, Edward Augustus Croslear (c. 1820–1915), a deacon of the A. M. E. Church, was a hard-working farmer amidst an enclave of Blacks living on Berkshire School Road in Sheffield. Descended from New York state slaves, he was held in high esteem for his good citizenship and Christian character, according to his obituary notice. His wife, Lucy (died 1905), was a native of Sheffield.

Croslear purchased a one-acre farm in 1854, and expanded it by 5 acres in 1867. A Civil War veteran, he was a charter member of Barnard post, Grand Army of the Republic of Sheffield. When it disbanded, he joined D. G. Anderson post of Great Barrington.

Croslear wanted it known that Black people were respectable and newsworthy. He sent an item to *The Berkshire Courier*. The editor, who apparently couldn't abide poor spelling and grammar, made an example of it: "Sheffield Mass Saterday Nov 16 1867 Mr Edeter Dear Sir I wish to inform you of the

Edward Augustus Croslear, Civil War veteran, 54th Massachusetts Regiment, standing in partial Civil War uniform in front of the General Store, Sheffield, now the Old Stone Store, an exhibit space for the Sheffield Historical Society. Photo c.1890–1900. Photo courtesy of Sheffield Historical Society, Mark Dewey Research Center, Carrie Smith Lorraine photo.

festable that our Colard lady held here on thursday of last Week for the benefit of our Colard Minster Mr. Thomson there Was a very good attendance for allthough the Wether Was unfavorable there Was a ver Good atendance some from Bridgeport and Stockbridge the Colard People of Sheffield are having a very Nice Relegeaus Meeting in Sheffield and are in hopes of Buelding themselves up Dear sir Please to Print this in your Next Paper that they may see that the Colard People are trying to bee some body. truly yours EAC" (Croslear 1867). Still, Croslear made his point.

Bernard A. Drew

Edward Augustus and Lucy Croslear of Sheffield, c. 1890–1900. Photo courtesy of Sheffield Historical Society, Mark Dewey Research Center, Carrie Smith Lorraine photo.

Civil War: Other Massachusetts Units and Service

While many people are familiar with the glorious and brave achievements of the 54th Regiment, there are several other less-known units that Black men from Berkshire County served in. These include the 55th Massachusetts Infantry; 5th U.S. Colored Heavy Artillery; 5th Regiment, Massachusetts Volunteer Cavalry; 52nd U.S. Colored Infantry; and the U.S. Colored Troops (USCT). Most served in the 5th Regiment, Massachusetts Volunteer Cavalry, which was mustered in early 1864 and saw action in Virginia, although at first as an infantry unit. After the close of the Civil War, the unit was stationed briefly in Texas before the men were mustered out.

Not only did Black troops serve on land but several served on the sea, in the Union navy:

- John Bowen, Kent, 26 years old, seaman
- Daniel Collier, Stockbridge, 18 years old, seaman
- Joshua Foster, Pittsfield, 20 years old, landsman
- Theodore Gunn, Pittsfield, 18 years old, ordinary seaman
- Henry Hector, Salisbury, 21 years old, landsman
- Ira E. Jackson, Stockbridge, 27 years old, seaman
- Mason Jones, Pittsfield, 22 years old, landsman
- Andrew Langston, Canaan, 21 years old, landsman
- John M. Pierce, Norfolk, 26 years old, landsman

- Anthony Van Alstyne, Sheffield, 22 years old, landsman
- Isaac William, Berkshires, 34 years old, landsman and second class fireman

A rating of seaman meant the individual had five years' experience. In addition, John Richards of Pittsfield had served as a crewman in the Pacific on the whaler Rebecca Sims out of New Bedford from 1828 to 1832.

Susan Denault, Deb Calderara, Tim Herene, and Jonathan Olly

Men from Berkshire County Who Served in the 5th Regiment, Massachusetts Volunteer Cavalry

Name	Age	Occupation	Enlistment/muster date
Great Barrington			
John Carr	22	laborer	6/03/1864
Othello Jackson	21	waiter	3/04/1864
John McArthur	22	laborer	3/12/1864
Timothy Pelton	21	clerk	8/01/1865
George W. Suma	26	teamster	3/04/1864
Jacob H. Thomas	26	farmer	3/30/1864
Hinsdale			
William Michaels	35	gardener	3/04/1864
William F. Thompson	36	farmer	10/31/1865
Lanesboro			
Sylvester Moores	26	laborer	3/04/1864
Lee			
George R. W. Chadwell	24	laborer	1/29/1864
Frederick B. Randolph	18	laborer	1/29/1864
Thomas Watson	21	farmer	6/03/1864
Henry Weaver	20	laborer	6/15/1864
Lenox			
Alexander Adams	18	farmer	9/021864
Alfred Michael	19	farmer	9/03/1864
Pittsfield			
Richmond Birdsound	25	farmer	3/01/1865
Augustus Fields	19	laborer	12/17/1863
John E. Gillard	30	barber	3/04/1864
Benjamin F. Porter	21	barber	3/12/1864
John A. William	37	laborer	1/29/1864
New Ashford			
Isaac Johnson	37	hostler	3/04/1864

New Marlborough

Edward B. Benton	36	laborer	2/29/1864

Otis

Homer C. Dolphin	36	farmer	3/10/1864
Joshua Rodman	25	farmer	1/29/1864
Charles Van Hoesen	30	farmer	1/29/1864

Sheffield

Frances Boyd	25	laborer	4/22/1864
Daniel Brown	23	teamster	1/29/1864
Albert Frasier	18	farmer	4/12/1864
George Hicks	25	laborer	1/09/1864
Edward Johnson	21	laborer	11/18/1864
George Mars	30	laborer	1/29/1864
Robert Millier	24	laborer	4/29/1864
Benjamin Simons	18	laborer	5/05/1864

Stockbridge

Theodore Martin	33	farmer	1/29/1864

West Stockbridge

Robert H. Roberson	18	laborer	1/02/1864
Albert (or Henry) M. Rogers	40	laborer	1/29/1864

Men who served in other units were
(note that some men served in more than one unit):

Anthony L. King	Becket	55th Mass.	21	gentleman	8/24/1864
Milton M. Gardner	Dalton	55th Mass.	37	teamster	8/30/1864
Dexter M. Jackson	Lee	55th Mass.	30	farmer	1/29/1864
Richmond Birdsound	Pittsfield	U.S. Col. Artillery	25	farmer	3/01/1865
Daniel F. Philips	Pittsfield	55th Mass.	30	cook	6/22/1863
Abraham Reynolds	Pittsfield	52nd Mass.	36	farmer	3/04/1865
Franklin J. Dickerson	Richmond	55th Mass.	25	laborer	12/08/1863

Civil War: The 29th and 31st
Connecticut Volunteer Infantry Regiments

Reflecting improved attitudes, but still segregated thinking, toward African Americans, Connecticut followed Massachusetts's lead in forming units of Black soldiers commanded by white commissioned officers. Fifty-two men from northwest Connecticut served during the war, predominantly in the 29th and 31st Connecticut Volunteer Infantry Regiments. Each community contributed the following: Canaan, five; North Canaan, one; Colebrook six; Cornwall, four; Kent, one; Norfolk, seven; Salisbury, twelve; and Sharon, sixteen. Half were wounded or killed. William Bush of Sharon served in the 14th Connecticut Regiment, an all-white unit, perhaps because of his light skin color.

Jonathan Olly

This plaque from the Civil War monument in Sharon, Connecticut, lists Charles Reed and Charles Treadway, who served with the 29th Connecticut Volunteer Infantry Regiment. Photos by Constance Brooks.

Honoring Those Who Fought for Freedom

In his "Address to the Nation, delivered on 16 August 1900 at the Second Annual Meeting of the Niagara Movement in Harper's Ferry, West Virginia, W. E. B. Du Bois delivered a stirring speech—still considered a classic in the art of rhetoric. Below is an excerpt from that address.

And we shall win. The past promised it, the present foretells it. Thank God for John Brown! Thank God for Garrison and Douglass! Sumner and Phillips, Nat Turner and Robert Gould Shaw, and all the hallowed dead who died for freedom! Thank God for all those today, few though their voice be, who have not forgotten the divine brotherhood of all men, white and black, rich and poor, fortunate and unfortunate.

Source: Du Bois, W. E. B. "Address to the Nation." (16 August 1900). http://www.wfu.edu/%7Ezulick/341/niagara.html (accessed 19 April 2006).

Northwest Connecticut Volunteers in the 29th and 31st Regiments

Name	Regiment	Enlistment/muster date
Canaan		
Frank Hamilton	29th	3/08/1864
Joseph Parks	29th	8/18/1864
James Royce	29th	3/08/1864
Joseph Vance	29th	9/19/1864
Edward C. Wooster	29th	3/08/1864
North Canaan		
Sylvester Lee	29th	3/08/1864
Colebrook		
Walter A. Arnum	29th	3/08/1864
Elias Hickox	29th	3/08/1864
Samuel Hickox	29th	12/08/1863
Warren Nelson	29th	3/08/1864
Charles St. John	29th	3/08/1864
Henry L. White	29th	3/08/1864
Cornwall		
George H. Green	29th	3/08/1864
Peter Howard	29th	died during training
John Lepyon	29th	3/08/1864
John L. Watson	29th	3/08/1864
Kent		
Henry H. Fitch	29th	3/08/1864
Norfolk		
Chauncey Crossley	54th (MA)	7/02/1863
Alanson Freeman	29th	3/08/1864
Henry Freeman	29th	3/08/1864
Edward Hines	54th (MA)	3/30/1863
Joseph Prime	29th	3/08/1864
Ensign Prince	29th	3/08/1864
Samuel Smith	29th	3/08/1864
Salisbury		
John S. Addison	29th	3/08/1864
Charles Brown	29th	3/08/1864
Charles Brown	29th	3/08/1864
John Brown	29th	3/08/1864
Jesse W. Davis	29th	3/08/1864
Simon M. DeWitt	29th	3/08/1864
George H. Foote	29th	3/08/1864
Henry A. Freeman	29th	3/08/1864

William Glasco	29th	3/08/1864
Joseph Hydre	29th	3/08/1864
Edward Jackson	29th	3/08/1864
Abram Wethington	31st	4/08/1864
Sharon		
Henry E. Bush	n.a.	not available
William Bush	14th (CT)	not available
James Carl	29th	3/08/1864
George Dunbar	n.a.	not available
William H. Gaul	29th	3/08/1864
David Hector	31st	2/12/1864
James B. Johnson	29th	3/08/1864
William H. Logan	29th	3/08/1864
Charles Loretta	31st	3/15/1864
John Lynch	29th	3/08/1864
Miles Pedro	29th	3/08/1864
Charles E. Reed	29th	3/08/1864
Josiah Starr	29th	3/08/1864
Lewis H. Starr	29th	3/08/1864
Charles H. Treadway	29th	3/08/1864
Almon L. Wheeler	29th	3/08/1864

The Sharon, Connecticut, Soldiers' Monument, erected in 1885. Four names on the monument are of African Americans who served in the Civil War: Henry Bush, William Gaul, Charles Reed, and Charles Treadway. Photos by Constance Brooks.

The Fall of Richmond: A Black Soldier's Perspective

J. J. Hill, orderly for Col. W. B. Wooster, commander of the 29th Connecticut Colored Infantry Regiment, describes the capture of the Confederate capital in April 1865, and the brief visit there by President Abraham Lincoln in his book *A Sketch of the 29th Regiment of Connecticut Colored Troops*. Part of the description is reprinted below.

All was quiet here until the 1st of April, when all was in readiness, and the order was given to strike tents and move on to Richmond. During Sunday night the brigade was out in line of battle, and at three o'clock in the morning the rebels blew up three gun boats and commenced vacating their works in our front. At 5 A.M the troops commenced to advance on the rebel works—the 29th taking the advance, the 9th U.S.C.[olored] troops next. Soon refugees from the rebels came in by hundreds. Col. W. B. Wooster passed them about, and made them go before the regiment and dig up the torpedoes that were left in the ground to prevent the progress of the Union Army. They were very numerous, but to the surprise of officers and men, none of the army were injured by them.

On our march to Richmond, we captured 500 pieces of artillery, some of the largest kind, 6,000 small arms, and the prisoners I was not able to number. The road was strewed with all kinds of obstacles, and men were lying all along the distance of seven miles. The main body of the army went up the New Market road. The 29th skirmished all the way, and arrived in the city at 7 A.M., and were the first infantry that entered the city; they went at double quick most of the way. When Col. Wooster came to Main St. he pointed his sword at the capitol, and said "Double quick, march," and the company charged through the main street to the capitol and halted in the square until the rest of the regiment came up.

Very soon after the arrival of the white troops the colored troops were moved on the outskirts of the city, and as fast as the white troops came in the colored troops were ordered out, until we occupied the advance. The white troops remained in the city as guards. We remained on the outpost.

[On April] 3d President Lincoln visited the city. No triumphal march of a conqueror could have equalled in moral sublimity the humble manner in which he entered Richmond. I was standing on the bank of the James river viewing the scene of desolation when a boat, pulled by twelve sailors, came up the stream. It contained President Lincoln and his son... In some way the colored people on the bank of the river ascertained that the tall man wearing the black hat was President Lincoln. There was a sudden shout and clapping of hands. I was very much amused at the plight of one officer who had in charge fifty colored men to put to work on the ruined buildings; he found himself alone, for they left work and crowded to see the President. As he approached I said to a woman, "Madam, there is the man that made you free." She ex-claimed, "Is that President Lincoln?" My reply was in the affirmative.

She gazed at him with clasped hands and said, "Glory to God. Give Him praise for his goodness," and she shouted till her voice failed her.

Source: Hill, J. J. *A Sketch of the 29th Regiment of Connecticut Colored Troops*. Baltimore, 1867, 25–27.

World War I

On 6 April 1917 the United States declared war on Germany and officially entered the Great War. On 18 May 1917 the Selective Service Act was passed, which authorized the president to increase military forces. This act required every male living in the United States between the ages of eighteen and forty-five to register for the draft. However, not all the men who registered necessarily served in the military, and also there were many who served but did not register for the draft.

Black leaders and others supported and encouraged Black men to enlist in the military despite racial tensions in the United States. W. E. B. Du Bois stated in the July 1918 issue of *The Crisis* (journal of the National Association for the Advancement of Colored People): "[We] close our ranks shoulder to shoulder with our fellow citizens and the allied nations that are fighting for democracy. . . . We make not ordinary sacrifice, but we make it gladly and willingly with our eyes

Charles Persip of Pittsfield (second from left) marching in Memorial Day Parade in the 1970s. Photo courtesy of Mrs. Frances Persip Duval Collection and *Berkshire Eagle*.

lifted to the hills" (Lanning 1997, 130). But the American public was not willing to accept Black soldiers into the service, nor Black units during World War I. Alfred Persip's experience in World War I described in the entry that follows reflected this reality.

Record searches in the Ancestry World War I Draft Registration Cards 1917–1918 database indicate there were two draft registration boards that served central and southern Berkshire County. Pittsfield and Lee were the designated centers for registration. Some of the registrants may have been born outside of Berkshire County, but were living or working in Berkshire County at the time of registration and were included. Searching Ancestry.com's World WarI draft registration database indicates that the total number of eligible men from Berkshire County who registered numbered around 15,739. Of that total number 176 Black males registered for the draft, but it is not yet known how many served.

Susan Denault and Dawn Morin

Charles Persip (left) with a World War I comrade. Photo courtesy of The Berkshire County Historical Society Collections.

The Persips in World War I

Alfred K. Persip Sr. (1895–1983) continued the tradition of military service begun by the Black enlistees in the famed Massachusetts 54th Regiment during the Civil War. (His maternal grandfather, Charles Hamilton of Lanesboro, had served in that regiment.) Alfred was the first Black from Berkshire County to enlist at the outbreak of World War I. He was assigned to the 372nd Regiment, which was lent to the French 157th Division, the "Red Hand," since the American army did not want a Black unit under its command. His unit was at the front during the Allied Meuse-Argonne offensive in the autumn of 1918. The all-Black unit earned the Croix de Guerre with palm leaves, the highest unit decoration bestowed by the French military.

Back home, Alfred Persip was a landscape gardener and an active member of the American Legion, serving three times as commander of Pittsfield Post 68. That post in 1983 was named for his brother Charles (1892–1982), a charter member, one-time commander, and first life-member. Charles, a farmer and caretaker, nicknamed "Mr. American Legion" by his comrades, was also a veteran of World War I, as was another brother, John "Popeye" Persip (1887–1983), a cook and caterer. All of the Persips were active in community and veterans' affairs.

Persip Park, above the railroad tracks on North Street, Pittsfield, was dedicated to the Persip family in March 1983. It is near the railroad station, which is appropriate, since the Persip brothers frequently went there during World War II to see off draftees heading to boot camp. The Berkshire Historical Society has Alfred Persip's recollections on tape in its oral history collection.

Bernard A. Drew

John Persip of Pittsfield in the 1950s. Photo courtesy of Mrs. Frances Persip Duval Collection.

Charles Persip marching in a Memorial Day Parade in Pittsfield in the 1970s. Photo courtesy of Mrs. Frances Persip Duval Collection and *Berkshire Eagle*.

Charles Persip receiving the American Legion Pendill Trophy, c. 1970s in Pittsfield. Photo courtesy of Mrs. Frances Persip Duval Collection and *Berkshire Eagle*.

World War II

The Selective Service Training Act of 1940(the nation's first peacetime conscription), opened the military to Black men. Approximately 909,000 African American men and women (after 17 March 1942) served in the army. The Service Act limited Black personnel to a proportionate number of the Black population of the country (10.6 percent), and Black units would be established in each major branch of the army. There would be, however, no intermingling of "colored and white" enlisted personnel in the same units (Moore 1996, 29).

According to the Ancestry.com U.S. World War II Army Enlistment Records 1938–1946 database, approximately 8,944 men from Berkshire County enlisted, 81 of whom were Black men, as follows:

Black Men Living in Berkshire County Who Served from 1938 to 1946

Name	Date of birth	Draft/enlistment date	Occupation
Russell J. Amos	1923	1943	railroad sectionhand
Edward L. Anderson	1919	1945	n.a.
Andrew N. Bailey Jr.	1922	1943	geographer
Charles W. Bateman	1923	1942	n.a.
Robert E. Blackwell Jr.	1921	1942	motorcycle mechanic
Arvern Brinson	1919	1946	light-truck driver
Archie D. Caesar	1919	1942	gas and oil man
Franklyn I. Caesar	1926	1945	postal clerk/ photographer
Lawrence A. Caesar	1924	1943	n.a.
Samuel L. Caesar	1929	1946	n.a.
Benjamin Carter	1910	1942	student
John P. Chadwell	1926	1946	warehouseman
John H. Chambers	1924	1945	electroplater
Ellsworth L. Coffin	1904	1942	actor
Peter F. Crawford	1926	1945	student
Walter E. Crisp	1918	1941	truck driver/chauffeur
James E. Crosrer	1916	1943	quarryman/miner
James P. DeGroat	1907	1943	blacksmith/ bandleader
Snlven Dean Jr.	1922	1943	cook
Lester S. Dewitt	1926	1945	n.a.
Frederick A. Dillard	1917	1942	pump operator
Charles W. Evans	1923	1942	welder
Winthrop C. Evans	1921	1943	truck driver/chauffeur
Irving Fisher	1906	1942	truck driver/chauffeur
M. Fowler Jr.	1924	1943	student
Albert Gibson	1912	1942	engineering aide/sales clerk
Charles H. Glass	1920	1945	cook
Romaine H. Goldsborough	1921	1942	gas and oil man
Gordon A. Greene	1924	1945	n.a.
Clarence S. Gunn	1920	1943	n.a.
Norman L. Hall	1924	1943	actor
Albert L. Hamilton	1911	1943	n.a.
Thomas Hart	1919	1942	student
William H. Hicks	1906	1942	shoe repairman
Clifford M. Hill	1916	1944	n.a.

Floyd A. Hill	1919	1941	n.a.
John E. Jackman	1910	1942	n.a.
Calvin Z. Jackson	1907	1941	n.a.
Warren H. Jacobs	1921	1942	student
Reuben H. Johnson	1908	1942	n.a.
Eddie Lee	1921	1943	bridge builder
Loren C. Malone	1910	1943	blaster/powder man
Bert A. Mayes	1915	1943	truck driver/chauffeur
David McArthur	1919	1944	toolroom keeper
Claude A. McCollom	1916	1943	surveyor
William E. Moore	1916	1943	shoe repairman
Frederick A. Nichlen Jr.	1920	1941	blacksmith/ bandleader
Jerry Oakley	1909	1943	switchboard installer
Patrick Copeland	1918	1946	automobile mechanic
Frank Patrick	1915	1944	laundry machine operator
Earl G. Persip Jr.	1912	1943	truck driver/chauffeur
Edward L. Persip	1922	1943	truck driver/chauffeur
Kenneth E. Persip	1922	1943	n.a.
Howard A. Porter	1919	1942	actor
Thurston E. Porter	1922	1942	n.a.
Merritt F. Powers	1913	1942	n.a.
Joseph A. Reid	1923	1943	n.a.
Lawrence E. Richards	1913	1942	n.a.
William L. Richards	1906	1942	truck driver/chauffeur
Arthur E. Robinson	1916	1944	laborer
Robert L. Robinson	1922	1943	n.a.
William T. Robinson	1909	1942	laundry machine operator
Charles B. Smith	1924	1946	n.a.
Walter T. Spatjuzeg	1909	1943	equipment technician
Albert C. Thompson	1922	1943	truck driver/chauffeur
George E. Thompson Jr.	1920	1942	surveyor
Kenneth F. Todd	1918	1942	truck driver/chauffeur
John O Tucker	1920	1943	truck driver/chauffeur
Frederick W.Tuggle	1922	1942	n.a.
Floyd J. Walker	1926	1945	motorcycle mechanic
Lafayette W. Walker	1925	1943	student
Elliott Ward	1927	1946	automotive mechanic
Kenneth N. Washington	1925	1943	student
Elliott White	1905	1942	n.a.

Charles A. Williams	1912	1941	truck driver/chauffeur
Charles A. Williamson	1918	1943	equipment technician
Walter W. Wright	1924	1943	ship fitter

As in World War I, the Persip family distinguished itself with three men enlisting. So, too, did the Caesar family, which sent four men into service. In January 1943 the Second Congregational Church in Pittsfield held a ceremony honoring twenty-one Black men who had served in the military, including those currently serving and those who served in the past.

Dawn Morin and Susan Denault

Hubert Butler of Lenox in 1943. Photographed by James VanDerZee in his New York City studio. Photo gifted from Hubert Butler to George Darey. Copyright Donna Mussenden VanDerZee.

Berkshire Women in World War II

Since World War I, several attempts were made to allow women in the military, but all failed. On 17 March 1942 the Women's Army Auxiliary Corps (WAAC) was established. African American women were accepted into the WAACs due to the pressure placed on the War Department by Black political organizations demanding racial equality. Over 150,000 women served in the WAAC (changed in 1943 to WAC, or Women's Army Corps), but only 4 percent were African American.

Enlistment records provide details for three of the four women from the Berkshires known to have served. Hannah G. E. Hoose was the first to enlist, as an Inactive Reserve/Aviation Cadet on 30 January 1943. She was born in 1913 in New York and was working as a cook at the time. Ten days later, on 9 February, Myr E. I. Thompson enlisted as a WAC/Aviation Cadet. Born in 1917 in Rhode Island, she was employed as a submarine cable station operator, presumably not in the Berkshires. Arlene V. Greene (born 1921) enlisted as a WAC on 21 September 1943. She had attended college for two years and was employed as a clerk at that time. The fourth enlistee was Lillian E. Battle of Robbins Avenue in Pittsfield; she was a graduate of Tuskegee Institute when she joined the WAC.

Susan Denault

90

Sources

American Revolution

Crissey, Theron Wilmont. *History of Norfolk, Litchfield County, Connecticut, 1744–1900.* Everett, MA: Massachusetts Publishing Co., 1900.

History of Litchfield County, Connecticut. Philadelphia: J. W. Lewis & Co., 1881.

History of Berkshire County, Massachusetts. Vol. 1. New York: Beers, 1885.

Jones, Electa. *Stockbridge Past and Present.* Springfield, MA: Samuel Bowles & Co., 1854.

Massachusetts Office of the Secretary of State. *Massachusetts Soldiers and Sailors of the Revolutionary War.* 17 vols. Boston: Wright and Potter, 1896–1908.

Mullen, Robert W. *Blacks in America's Wars.* New York: Anchor Foundation, 1973.

National Society of the Daughters of the American Revolution. *Minority Military Service: Massachusetts, 1775–1783.* Washington, DC: D.A.R., 1989.

National Society of the Daughters of the American Revolution. *Minority Military Service: Connecticut, 1775–1783.* D.A.R., 1988.

Piper, Emilie S. *Town of Pittsfield: Original Papers (1739–1843).* Pittsfield, MA: Berkshire Athenaeum, 1999.

Smith, J. E. A. *History of Pittsfield, Berkshire County, Massachusetts, 1734–1860.* Boston: Lee and Shepard, 1869.

Starr, Edward C. *A History of Cornwall, Connecticut.* New Haven, CT: Tuttle, Morehouse & Taylor, 1926.

White, David C. *Connecticut's Black Soldiers, 1775–1783.* Chester, CT: Pequot Press, 1973.

Agrippa Hull, American Revolution Veteran and Caterer

Chapman, Gerard. "Agrippa Hull: Stockbridge Immortal." *Berkshire Eagle,* 15 July 1980.

Egleston, Thomas. *Life of John Patterson, Major General in the Revolutionary Army.* New York: 1894.

Parkman, Francis. *The Journals of Francis Parkman.* Ed. by Mason Wade. New York: Harper, 1947.

Sedgwick, Catharine M. *Life and Letters.* Ed. by Mary E. Dewey. New York: Harper & Brothers, 1871.

Civil War: The 54th Massachusetts Volunteer Infantry Regiment

Atkinson, Edward, ed. *The Monument to Robert Gould Shaw: Its Inception, Completion and Unveiling, 1865–1897.* Boston: Houghton, Mifflin and Co., 1897.

Berlin, Ira, Joseph P. Reidy, and Leslie S. Rowland, eds. *Freedom's Soldiers: The Black Military Experience in the Civil War.* Cambridge, England: Cambridge University Press, 1998.

Black Sailors database. http://www.itd.nps.gov/cwss/sailors_index.html (accessed 17 March 2006).

Blight, David. "The Meaning of the Fight: Frederick Douglass and the Memory of the Fifty-Fourth Massachusetts." *The Massachusetts Review* 36, no. 1 (1995): 141–53.

Briggs, Walter DeBlois. *Civil War Surgeon in a Colored Regiment.* Berkeley and Los Angeles: University of California Press, 1960.

Burchard, Peter. *One Gallant Rush: Robert Gould Shaw and His Brave Black Regiment.* New York: St. Martin's Press, 1965.

Civil War Soldiers and Sailors System. http://www.Ancestry.com.

Coffin, William and Thomas Wentworth Higginson. "The Shaw Memorial and the Sculptor St. Gaudens." *Century Magazine* 54, no. 2 (1897): 176–200.

Doughton, Thomas L. "Men Listing Massachusetts Towns as Their Place of Residence Who Enlisted in the 54th Regiment." 1999. http://www.geocities.com/afroyankees/Military/54mass2.html (accessed 7 Nov. 2004).

Emilio, Luis F. *A Brave Black Regiment: History of the Fifty-Fourth Regiment of Massachusetts Volunteer Infantry, 1863–1865.* New York: Arno Press, 1969.

Gooding, James Henry. *On the Altar of Freedom: A Black Soldier's Civil War Letters from the Front.* Ed. by Virginia Adams. Amherst: University of Massachusetts Press, 1991.

Greene, Robert Ewell. *Swamp Angels: A Biographical Study of the 54th Massachusetts Regiment, True Facts about the Black Defenders of the Civil War.* Fort Washington, MD: Bo Mark/Greene Publishing Group, 1990.

Savage, Kirk. *Standing Soldiers, Kneeling Slaves: Race, War, and Monument in 19th-Century America.* Princeton, NJ: Princeton University Press, 1997.

Shaw, Robert Gould. *Blue-Eyed Child of Fortune: The Civil War Letters of Robert Gould Shaw.* Ed. by Russell Duncan. Athens: University of Georgia Press, 1992.

Silvio O. Conte Archives. *Civil War Muster Rolls.* Pittsfield, MA.

Milo J. Freeland, First to Fulfill His Term with the Massachusetts 54th Regiment

Bartomioli, Karen. "Day of Contrasts Brings Honor to Memory of Black Soldier." *Lakeville Journal*, 25 April 1996.

Edward Augustus Croslear, Civil War Veteran and Farmer

Croslear family file, Dewey Research Center, Sheffield Historical Society.

EAC (Edward A. Croslear). Letter to the editor. *Berkshire Courier*, 21 Nov. 1867.

"Edward A. Croslear." *Berkshire Courier*, 28 Jan. 1915.

"Lucy Croslear." *Berkshire Courier*, 13 July 1905.

Civil War: Other Massachusetts Units and Service

Adjutant General's Office, Boston, MA. *Record of the Massachusetts Volunteers, 1861–1865*. Boston: Wright & Potter, 1868–1870.

Civil War Soldiers & Sailors System database. http://www.Ancestry.com.

National Parks Service. "Civil War Soldiers & Sailors System." http://www.itd.nps.gov/cwss/sailors_index.html.

New Bedford Free Public Library. "Whalemen's Shipping List." http://www.ci.new-bedford.ma.us/SERVICES/LIBRARY/whalingproject/Whaling.htm

Silvio O. Conte Archives. Pittsfield, MA. *Civil War Muster Rolls*.

Civil War: The Connecticut 29th and 31st Volunteer Infantry Regiments

Adjutant General's Office. Boston, MA. *Record of the Massachusetts Volunteers, 1861–1865*. Boston, MA: Wright & Potter, 1868–1870.

Adjutant General's Office. Hartford, CT. *Record of Service of Connecticut Men in the Army and Navy of the United States during the War of the Rebellion*. Hartford, CT: Case, Lockwood & Brainard Co., 1889.

National Parks Service. "Civil War Soldiers & Sailors System." http://www.itd.nps.gov/cwss/sailors_index.html (accessed 17 March 2006).

Town of Sharon, CT. Vital records, 1739–1855/1867. http://www.rootweb.com/-ctlitch2/towns/sharon/sharon.htm

Van Alystyne, Lawrence. *Burying Grounds of Sharon, Connecticut, Armenia and North East New York: Being an Abstract of Inscriptions from Thirty Places of Burial in the Above Named Towns*. Amenia, NY: Walsh, Griffen & Hoysradt, 1903.

White, David O. "Blacks in Connecticut." http://www.ctheritage.org/encyclopedia/topicalsurveys/blacks.htm (accessed 17 March 2006).

White, David O. *Connecticut's Black Soldiers, 1775–1783*. Chester, CT: Pequot Press, 1973.

World War I

Lanning, Michael Lee, Lt. Col. (Ret.) *The African-American Soldier, from Crispus Attucks to Colin Powell*. Carol Publishing Group 1997. http://www.redstone.army.mil/history/integrate/CHRON3.html (accessed 9 Feb. 2006)

World War I Draft Registration Cards 1917–1918 database. http://www.Ancestry.com.

The Persips in World War I

"Alfred Persip Sr. Dies at Age 87; Was Longtime Leader of Veterans." *Berkshire Eagle*, 6 April 1983.

Carmen, Linda. "Youths Told of Contribution of Blacks in World War I." *Berkshire Eagle*, 10 July 1980.

Chapman, Gerard. "Remembering the Persips." *Berkshire Eagle*, 21 May 1994.

Overmyer, James E. "Persip, U.S. Black Soldier in World War I, Questions Move That Put Him in French Army." *Berkshire Eagle*, 15 Sept. 1977.

World War II

Buckley, Gail. *American Patriots: The Story of Blacks in the Military from the Revolution to Desert Storm*. New York: Random House, 2001.

"Second Church to Honor Negro Servicemen," *Berkshire Evening Eagle*, 23 Jan. 1943.

World War II Army Enlistment Records, 1938–1946, for "Negroes" living in Berkshire County, MA. http://www.Ancestry.com.

Berkshire Women in World War II

"First Local Negro Girl Enters WAC." *Berkshire County Eagle*, 27 Sept. 1944.

"Inducted Into WAAC." *Berkshire Evening Eagle*, 1 Feb. 1943.

Moore, Brenda L. "To Serve My Country, to Serve my Race: The Story of the Only African American WACS Stationed Overseas during World War II." New York: New York University Press, 1996.

World War II Army Enlistment Records, 1938–1946 for "Negroes" living in Berkshire County, MA. http://www.Ancestry.com.

Religion

Religion and religious institutions have played a central role in African American life in the region since the mid-nineteenth century. Churches established first in Pittsfield and then Lee, Great Barrington, and Sheffield provided religious freedom (the roles of Blacks in white churches were often restricted) and also became the centers of community social and political life. The pastors of these churches more often than not became leaders and spokesmen for the Black community.

Religious Institutions

Distinctly Black religious institutions first appeared in the Berkshires in the middle of the nineteenth century. Prior to then, Blacks who attended church did so at white churches, mainly the Congregational and Episcopal churches. In northwest Connecticut, where slavery lasted much longer than in Massachusetts, some slaves were baptized and attended church, usually seated in segregated pews in the back of the church or in a balcony. The earliest-known Black church member in the Berkshires was a man identified as "Simon, a Negro," who joined the Great Barrington (Massachusetts) Congregational Church on 25 May 1746. The records show he joined after leaving another church and that he joined with another man, who may have been his master or employer. Before the establishment of their own churches, Blacks were sometimes served by visiting Black clergy from other towns, most of whom were seeking converts for the expanding Black Methodist churches. In 1861 the Black clergyman, Rev. Jacob Mitchell of New Haven, Connecticut, was reported in the *Berkshire Courier* to be the presiding elder in the Methodist Church for Norwich, New Haven, and Bridgeport, Connecticut, as well as for Great Barrington and Lee, Massachusetts, in the Berkshires.

As Black churches appeared across the United States in the middle years of the nineteenth century, several established themselves in the Berkshires. The first was the Second Congregational Church in Pittsfield, Massachusetts, founded in 1846 by seven men and women who faced discrimination in the city's First Congregational Church. Six years later, in 1852, came the African Methodist Episcopal Church in Lee and then the African Methodist Episcopal (A. M. E.) Zion Society in Great Barrington in the 1860s. A second Black church, also of the A. M. E. Zion denomination, was also established in Lee. Both Lee churches had closed by the 1920s, since the Black population there declined. A small, nondenominational chapel was built in

Worshippers leaving buses to attend the Moorish Science Temple in Great Barrington in the 1940s. Photo courtesy of the Great Barrington Historical Society's *Newsletter*, 34 (winter 2000).

Sheffield, Massachusetts, in the 1880s; it closed in 1915. In 1884 the A. M. E. Zion Society in Great Barrington became the Clinton A. M. E. Zion Church; later it became the mother church of the Macedonia Baptist Church in Great Barrington (1944) and the Price Memorial A. M. E. Zion Church in Pittsfield (1958). In 1944 a Moorish Science Temple was established in Great Barrington; it drew few local members, with followers bused in from other locations. Subsequent to difficult relations with town officials over taxes, the temple closed in 1949. Founder of the Price Memorial Church, Rev. Fanny Cooper also established the Warren Brown Chapel, A. M. E. Zion, in North Adams, Massachusetts, in 1977, which, for a lack of members, closed some years later. The Good Samaritan A. M. E. Zion Church, led by Rev. John Parron, also operated in Pittsfield in the 1980s. There is no record of distinctly Black churches being formed in northwest Connecticut, perhaps because the Black population in the towns was often small and declined after the Civil War, many people moving to cities such as Hartford, with large, active Black churches.

In 2006 the Black churches in the region and their pastors were the Second Congregational Church (no pastor), Price Memorial A. M. E. Zion Church (Rev. Surgest Aker), and Victory Church of God in Christ (Rev. Charles Pratt) in Pittsfield and the Clinton A. M. E. Zion Church (Rev. Esther Dozier) and the Macedonia Baptist Church (Rev. Joseph Forte) in Great Barrington.

Not all African Americans, however, were or are members of these churches. Some chose to join predominantly white churches, and others did not attend at all. In her personal essay elsewhere in this volume, Mae Brown of Great Barrington tells of her decision to leave the Clinton A. M. E. Zion Church in 1960 and join the First Congregational Church. David Gunn Sr. was a deacon of the First Congregational Church in Stockbridge, and that church was a center of civil rights activity in the 1960s. Cooperation among the churches, both Black and white, has been the rule, with frequent visits by choirs and guest sermons by pastors. Great Barrington has seen substantial cooperation among its Black and white churches since the 1940s, and the Clinton Church in Great Barrington and Price

Rev. Joseph Forte of the Macedonia Baptist Church in Great Barrington, c. 1999. Photo by Erik Callahan.

Memorial in Pittsfield frequently participate in services and other events together.

In *The Souls of Black Folk*, W. E. B. Du Bois (1903) wrote that "the Negro church of to-day is the social center of Negro life in the United States, and the most characteristic expression of African character. . . . Thus one can see in the Negro church to-day, reproduced in microcosm, all the great world from which the Negro is cut off by color-prejudice and social condition." This was certainly true of the Black churches in the Berkshires, and Du Bois likely first witnessed this as a youth when he attended events of the A. M. E. Zion Society in Great Barrington. Beyond worship and spiritual fulfillment, they offered education for the children, served as community centers, and provided entertainment for members and often the entire community. Church leaders represented the interests and concerns of the Black community. Several churches were also active in the civil rights movement, raising money, hosting events, and sending members to events. Members of the clergy who were influential in their communities include Reverends Samuel Harrison, Thomas Nelson Baker, Alexander Jamison Sr., and Willard Durant in Pittsfield; Robert Jeter in Lee; and Reverends J. F. Waters, Henry Morrison, William Durante, and Esther Dozier in Great Barrington.

David Levinson

Sunday School Convention Stirs Great Barrington

In September 1895, the annual convention of the Sunday Schools of the New England Conference of the A. M. E. Zion Church was held at the Clinton Church. The event, which drew several dozen pastors and teachers, was of sufficient local importance to garner front-page coverage in the *Courier*. One report issued by the conference on civil rights and lynching and was quoted in the *Courier* (5 Sept. 1895, 1).

Although there is reported to be a revival of industry throughout the land, and this year's grain crop is tremendous in its proportions, the condition of the Negro citizen in this nation continues to be one of anxious solitude. The deplorable spirit of lawlessness, as manifested in lynchings, seems no longer to continue itself within its former well understood limits, but, while still controlling action in its old familiar haunts, is spreading itself over the land, entering even that splendid commonwealth, which gave to our nation the immortal president, Abraham Lincoln. What we need in this critical condition of public affairs is just what we needed in the dark days of slavery—men to "stand on the wall."

As did Garrison, Phillips, Sumner and Douglass, hurling their thunderbolts at the citadel of injustice, and swaying the rulers and people of the American nation into a recognition and practice of the principles of the constitution of the United States. God's blessing cannot long continue with a nation whose people are indifferent to, or careless of the claims of justice to each and all of its citizens. The future of our country depends upon our activity along the lines laid down in the great command, "Thou shalt love the Lord thy God with all thy heart; and thy neighbor as thyself."

Women as Religious Leaders

Rev. Esther Dozier of the Clinton A. M. E. Zion Church, Great Barrington, c. 1999. Photo by Erik Callahan.

Women in the United States have played a greater part in the founding and development of religions and denominations than in most other parts of the world. Three religions founded or developed in the United States—the Shakers, Seventh-day Adventists, and Christian Science—were founded by women. The history of Black churches also shows the significant role often played by women, and the history of Black churches in the Berkshires is no different. In 1846 three women (Catherine Fields, Mary Richards, and Delilah Potter) and four men (Morris Potter, John L. Brown, William Potter, and Davis S. Thomas) founded the Second Congregational Church in Pittsfield to escape discrimination in the predominantly white First Congregational Church. In 1881 five couples—Jason and Almira Cooley, Manuel and Emily Mason, Daniel and Sarah Brown, Egbert and Rebecca Lee, and Jefferson and Margaret McKinley—signed the deed for property on Elm Court purchased by the African Methodist Episcopal Zion Society. Its church was built there in 1887. The business entrepreneur (Mrs.) Martha Crawford was the driving force in founding the Macedonia Baptist Church in Great Barrington in 1944 and held leadership positions for many years. In 1958 Rev. Fanny Cooper founded the Price Memorial A. M. E. Zion Church in her home in Pittsfield, and in 1977 the Warren Brown Chapel, A. M. E. Zion, in North Adams. Much of the women's work, however, was less dramatic—teaching Sunday school, running fund-raising events, singing in the choir, cooking and hosting church suppers and socials, regularly attending services, keeping the roll and ledger books, and helping the poor and sick.

Public leadership positions came much later. Reverend Cooper served as a pastor of the chapel she founded in North Adams. In 1999 the A. M. E. Zion Church appointed Rev. Esther Dozier the first female pastor of the Clinton A. M. E. Zion Church in Great Barrington. Reverend Dozier was married in the church in 1965 and served as exhorter before her appointment as pastor. The Second Congregational Church also has had a female pastor, the Rev. Carol Towley, who served as interim pastor from 2003 to 2005.

Also of significance is Eliza Ann Gardner (1831–1922). Although she was from Boston and lived there, she had a local connection as a member of the Great Barrington Gardner family (several of whom were early members of the Clinton A. M. E. Zion Church), and she was a cousin of W. E. B. Du Bois. A founder of the A. M. E. Zion's missionary effort, she also held leadership positions in the New England Conference, along with being a staunch abolitionist. In the 1920s the Eliza Ann Gardner Day School in Ghana was built in her honor.

David Levinson

> In 1899, Meriah Harris wrote in the *Zion* journal (p. 22):
>
> *That woman, the gentler half of God's creation, was an important, even though invisible, factor in the pioneer work of the Church cannot be doubted.*

Freeborn Garretson and "Black Harry" Hosier in Northwest Connecticut

The Methodist faith flourished in America in the years following the Revolution, having been introduced from England a few decades prior. Itinerant preachers traveled the country speaking in homes, town halls, and outdoors in any community where they hoped to draw a crowd. Two such ministers entered northwestern Connecticut in the summer of 1790: Freeborn Garretson and Harry Hosier. Garretson was from Maryland and a former slave owner. His partner, "Black Harry" Hosier, was a former slave, probably from North Carolina. Together they worked their way up through the Atlantic states spreading the gospel. Entering Connecticut at Sharon on 20 June, they proceeded to Cornwall (21 June), Litchfield (23 June), Hartford (28 June), then Worcester (30 June), Boston (1 July–7 July), and then Providence (8 July).

From there they moved west, passing through Hartford (13 July), Cornwall (24 July), Canaan (25 July), and Salisbury (25 July) before reaching New York state at the end of July.

Upon entering a community Garretson would speak before a crowd first, followed by Hosier. Said a contemporary of Hosier, "Harry was very black, an African of the Africans. He was so illiterate he could not read a word. He would repeat the hymn as if reading it, and quote his text with great accuracy. His voice was musical, and his tongue as the pen of a ready writer. He was unboundedly popular, and many would rather hear him than the bishops" (McEllhenny n.d.). No doubt many Black people, who had probably never met a Black minister, warmly received Hosier in their communities as someone who could personally relate to their experiences. And as someone who had escaped bondage and was now in a position of power and respect, he made for a strong role model. While not every community—white or Black—welcomed the ministers, their work nonetheless helped eventually establish Methodist churches in nearly all of these communities.

Garretson and Hosier preached in Sharon on 20 June 1790. One source records that they preached under a tree to about one thousand people—nearly half of the town's population. A town history written in 1877 recalls that Hosier, either on 20 June or at a later date, was arrested and charged with a "crime against the peace and good order of society. . . . The crowd assembled to witness the proceedings was so great that the court was held in the Congregational Church on the public green." Eventually the trial ended with Hosier found not guilty (Sedgwick 1898, 87). Interestingly, the Congregational minister at the time, and probably the man who presided over Hosier's trial, was Cotton Mather Smith, a descendant of the famous Puritan minister.

In the summer of 1790 Garretson and Hosier passed through Cornwall twice—on 22 June and 24 July. The second time Garretson remarked of their reception, "I found that the Lord had begun a blessed work in this town when I preached here before, so I rode to Canaan, where I was comfortable" (Stevens 1864–1867, 67).

The preachers entered Salisbury on 25 July 1790, on their way back to New York. Garretson recalled, "I rode in the afternoon and preached in Salisbury, in a part of the town in which I had never before been, and I think I have never seen so tender a meeting in this town before, for a general weeping ran through the assembly, especially when Harry gave an exhortation. The Lord is carrying on a blessed work here" (Stevens 1864–1867, 67).

Jonathan Olly

The Trial of "Black Harry" Hosier

A colored man, Black Harry, as he was called, a local preacher, often accompanied Mr. [Freeborn] Garretson in his travels. Harry once spent two or three weeks in Sharon, and made himself very useful in preaching. Some unprincipled person invented and circulated an infamous story about him, and as it involved an alleged crime against the peace and good order of society, he was arrested and brought to trial before the civil authorities. The crowd assembled to witness the proceedings was so great that the Court was held in the Congregational Church on the public green. The result was that not a shadow of criminality was proved against him, and he was honorably discharged. Andrew Harpending, a traveling preacher of some note, happened to be present, and as the people began to leave the church, he procured a table and taking his stand upon it in the open air, preached one of his characteristic sermons, loud, fearless and earnest. A young lady, living half mile south, not being, permitted to attend the meetings, stood at an open upper window, and there distinctly heard the preaching and under its influence was brought to a saving knowledge of God. So God often works in unexpected ways and "makes the wrath of man to praise him."

Source: Sedgwick, Charles F. *General History of the Town of Sharon.* Amenia, NY: n.p., 1877, 87.

Lemuel Haynes, Pioneer Minister

Lemuel Haynes as shown on the frontispiece of: Cooley, Timothy Mather, *Sketches of the Life and Character of the Rev. Lemuel Haynes, A.M.* New York: Harper & Brother, 1837. The title page is shown below. Photos courtesy of Berkshire Athenaeum Collection.

SKETCHES

OF THE

LIFE AND CHARACTER

OF THE

REV. LEMUEL HAYNES, A.M.,

FOR MANY YEARS PASTOR OF A CHURCH IN RUTLAND, VT., AND LATE IN
GRANVILLE, NEW-YORK.

BY TIMOTHY MATHER COOLEY, D.D.,

PASTOR OF THE FIRST CHURCH IN GRANVILLE, MASS.

WITH SOME INTRODUCTORY REMARKS BY

WILLIAM B. SPRAGUE, D.D,

PASTOR OF THE SECOND PRESBYTERIAN CHURCH IN ALBANY

Nil desperandum Christo duce.

NEW-YORK:

HARPER & BROTHERS, 82 CLIFF-ST.

1837.

Lemuel Haynes (1753–1833), who began training as a clergyman by learning Latin from the Rev. Daniel Farrand in North Canaan, Connecticut, in 1779, is believed to be the first Black man to be ordained by any religious sect in North America. Born a free man of a white mother and Black father in West Hartford, Connecticut, he was bound out in service in Granville, Connecticut. As a young man he worked on Farrand's farm. Following his indenture, in 1774 he enlisted as a minuteman and served at Lexington, Massachusetts, and during the siege of Boston. During this time he became involved in antislavery activities and argued not only for the end of slavery and the slave trade but also for full equality. After serving on the Ticonderoga expedition, he began his theological studies and was ordained as a Congregational minister in Litchfield, Connecticut, in 1785. He encountered some prejudice during his time as a supply preacher at white churches in Middle Granville and Torrington, Connecticut, and so accepted a call to a church in West Rutland, Vermont, where he remained for three decades. Reverend Haynes married a white woman, Elizabeth Babbitt. With only a rudimentary education, he nonetheless wrote religious tracts, including one—perhaps the first by a Black in the United States—*Liberty Further Extended*, in which he declared, "that an African . . . has an undeniable right to his Liberty." He noted the irony of slave owners fighting for freedom during the Revolutionary War while still denying it to others. Reverend Haynes wrote numerous religious and social tracts and may have been the first Black political philosopher in North America. He was presented with an honorary master of arts degree from Middlebury College, in Vermont, in 1804—said to have been the first bestowed on a Black. The pastor spent the last decade of his life in upstate New York.

Emilie Piper and Bernard A. Drew

"Liberty is equally as precious to a Black man, as it is to a white one, and bondage as equally as intolerable to the one as it is to the other." Lemuel Haynes, 1770s.

The Second Congregational Church, Pittsfield

Prior to 1846 the First Congregational Church, United Church of Christ (UCC) in Pittsfield was the principal religious institution for Blacks living in the area. Owing to racial intolerance, however, there came a time when seven of the Black congregants decided they should form their own religious institution, one that would be free of the racism they experienced. John L. Brown, Morris Potter, William Potter, David S. Thomas, Catherine Fields, Delilah Potter, and Mary Richards established the first of the region's Black churches in February 1846. It is reportedly the second oldest UCC-affiliated church in Massachusetts and the eighth in the nation to continuously serve a predominantly African American congregation.

Through the efforts of the Rev. John Todd, pastor of the First Congregational Church, and the Honorable E. A. Newton, the group reconstructed a dilapidated Wesleyan Methodist Church building that was relocated to First Street. It was dedicated as the Second Congregational Church on 20 February 1846.

Reverend Henry Highland Garnet (the first pastor of the Liberty Street Presbyterian Church in Troy, New York, until 1848 and a noted Black abolitionist) supplied pulpit services during the initial four years of the church.

The Rev. Thomas P. Hunt also filled the pulpit on occasion until the coming of Rev. Samuel Harrison in 1850.

Reverend Harrison was born of slave parentage in 1818. He was called to be the first pastor of the Second Congregational Church in 1850. There he ministered until 1862, when, because of a rift in the church, he tendered his resignation; but later returned in 1872 and remained until the time of his death in 1900. Reverend Harrison served a total of forty years ministering to the needs of the Pittsfield community and in particular its Black residents.

In August 1901 the Rev. Dr. Thomas Nelson Baker became the second pastor. Dr. Baker, a learned and humble man, was a graduate of Boston University (BA), Yale Divinity School (STB, 1896), and Yale Graduate School (PhD, 1903). Reportedly, Dr. Baker was the first African American and former slave to receive a PhD in philosophy.

The first building of the Second Congregational Church of Pittsfield, built in 1846. Photo courtesy of Michael Kirk.

Church membership rose from 88 in 1917 to 120 by 1936. During his 38 years of continuous service, he guided the congregation in remodeling the original church building and celebrating its sixtieth and ninetieth anniversaries. Also during this period 25 young people from the church went to college. In January 1939, after tendering his resignation, Reverend Baker was elected minister emeritus. He held this honorary title until his accidental death on 22 February 1940.

The third pastor to fill the pulpit was Rev. Harold Leslie Nevers, also a graduate of Yale Divinity School, who began his service in September 1939, with Reverend Baker serving as minister emeritus. Reverend Nevers observed that his church was "sandwiched in between two barrooms" and that there was the need "to establish a church more accessible to its members." He guided the congregation in selling the church property on First Street and purchasing another building, a 13-room homestead, owned by John A. White, and an adjacent vacant lot at the corner of Columbus Avenue and Onota Street. The home was to be used as a parsonage and temporary church until they were able to build one on the adjoining lot. After extensive renovations he led the congregation in its first service on 1 May 1941 and the dedication of its sanctuary on 15 March 1942. By 1945 church membership had risen to 166. Reverend Nevers died in January 1965, after 26 years of continuous service and before the church edifice he envisioned could be constructed. Quinlan Peacock, of the First Congregational Church, occasionally provided pulpit services during the remainder of 1965 until the next pastor, Isaiah Jenkins, was called.

In 1958 Fannie Cooper, a member of the church since 1925, became an ordained elder in the A. M. E. Zion Church and began Price Memorial A. M. E. Zion Church out of her home. She later pastored Warren Brown Chapel A. M. E. Zion in North Adams, Massachusetts.

In January 1966 Rev. Isaiah Jenkins, a graduate of Boston University School of Theology, was called

to be the fourth pastor to fill the pulpit. During this decade of nationwide racial turmoil and Black frustration, Reverend Jenkins brought a sense of solidarity to Pittsfield's Black populace. Construction of the church edifice envisioned by Reverend Nevers began in July 1967 under Reverend Jenkins's leadership, but not without opposition, confusion, and misunderstanding. Owing to rancorous discord with members of the community (both Black and white), Reverend Jenkins departed in 1968. Completion of the church was accomplished under the able leadership of Wilbert N. Stockton, Willie Singleton, Clifford Potter, and Sammy Kennedy. The first service of worship in the new church building occurred on 21 Dec. 1969 with the Rev. Simeon Bankole-Wright serving as the fifth pastor to fill the pulpit, from June 1970 until May 1972. Reverend Randolph Smith frequently provided pulpit services until the next pastor, Robert Mason, was called.

In September 1973 Rev. Robert Lewis Mason, a Yale graduate with a Memphis, Tennessee, Baptist background, was called to be the sixth pastor to fill the pulpit. Under his leadership the church flourished with renewed vigor and an enthusiasm that had not been experienced in many years. Reverend Mason led the congregation in celebrating its 128th anniversary and engaged the Rev. Martin Luther King Sr. to be the guest speaker. In May 1977 Reverend Mason resigned.

Four years passed before the congregation summoned the next minister to pastor the church. In the interim several individuals provided pulpit services to the congregation: Reverends Arthur Teikmanis; James Trefry (director of Religious Education at the First Congregational Church); Dennis Dickerson (a professor of African American history at Williams College, in Massachusetts); Joseph Forte (then of Albany, New York); Clyde H. Miller Jr. (president of the City Missionary Society of Boston, Massachusetts); and Jeffrey Lewis (of Springfield, Massachusetts).

The seventh pastor to serve the congregation was the Rev. Leonard D. Comithier Jr., who came in

October 1981. Under his leadership the church again flourished and grew. A community scholarship fund was established in support of college-bound students. The Gospel Ensemble Choir was established, along with a young peoples choir (the Angels Without Wings). He established a dropout prevention and tutoring program called Project Life for at-risk students. With Dr. Dennis Dickerson as guest speaker, he led the church in celebrating its 135th anniversary. An annual Martin Luther King Memorial Service was established and is still enjoyed by the community after the turn of the twenty-first

Rev. Harrison on Returning to His Church

In his 1899 autobiography, Rev. Samuel Harrison wrote about his beliefs and also how his experience during Civil War service influenced his later thought and actions.

I have to say in the first place that if, under God, I am anything or have become anything in this world, it is through a godly mother's influence.

But, in all these years, the Lord helped me, and when I look back I am surprised at the way in which I have gotten along; myself and family have had shelter, food, raiment and fuel. God has withheld nothing from us which was needed, and now that I have reached old age, I can use the words of David, the sweet singer of Israel, "I have been young, now I am old, yet have I never seen the righteous forsaken nor his seed begging bread. "

I believe in helping people to help themselves. They appreciate such help.

Mine was not an isolated case of a minister being away from a church for some years and then returning to his old charge. There is a great deal in adaptation. I think that a man rarely loses interest in his first charge. There is a great deal in early associations. Then, the most of my children were born here and the most of them were buried here. No warmer friends have I had anywhere than in Pittsfield. I seemed to begin life anew. It was here where my expectation took a tangible form in the culmination of the ministry, upon which I had entered after a zigzag course in my earlier life. I was welcomed back.

I concluded not to return south if I could get my discharge; so I wrote my resignation, endorsed by my physician, and forwarded it to Governor Andrew and he secured my honorable discharge. I also told him the paymaster had declined to pay me because of my being of African descent. I was not able for some time to do anything, but, when I became able, I resumed my old employment in behalf of the Freedmen, more successfully because I had been among them and knew from personal observation what I was talking about.

Three months passed and no pay. I knew that my family's means were nearly used up. What to do I hardly knew, but bore up under it as well as I could. My wife and six children, a debt of three hundred dollars on my house, and grocery bills. I had a hard burden to carry. I grew sick under the pressure. But that promise kept me up, "I will not 1eave thee nor forsake thee." God had his way in all this thing, though I did not see it then, and I more and more observe that good Providence.

Source: Harrison, Samuel. *Rev. Samuel Harrison, His Life Story, as Told by Himself.* Pittsfield, MA: Privately printed, 1899. [Available at the Berkshire Athenaeum, Pittsfield, MA.]

century. Reverend Comithier recognized a need for the church to embrace its history and to fellowship with a true sense of community. He faithfully served the congregation as its pastor until 16 October 1986.

In March 1987 Rev. Alexander Jamison Sr., a student at Andover Newton Theological Seminary (Andover, Massachusetts) was called to become the eighth pastor to serve the congregation as its minister and the first in twenty years to come with a strong background in the United Church of Christ. Reverend Jamison led the transition of the Project Life program from a church-based to a community-based program at the Christian Center and renamed it Education Project Life. Under the new moniker the purpose of the project was expanded and served over a period of ten years to expose at-risk students to the benefits of a college education through campus tours. Reverend Jamison pastored the congregation until his departure in 1992.

Rev. Jerome T. Edgerton served as the ninth pastor, from 1993 until 1994. Reverend Edgerton's concern for the youths in the community led to a revitalization of the church Sunday school, sponsorship of a Boy Scout and a Girl Scout troop, and a television ministry on the local cable network to provide worship services to the sick and shut-in. In 1994 Rev. Edgerton resigned. Thereafter the pulpit was filled by several guest ministers, notably Rev. John Killikelly and Rev. Frank Turner, both from Albany, New York.

Rev. John McFarland served as the tenth pastor, from 1995 until 1996. During his brief ministry Rev. McFarland recognized that the pastor of this congregation had since its inception been a focal point and a driving force in this community. He recognized that for most of its history Second Congregational Church needed no direct outreach for growth because it was the only predominantly African American congregation in Pittsfield, providing both spiritual and social activities for the populace. For many years those coming to Pittsfield lived with family already residing in the area and by association attended the same church. Rev. McFarland's interests in a communal parenting ministry to address the burgeoning needs of those in recovery, former inmates desiring to rebuild their lives, and women who were victims of domestic violence did not align with the desires of the congregation. He pastured the congregation until his departure in 1996.

During the decade after 1996 the church was without a full-time pastor. However, two interim ministers have ably served the congregation during the four years up to 2006: Rev. John G. Wightman, the eleventh pastor, serving from 13 February 2000 until February 2002; and Rev. Carol K. Towley, the twelfth pastor, serving from February 2003 (installed 2 May 2004) until 12 June 2005. Notably, Rev. Wightman was the first non-Black minister called to pastor the congregation. Reverend Towley, the second non-Black minister, was also the first female called to serve the congregation.

The congregation was in search of a pastor as of 2006. In the interim and as had occurred on numerous prior occasions, pulpit services were being provided by guest ministers supplied by the Diaconate Board, then under the able leadership of Catherine Rickard.

Ivan Newton

Samuel Harrison, Minister and Activist

Samuel Harrison (1818–1900), a minister and former slave, was one of Berkshire County's most ardent abolitionists. He was born in Philadelphia, the son of slaves owned by the Bolton family. Shortly after his birth the Boltons granted his widowed mother and her son their freedom, and the two moved to New York City. When Harrison was nine years old, his mother sent him to live with an uncle in Philadelphia, to remove him from an abusive and alcoholic stepfather. A few years later his mother joined for the same reason.

Throughout his childhood, Harrison worked as an apprentice to his uncle in a shoemaking shop, learning a trade that would support him for years. He also attended church services with his mother regularly, and it was during his adolescence that Harrison received his calling to the church. "I became deeply interested and I was impelled, by some unseen power, to follow up those [church] meetings," Harrison (1899) wrote in his autobiographical sketch.

Harrison tried hard to educate himself. In 1836 he enrolled in a manual-labor school run by the abolitionist Gerrit Smith in Peterboro, New York. After only a few months he transferred to Western Reserve College in Hudson, Ohio (now Case Western Reserve University, in Cleveland), which took a pro-abolition stance some twenty years before the Civil War. Financial difficulties forced him to return to Philadelphia in 1839.

In Philadelphia, Harrison married Ellen Rhodes, whom he had known when the two were children. Over the next twenty years Ellen gave birth to thirteen children; sadly, seven died in early childhood.

Harrison and his family moved from Philadelphia to Newark, New Jersey, in 1848, after a former classmate and fellow clergyman, E. P. Rogers, secured Harrison a place with the Newark Presbytery. He took a preliminary examination and earned a license to preach but still needed

Samuel Harrison, first minister of the Second Congregational Church of Pittsfield. Photo courtesy of Samuel Harrison Society, Inc.

more study before being ordained. Harrison worked with Rogers for two years in Newark prior to receiving word of an opportunity to preach as the pastor of a new congregation in Pittsfield, Massachusetts. In 1850 Harrison made the move to Massachusetts, where he was ordained as a preacher by the Berkshire Association of Congregational Ministers and became the first minister of the Second Congregational Church of Pittsfield, the first Black church founded in the county.

Harrison settled into his position and became well known in the area for his fiery sermons and outspoken criticism of slavery. He was invited to speak at a number of different churches in the region on contemporary political issues, such as

Blacks serving in the army, war in eastern Europe, and the history of the city of Pittsfield. In 1862 he delivered to a Williamstown congregation the lecture "The Cause and Cure for the War," a fiery oration in which he trumpeted support for enlistment of Black troops. He retired from his Pittsfield pulpit in 1862 and began working with the National Freedmen's Relief Association to solicit aid for former slaves on the South Carolina Sea Islands. In July of 1863 Harrison journeyed to Boston and met with John A. Andrew, the abolitionist governor of Massachusetts, who requested that he travel to South Carolina and "express the sympathy of the Commonwealth" to the surviving members of the 54th Massachusetts Regiment, the first Black unit mustered in the North, which fought valiantly at Fort Wagner. Harrison set off in August 1863. He preached to soldiers and freedmen for six weeks before returning to the North, only then to be officially appointed chaplain of the 54th Regiment by Governor Andrew. He reported for duty at Morris Island, South Carolina, in November 1863. Immediately, the issue of discriminatory pay practices drew protest from Harrison, who demanded that he receive the same wages as white chaplains. Governor Andrew and Attorney Gen. Edward Bates penned letters to Lincoln on Harrison's behalf.

Taken ill in March 1864, Harrison was honorably discharged from the army. After rejoining the National Freedmen's Relief Association and attending, along with Frederick Douglass, the Syracuse, New York, National Convention of Colored Men in October 1864, Harrison ministered to Black congregations in Newport, Rhode Island (1865), Springfield, Massachusetts (1866–1870), and Portland, Maine (1870–1872) before resuming the pastorship of the Second Congregational Church in Pittsfield. He served as chaplain of the W. W. Rockwell Post 125, G. A. R. (1882, 1883, 1885–1894). An impassioned orator and writer, Harrison published a variety of tracts on racial equality, enfranchisement, reconstruction, and "historical perspectives," including *Pittsfield Twenty-five Years Ago* (1876), *A Centennial Sermon* (1876), *An Appeal of a Colored Man to His Fellow-Citizens of a Fairer Hue in the United States* (1877), *Pittsfield Then and Now* (1886), and *Rev. Samuel Harrison: His Life Story* (1899).

After he returned to his congregation and home in Pittsfield, Harrison continued to preach and to make political speeches. He worked passionately for the temperance movement, the Freedman's Society, and the Republican Party. Working, preaching, and writing up until the year he died, Rev. Samuel Harrison defied the roles usually assigned to an ex-slave. He was a well-known and well-loved political activist in western Massachusetts and an inspiration to other Blacks. Harrison died in 1900. Two years later a tablet commemorating his forty years of ministering to Pittsfield African Americans was placed at the Second Congregational Church, with the inscription: "A Wise Leader, an Honored Citizen, an Ardent Patriot, a Beloved Messenger of the Lord, he wrought well for his people, his Country and his God."

Rev. Harrison's house stands at 82 Third Street, although it is in great need of repair. The Samuel Harrison Society is raising funds to restore the house as a museum of African American history. The house was given to the society by Ruth Edmonds Hill, great granddaughter of Rev. Harrison and Oral History Coordinator, The Arthur and Elizabeth Schlesinger Library on the History of Women in America at Radcliffe College.

Frances Jones-Sneed and Randy Weinstein

Samuel Harrison and Harrison House Photo Essay

The gravestone of Reverend Samuel Harrison and Wife, Pittsfield Cemetery. Photo by Pat Cotton, courtesy of the Samuel Harrison Society, Inc..

The gravestone of the wife of Reverend Samuel Harrison, Pittsfield Cemetery. Photo by Pat Cotton, courtesy of the Samuel Harrison Society, Inc.

The Samuel Harrison House in Pittsfield in 2004. Photo by Pat Cotton, courtesy of the Samuel Harrison Society, Inc.

The Samuel Harrison House in Pittsfield in 2005. Photo by Rachel Fletcher.

Interior of the Rev. Samuel Harrison House in Pittsfield in 2005. Photo by Rachel Fletcher.

A press conference at the Rev. Samuel Harrison House in Pittsfield in 2005. Congressman John Olver, center, is presenting a $250,000 preservation award to Councilwoman Linda Tyer, right, and Ivan Newton, left. Photo by Rachel Fletcher.

A press conference at the Rev. Samuel Harrison House in Pittsfield in 2005. Congressman John Olver, right, is presenting a $250,000 preservation award to Councilwoman Linda Tyer. Photo by Rachel Fletcher.

Thomas Nelson Baker, Minister and Philosopher

Dr. Thomas Nelson Baker, second minister of the Second Congregational Church of Pittsfield. Photo courtesy of Second Congregational Church of Pittsfield.

A minister and former slave, Thomas Nelson Baker (1860–1941) is reportedly the first former slave to receive a PhD in philosophy. He was born in Eastville, Virginia, the son of Thomas and Edith Baker, both slaves of Robert Nottingham. He attended public school until the age of twelve, when economic necessity forced him to leave to work on local farms to help support his parents and siblings. Later, at the age of twenty-one, he enrolled at Hampton, a normal school established by Gen. Samuel Armstrong for the education of freed slaves and their children. His tuition was paid in part by John Denison, a supporter of Armstrong and pastor of Williams College (in Williams, Massachusetts). Denison, who "was particularly struck by Baker's intelligence and drive to educate himself as well as his interest in the ministry," arranged for Baker to attend Mount Hermon for Boys (in Northfield, Massachusetts) (Weis, 2003). With the financial support and recommendation of John Denison, Baker, in 1885 at the age of twenty-five, entered Mount Hermon, where he distinguished himself academically. He "finished the four-year course in a shade over three years" and thereafter enrolled at Boston University, where he continued to excel academically (Weis, 2003). He was chosen by the faculty to be the commencement speaker at his graduation in 1893.

Baker then attended Yale Divinity School (New Haven, Connecticut), where he received a master's degree after three years. Reverend Baker served first at Dixwell Congregational Church in New Haven and later as the second pastor of the Second Congregational Church in Pittsfield, Massachusetts (1901–1939). He earned his PhD from Yale in 1903, during the early years of his ministry in Pittsfield. In January 1939, after tendering his resignation, Reverend Baker was elected minister emeritus. He held this honorary title until his accidental death in 1941.

Ivan Newton

Clinton A. M. E. Zion Church, Great Barrington

An African Methodist Episcopal Zion Society was formed in Great Barrington in 1870 or perhaps a few years earlier. The founding and early members included some local Black families and others who had arrived recently from the south. The group met at first in members' homes and then in public halls. It was served by a visiting pastor who came four times a year. Soon the society became the central institution for the Black community and formed a sewing society, literary society, and children's society. In 1884 the society incorporated as the Clinton African Methodist Episcopal Zion Church and in 1886–1887 built a small wooden church on Elm Court in Great Barrington. The church building was dedicated on 6 Feb. 1887 and by 2006 was the oldest building in continuous use by a Black organization in the county. Reverend Joseph G. Smith was pastor when the church was built. Although it was the smallest church in town, it was active in town life through its many church suppers, literary readings, musical and dramatic performances, and guest speakers and preachers. Over the

A group of Black people at a summer lake outing. The photographer's tag shows that the photo was taken by Rev. Chauncey Hatfield of the Clinton A. M. E. Zion Church in Great Barrington. It probably dates to 1894–96 and was taken at Lake Buel in Great Barrington. The group were likely members of the church who held an annual outing at the lake. Photo courtesy of Gary Leveille Collection, Great Barrington Historical Society.

The Belmont Street A. M. E. Zion Church Choir (from Worcester, Massachusetts) singing at the 114th Anniversary celebration of the Clinton A. M. E. Zion Church in Great Barrington. Photo courtesy of Clinton A. M. E. Zion Church, Great Barrington.

years the church attracted such luminaries as W. E. B. Du Bois, Bishop J. W. Hood, and NAACP leader Bishop Stephen Gill Spottswood to town. In 1890, during the pastorate of J. F. Waters, the church hosted a New England supper that attracted over four hundred people. Providing meals and entertainment was necessary because the church membership was always small and poor, requiring that funds had to be raised from the general community to supplement members' offerings. In 1895 and 1896 entertainment was provided by the pastor, Rev. Chauncey Hatfield, who showed "moving pictures" with his light-box projector; tragically, the box set his clothes on fire one evening, and he died a week later. In 1895 the New England Conference held its annual Sunday School Convention at the church. In 1899 Rev. Isaac Watkins held the church's first camp meeting. Wagons picked people up three times a day in front of the post office to take them to the meeting grove in Van Deusenville.

The membership grew and then declined in the early years of the twentieth century as Blacks moved away from Great Barrington in search of better jobs. In December 1913 the church membership split into two factions, and one decided to end affiliation with the A. M. E. Zion Church, reincorporating as the Second Congregational Church of Great Barrington. In May 1914 the decision was reversed and the Clinton Church was reestablished in its home on Elm Court. As the Black population grew in the 1920s, so, too, did the church membership. Reverend Byron Scott, who served as pastor for twelve years between 1917 and 1931, was in the pulpit during much of this growth. In 1939, under the direction of Rev. Edward H. Coleman, a parsonage was added to the back of

"The preacher is the most unique personality developed by the Negro on American soil. A leader, a politician, an orator, a "boss," an intriguer, an idealist,—all these he is, and ever, too, the centre of a group of men, now twenty, now a thousand in number." W. E. B. Du Bois, *The Souls of Black Folk*, 1995. [First pub. 1903]

the church, which made it easier to retain pastors for several years at a time. The Rev. Henry Morrison went before the Board of Selectmen in 1943 to complain about poor housing conditions endured by the Black community.

The men of the church, in 1951, dug out the basement and converted it into a dining hall, and the Quarterly New England Conference was held in the new facility. In the 1950s the church grew to its greatest number of members, with seventy-seven in 1954. Reverends Raleigh Dove (1946–1951), Alexander W. Johnson (1951–1954), and David Woodson (1954–1957) were popular pastors and provided stable leadership during these years. Ruth D. Jones, Reverend Dove's daughter, was an early participant in the civil rights movement and a promoter of Du Bois's legacy in town. In the 1950s and 1960s the church was a meeting place for the NAACP and was also an early home for Construct, Inc., the affordable-housing agency. Several members were also active in the Red Cross, and the United Church Women and the church regularly participated in ecumenical services in town.

Serving as pastor from 1962 to 1972 was Rev. William Durante. (His son, Willard Durant, was later pastor of the Price Memorial A. M. E. Zion Church in Pittsfield.) The church established rela-

tionships with other A. M. E. Zion churches, including Price Memorial in Pittsfield and churches in Worcester and Springfield, Massachusetts. It also took pride in being the "Mother Church" for both the Macedonia Baptist Church in Great Barrington and the Price Memorial Church. In 1975 (Mrs.) Pinkie Brooks, an active member and leader since joining in 1929, was honored as "Mother of the Church," and Wray Gunn, chairman of the Trustee Board, became head of Construct, Inc., the affordable-housing organization. In that same year, the church was remodeled and the facilities upgraded.

The Rev. Esther Dozier was appointed the first female pastor of the church in 1999, following forty-eight men who had so served. Under her leadership the church was prominent in preserving the legacy of W. E. B. Du Bois, who attended the church as a youth, and local Black history. At the same time, as of 2006 it was continuing to maintain its identity as a traditional rural church drawing a membership that sees its church as a refueling place, that believes prayer changes things, that has a desire to praise God, and that seeks to "live holy" so as to experience the Holy Ghost.

David Levinson

Willard H. Durant, Pastor and Community Leader

From the 1960s on, Willard Durant (born 1935) was a community leader, child advocate, community activist, and religious leader in Pittsfield, Massachusetts. In his work he often partnered with his wife, Rosemary (Morehead) Durant. Ivan Newton, historian of the Second Congregational Church, told journalist Lesley Ann Beck in 2002: "He's been a pillar in the community ever since I've been here, and I've been here 25 years. I would call him a centerpiece."

Durant was born in Ansonia, Connecticut. His father, William Durante, was pastor of the Clinton A. M. E. Zion Church in Great Barrington from 1962 to 1972. Willard Durant served in the U.S. Air Force and then worked at Pratt & Whitney, the aircraft engine manufacturer, before marrying Rosemary in 1958 and moving to Pittsfield, her hometown, the following year. The Durants had eight children (four adopted) and over the years opened their home to another fourteen additional foster children. Durant attended several colleges, earning a master's degree from Goddard College in Vermont.

In Pittsfield Durant worked for General Electric until 1965, when he left to become a neighborhood aide in Action for Opportunity, an antipoverty agency. The following year he was elected head of the Pittsfield chapter of the NAACP. After serving for several years as an assistant pastor at the Clinton and Price Memorial A. M. E. Zion churches, he became a pastor of Price Memorial in 1976, a position he held until 2002.

In 1982 Durant became director of the Christian Center, which he and Rosemary codirected until 1997. Established in 1896 as a mission by the Epworth League of the Methodist Church, the Christian Center is a nonprofit, educational, and social service agency. Under the Durants it was staffed mainly by volunteers. It provided food for the poor, ran after-school and housing programs, offered a clothing service, and constructed the Erworth Arms housing for senior citizens at 350 West Street.

In addition to these full-time positions, Durant volunteered on numerous committees and commissions, including Head Start and the Pittsfield Crime Prevention Council. Among the numerous honors he received for his work in the Pittsfield community and with its children were the Jaycee Distinguished Service Award, the Berkshire County NAACP Brotherhood Award, and, with Rosemary, the Helen Spurrier Howard Child Advocate Award from the Berkshire County Council for Children. In 2002 he was designated a "Berkshire Hero" by the *Berkshire Eagle.*

David Levinson

Rev. Willard H. Durant of the Price Memorial A. M. E. Zion Church in Pittsfield, c. 1999. Photo by Erik Callahan.

Sources

Religious Institutions

Beck, Lesley Ann. "A Pillar of the Community: The Rev. Willard H. Durant." *Berkshire Heroes.* http://63.147.65.2/heroes/new/default.asp?filename=durant (accessed 31 Oct. 2004).

Dozier, Esther. Personal communication with the author, 2005.

Drew, Bernard A. *Great Barrington: Great Town/Great History.* Great Barrington, MA: Great Barrington Historical Society, 1999.

Du Bois, W. E. B. "Early Writings: Columns from the *New York Independent.*" Reprinted in *The Seventh Son: The Thought and Writings of W. E. B. Du Bois.* Vol. 1, 1883–1885, ed. by Julius Lester, 154-69. New York: Vintage Books, 1971.

Du Bois, W. E. B. *The Souls of Black Folk: Essays and Sketches.* Chicago: A. C. McClurg & Co., 1903.

Early Records of the Congregational Church. [Typed manuscript available at the Mason Library, Great Barrington, MA.]

Harrison, Samuel. *Rev. Samuel Harrison, His Life Story, as Told by Himself.* Pittsfield, MA: Privately printed, 1899. [Available at the Berkshire Athenaeum, Pittsfield, MA.]

Levinson, David. *Sewing Circles, Dime Suppers, and W. E. B. Du Bois: A History of the Clinton A. M. E. Zion Church.* Great Barrington, MA: Berkshire Publishing Group, 2006.

Michaels, Julie. "AME Zion Comes of Age." *The Berkshire Sampler,* 25 March 1979.

Taylor, Richard H. *Historical Directory of the Congregational, Christian and United Church of Christ Congregations in Berkshire County, Massachusetts: 1734–1979.* Dalton, MA: Berkshire Association of the United Church of Christ, 1979.

Women as Religious Leaders

Du Bois, W. E. B. "Early Writings: Columns from the *New York Independent.*" Reprinted in *The Seventh Son: The Thought and Writings of W. E. B. Du Bois.* Vol. 1, 1883–1885, Ed. by Julius Lester, 154-69. New York: Vintage Books, 1971.

Du Bois, W. E .B. *The Philadelphia Negro: A Social Study.* Philadelphia: University of Pennsylvania Press, 1898.

Du Bois, W. E. B. *The Souls of Black Folk: Essays and Sketches.* Chicago: A. C. McClurg, 1903.

Du Bois, W. E. B., ed. *The Negro Church.* Atlanta, GA: Atlanta University Press, 1903.

Harris, Meriah E. "Women in the Pioneer Work of the Church." *A. M. E. Zion Quarterly Review* (April 1899).

Michaels, Julie. "AME Zion Comes of Age." *The Berkshire Sampler,* 25 March 1979.

Walls, William J. *The African Methodist Episcopal Zion Church; Reality of the Black Church.* Charlotte, NC: A. M. E. Zion Publishing House, 1974.

Freeborn Garretson and "Black Harry" Hosier in Northwest Connecticut

History of Litchfield County, Connecticut, with Illustrations and Biographical Sketches of Its Prominent Men and Pioneers. Philadelphia, PA: J. W. Lewis & Co., 1881.

McEllhenny, John G. "Harry Hosier, An African American Who Gave a Beat to Methodist Preaching, c.1750–c.1806." Retrieved from http://www.gcah.org/BulletinInserts/BI_Hosier.htm.

McEllhenny, John G. *200 Years of United Methodism: An Illustrated History.* Madison, NJ: 1984. Electronic edition: http://www.drew.edu.books/200Years/part2.020.htm.

Sedgwick, Charles F. *General History of the Town of Sharon, Litchfield County, Connecticut.* Amenia, NY: Charles Walsh, 1898.

Stevens, Abel. *History of the Methodist Episcopal Church in the United States of America.* New York: 1864–1867. Electronic edition: http://www.nnu.edu/wesleyctr/books/0201-0300/stevens/0219-247.htm.

Lemuel Haynes, Pioneer Minister

Duffy, John J., et al. T*he Vermont Encyclopedia.* Hanover, NH: University Press of New England, 2003.

Felton, Harold W. *Canaan: A Small New England Town during the American Revolutionary War.* Falls Village, CT: Bramble Co., 1990.

Haynes, Lemuel. *Black Preacher to White America: The Collected Writings of Lemuel Haynes, 1774–1833.* Ed. by Richard Newman. Brooklyn, NY: Carlson Publications, 1990.

Kaplan, Sidney. *The Black Presence in the Era of the American Revolution.* Amherst: University of Massachusetts Press, 1989.

Saillant, John. *Black Puritan, Black Republican: The Life and Thought of Lemuel Haynes, 1753–1833.* New York: Oxford University Press, 2003.

Sprague, William B. *Annals of the American Pulpit; or Commemorative Notices of Distinguished American Clergymen of Various Denominations*. New York: Robert Carter & Brothers, 1859.

WGBH Interactive. "Lemuel Haynes, 1753–1833." *Africans in America*. http://www.pbs.org/wgbh.aia/part2/2p29.html (accessed 9 Nov. 2004).

Second Congregational Church, United Church of Christ, Pittsfield

"Colored Race Started Church Back in 1846," *Berkshire Eagle*, 27 Jan. 1917.

Cade, Edward C., United Church of Christ, assistant archivist. E-mail, 9 Nov. 2001.

The 128th Anniversary Journal of the Second Congregational Church, United Church of Christ (5–9 June 1974). [Available at the Second Congregational Church, Pittsfield, MA.]

The 140th Anniversary Journal of the Second Congregational Church, United Church of Christ (21 Sept. 1986). [Available at the Second Congregational Church, Pittsfield, MA.]

The 150th Anniversary Journal of the Second Congregational Church, United Church of Christ (22 Sept. 1996). [Available at the Second Congregational Church, Pittsfield, MA.]

"Second Congregational Church to Celebrate 90th Anniversary of Its Founding Tomorrow," *Berkshire Eagle*, 29 Aug. 1936.

Samuel Harrison, Minister and Political Activist

Blassingame, John W. "Negro Chaplains in the Civil War." *The Negro History Bulletin*, Oct. 1963.

"Death of a Famous Colored Preacher." *North Adams Transcript*, 12 Aug. 1900.

Dickerson, Dennis. "Reverend Samuel Harrison: A Nineteenth Century Black Clergyman." In *Black Apostles at Home and Abroad: Afro-Americans and the Christian Mission from the Revolution to Reconstruction*, ed. by David W. Wills and Richard Newman. Boston: G. K. Hall & Co., 1982.

Harrison, Samuel. *An Appeal of a Colored Man to his Fellow Citizens of a Fairer Hue in the United States*. Pittsfield, MA: Chickering & Axtell, 1877. [Available at the Berkshire Athenaeum, Pittsfield, MA.]

Harrison, Samuel. *A Centennial Sermon Delivered in the Chapel of the Methodist Episcopal Church, July 2, 1876*. Pittsfield, MA: Chickering & Axtell, 1877. [Available at the Berkshire Athenaeum, Pittsfield, MA.]

Harrison, Samuel. *Pittsfield: Twenty-Five Years Ago*. Pittsfield, MA: Chickering & Axtell, 1876. [Available at the Berkshire Athenaeum, Pittsfield, MA.]

Harrison, Samuel. *Rev. Samuel Harrison, His Life Story, as Told by Himself*. Pittsfield, MA: Privately printed, 1899. [Available at the Berkshire Athenaeum, Pittsfield, MA.]

"Obtained Justice in Civil War Days for Pittsfield Man," *Berkshire Eagle*, 6 June 1925.

"Reverend Samuel Harrison." *Berkshire Eagle*. 11 Aug. 1900.

"Reverend Samuel Harrison." *Pittsfield Sun*, 11 Dec. 1902.

Smith, J. E. A. *The History of Pittsfield, Berkshire County, Massachusetts*. Springfield, MA: C. W. Bryan & Co., 1876.

Taylor, Richard H. *Historical Directory of the Congregational, Christian and United Church of*

Christ Congregations in Berkshire County, Massachusetts: 1734–1979. Dalton, MA: Berkshire Association of the United Church of Christ, 1979.

Thomas Nelson Baker, Minister and Philosopher

The 128th Anniversary Journal of the Second Congregational Church, United Church of Christ (5–9 June 1974). [Available at the Second Congregational Church, Pittsfield, MA.]

Weis, Peter. "No Slave to Fortune" *NMH Magazine* (Fall 2003).

Clinton African Methodist Episcopal Zion Church, Great Barrington

Du Bois, W. E. B. "Early Writings: Columns from the New York Independent." Reprinted in *The Seventh Son: The Thought and Writings of W. E. B. Du Bois*. Vol. 1, 1883–1885, Ed. by Julius Lester, 154-69. New York: Vintage Books, 1971.

Levinson, David. *Sewing Circles, Dime Suppers, and W. E. B. Du Bois: A History of the Clinton A. M. E. Zion Church*. Great Barrington, MA: Berkshire Publishing Group, 2006.

Willard H. Durant, Pastor and Community Leader

Beck, Lesley Ann. "A pillar of the Community: The Rev. Willard H. Durant." *Berkshire Heroes*. http://63.147.65.2/heroes/new/default.asp?filename=durant (accessed 31 Oct. 2004).

"The Durants Come Home," *Berkshire Eagle*, 20 Nov. 1982.

"Durants to Direct Christian Center," *Berkshire Eagle*, 17 Sept. 1982.

"Durant to Succeed Cooper as City AME Zion Pastor," *Berkshire Eagle*, 22 June 1976.

"Name in the News," *Berkshire Eagle*, 17 Dec. 1966.

Society, Arts, and Ideas

Black social life in the region has long existed along two dimensions. The first is social life in the Black communities, a subject of which relatively little has been written about but which is covered in several entries below. Second is Black involvement in and contributions to the region's and nation's artistic and intellectual life as covered in articles on the Harlem Renaissance and entertainment.

Kinship

The James VanDerZee women and children, Lenox, c. 1909. From left: Sister Mary, Walter's wife Catherine (called Kate) with son Reginald, Susan Elizabeth, Kate (first wife), Rachel (daughter), Jennie (sister). Back of photo says: "Van Der Zee Ladies. Wife, Daughter, Mother and Sisters." Photograph by James VanDerZee. Copyright Donna Mussenden VanDerZee.

One important element of African American culture, not addressed here in detail, is kinship, which includes marriage and family relationships. Based on ties of blood and marriage, these relationships are significant in regional African American life because they created and continue to create relationships within and across communities. They also help form personal identity, since it is important to individuals to be able to say, for example, that I am a Moorehead, Gunn, Caesar, Persip, or Burghardt descendant. Kinship is not addressed here in detail because the intensive and time-consuming genealogical research needed to study this topic is only in its early stages in the region. The fullest effort to date is Nancy Muller's genealogy of the Burghardt family in South County from the mid-eighteenth to the late nineteenth century. Her study shows much intermarriage between Burghardts and members of other early South County Black families including

Sadie and Sylvester Gunn, mother and father of Minietta, Maude, Maybelle, Charles, Clifford, Clarence, Mary and David. Photo courtesy of Wray Gunn Collection.

Tyringham and Monterey in the middle of the nineteenth century. And a recently published book provides genealogical information up to 1900 for the Starrs of Sharon and the Jacksons of Salisbury.

Although not yet fully documented, marriage between people from different towns was quite common and led to the dispersal of families and kin across several towns. As Elaine Gunn noted, it is something to think of people in the 1800s traveling by carriage from Sheffield to Williamstown to court, but it did happen. Kin ties were important in

the Newports, Jacksons, Van Nesses, Gardners, and Woosters. But, to show how kinship stretches over time and place, in 2006 there were no Black Burghardts left in South County, although there were Burghardt descendants in Pittsfield.

The Burghardts are not the only family studied intensively. There are also extensive but unpublished genealogies of the Gunn family dating from the 1700s up to the family members living in Sheffield, Great Barrington, and Stockbridge in 2006. Similarly, carefully compiled genealogies exist for descendants of Thomas Brister, William Egbert, and David L. Osterhout, and ancestors and family members of James VanDerZee in Lenox for the nineteenth and twentieth centuries. These genealogies, collected by Roberta M. Neizer, show links by marriage across these four Lenox families. Her research on the Mars family of northwest Connecticut and the Berkshires also shows links to the Brister and VanDerZee families beginning in the early nineteenth century. Clint Elliot has gathered detailed information about Black families in

Jefferson McKinley Remembered

Thomas Jefferson McKinley's reputation survived him in Great Barrington, as indicated by this announcement in the weekly *Courier* (11 August 1927, 5). The Chinn's had purchased the McKinley's home in the late 1800s before they relocated to New York City.

Mrs. William Chinn of New York has loaned to the Mason Library a flute, the property of Thomas Jefferson McKinley, colored, who died in Great Barrington December 21, 1896. At the time of his death Mr. McKinley was the oldest resident of Berkshire county. Though the exact date of his birth is not known, it is the popular belief that he had seen a hundred and twelve summers. He was a vegetable and fruit dealer and was known to the people of his time as "Old Jeff." Though he was brought in bondage and uneducated, his intellectual vision was remarkably clear, and, in his rude way, he was somewhat of a philosopher.

property transfers as well, with African Americans often buying and selling property from and to one another. For example, the Burghardt property on Route 23, which is now the W. E. B. Du Bois Homesite, passed from Burghardts to Pipers to Woosters and eventually to Du Bois himself (who was a Burghardt on his mother's side), all of whom were related through blood or marriage.

David Levinson

Five generations of Persips. From left (standing) Frances Persip Duval, Tara Taylor, and Frances Anderson; (seated) Francis Persip and Tatiana Taylor, 1987, Pittsfield. Photo courtesy of Mrs. Frances Persip Duval Collection.

Four generations of Pattersons, Gilmores, Marshalls, and Rollisons gather for one of their regular Sunday afternoon dinners in Pittsfield. Counterclockwise from the far right: Shirley Rollison (Clark), Henry Northrup Rollison, Estelle Rollison (Beckham), Amanda Marshall, Elizabeth Patterson, Margaret Gilmore, Ann Rollison (Penn), Myrtle Henderson Rollison, Henry Grant Rollison. Photo courtesy of John Garrett and Ann Rollison Penn Collection.

Guest Homes for African Americans

In 1897, recognizing the need for summer accommodations for visiting Blacks (who were barred from white-only establishments), pioneer restaurateurs Jason Cooley and his wife, Almira, leased rooms in the Marble Block in Great Barrington and rented them out.

Edgar Willoughby opened his Sunset Inn on Rosseter Street in Great Barrington in the 1920s specifically for Black patrons. His most famous guest was W. E. B. Du Bois, who stayed at the inn in 1928. In the 1940s Martha Wright Crawford opened Crawford's Inn on Elm Court in the same town. "It was predominantly for Blacks," recalled her son Isaac Crawford Jr. "She enclosed a porch and made an office for an employment agency, mainly for teachers and students in the summer" (Crawford Jr. 1998).

Charles H. Allen of Stockbridge won $11,000 in the Irish sweepstakes in the late 1920s and used his winnings to open a summer guest house on Park Street. He operated it as "a high-class place, and his patrons spent money in the town. Neighbors at first nearly had a panic, but they got over it, and when the tavernkeeper [*sic*] died, he held the respect of all the townspeople" (*Berkshire Eagle* 1946).

Perhaps the first crack in segregated visitor housing came in 1939 in Stockbridge. Jo Humphrey, daughter of Joseph Franz, who designed the Ted Shawn Theatre at Jacob's

The former Sunset Inn on 27 Rosseter Street in Great Barrington and the home of Clarence and Elaine Gunn for thirty-two years from 1953 to 1985. Photo courtesy of Elaine Gunn Collection.

Pillow, recalled when Dorothy Maynor was engaged to sing at Tanglewood in 1939. Tanglewood artists at that time were housed at the Red Lion Inn, but the inn was not yet open to Blacks. Consequently, arrangements were made for Maynor to stay at Allen's guest house on Park Street. Franz, who was a member of the Stockbridge Chamber of Commerce, somehow got wind of this development and was outraged. He went to his colleagues at the Red Lion Inn and demanded that they allow Maynor to break the color barrier at their establishment. The inn relented, and another milestone was reached.

And the fate of these early guest houses? The Marble Block still stands in Great Barrington; the Sunset Inn was demolished, and another house now stands on its site. Crawford Inn was razed to enlarge a bank parking lot, while in Stockbridge, Allen's hotel is now a private residence.

Bernard A. Drew

The following report in the *Berkshire Courier* (13 February 1886, 4) tells how the community would come together to support one another in the 1880s. Manuel Mason, a caterer and trustee of the Clinton A. M. E. Zion Church in Great Barrington, was well regarded in the white community.

Mr. Manuel Mason and family have recently moved into their new home, on the road leading to [the] reservoir. It is a neat and attractive house of two and a half stories, with parlor, hall, dining-room, and kitchen on the first floor, and above are three chambers and a large attic. The house has all the modern conveniences in the way of furnace, water, sewage, etc. It has a healthy location and commands a fine view of the valley.

Last Thursday a "house warming" was given Mr. and Mrs. Mason, from 4 to 10 o'clock, and a large number of friends testified their regard for the honest and industrious couple by nearly furnishing their new home, bringing a parlor set, rugs, curtains, lambrequins, vases, books, albums, stands, clothes, pictures, lamps, cut glass, silver, etc. Mr. and Mrs. Mason entertained all with a bountiful supper.

Entertainment and Social Life

Black singers, singing groups, dancers, actors, lecturers, dramatic readers, and preachers have been part of the Berkshire entertainment scene since the middle of the nineteenth century. Many of these entertainers were local amateurs, while others were professionals hired by Black churches and social clubs—and white ones also—to provide entertainment, often for the entire community.

In the nineteenth century and first few decades of the twentieth, churches were major providers of entertainment. Church suppers, socials, teas, festivals, fairs, and choir and Sunday school concerts were a regular feature of the monthly social calendar. Churches also raised income by bringing in outside entertainers, including choruses such as the Hampton Institute Chorus, well-known performers such as Blind Tom Number 2, and speakers. Churches put on plays and concerts as well, drawing on the talents of their members. An item in the *Berkshire Eagle* on 4 September 1901 reported that well-known local Black violinist, Billy Van Allen, regularly entertained the children of former president Grover Cleveland in Tyringham, when Cleveland lived there for the year. These entertainments were especially welcome in the long, cold winter months. During this period, white groups sometimes staged minstrel shows and racist performances of *Uncle Tom's Cabin*. (Minstrel shows continued to be staged by white groups as fundraising events in Pittsfield and Great Barrington into the early 1960s.)

In the twentieth century, with the growth in popularity of venues such as the Mahaiwe Theater in Great Barrington and the Colonial Theater in Pittsfield, and with the arrival of cinema and radio, church-sponsored events became less significant. One notable theatrical performance at the Colonial Theater was the 1926 staging of Eubie Blake's musical *Shuffle Along*, with an all-Black cast. Dances and balls, with music often provided by Black bands, also helped eclipse church events. Among the bands that performed were Johnny Hubbard and his Jazz Hounds and Charlie Gaulden's Rhythm Boys in the 1920s and 1930s, the Dixie Serenaders in the 1940s, the Charlie Gaulden Quartet in the 1950s, and the Chet Williams Band in the 1950s and 1960s.

An advertisement and ticket for a performance of *Uncle Tom's Cabin* in Sheffield in 1892. Photo from Coenen, Christopher. *Sheffield 1773–1983; A Pictorial Recollection.* Sheffield: Sheffield 250th Anniversary Committee, 1983.

Many Black social events were held at the St. John's Masonic Temple in Pittsfield and Walker and Sumner halls in Great Barrington. Some men from the county were active in St. John's Lodge #10 Ancient Free and Accepted Masons (A. F. & M.) in Pittsfield; and women, in the Beulah Chapter of the Order of the Eastern Star, also in Pittsfield. St. John's Lodge was chartered in Pittsfield in 1898 with Amos Hamilton, Josiah Gardner, and William H. Clarkson, the first

Local Entertainment

Before the appearance of mass media, local groups like churches provided entertainment for the town. This announcement was placed in the *Berkshire Courier* (20 August 1908, 3).

On Tuesday, Wednesday and Thursday evenings of next week, the Ladies' Sewing Circle of the local A.M.E. Zion church will hold a fair at the church. Wednesday evening there will be a musical and literary entertainment in which Mary A. Carter, wife of the pastor of the church at New Guinea, Sheffield, "Philadelphia's favorite elecutionist" will appear, supported by local talent and the church choir. The doors open at 4p.m. Admission 10 cents.

three officers. The lodge was always small (with less than fifty members) and relatively isolated from other Masonic lodges. The lodge owned its own room and by the 1950s had enough members that it could purchase its own building in 1954, at 173 Robbins Avenue in Pittsfield. The lodge then became a primary venue for African American dances, banquets, and civil rights meetings. It drew people from the entire county and beyond. A declining membership led the Grand Lodge to take ownership of the building and in 1993 it was sold to the Association for Basic Community Development, although St. John's Lodge continues to exist.

Early on, however, much of Black social life took place in private residences. In Great Barrington, two social clubs, the Progressive Club and the Jolly Club No. 12, were founded in the 1940s and remained active into the 1950s. Club members met regularly for dinners and card and game parties at one another's homes. The Progressive Club also hosted an annual dance for the entire South County. Black women in Great Barrington and Pittsfield founded the charitable Monday Nite Club in 1958, perhaps as an alternative to the all-white (at the time) Thursday Morning Club. In Pittsfield, Harry West owned a popular social club and pool hall on West Street, and Cliff Potter and

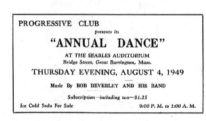

An admission ticket for the 1949 dance sponsored by the Progressive Club in Great Barrington. Photo courtesy of Clinton A. M. E. Zion Church, Great Barrington.

Luther Todd published *The Tattler*, which ran announcements of events and personal news. In the 1930s, Black social life became a bit more public as announcements of weddings and other events began to be reported regularly in the regional newspapers.

As a premier cultural resort, the Berkshires has attracted its share of professional Black musicians, singers, actors, and dancers. Photos of several of these musicians adorn the walls of the Castle Street Café in Great Barrington, which was once a tearoom owned by the Afro-Caribbean innkeeper Edgar Willoughby. Among the many notable African American entertainers who have performed in the Berkshires are the tenor Sydney Woodward, the dramatic reader Ada Bell Griffin, the actress Florence Mills, the soprano Catherine Van Buren, and musicians and composers Louis Armstrong, Duke Ellington, Count Basie, Billie Holiday, Sarah Vaughan, Coleman Hawkins, Miles Davis, Thelonious Monk, the Modern Jazz Quartet, and Wynton Marsalis. As for dance, Jacob's Pillow Dance Festival in Becket has featured and introduced several Black modern and contemporary dance companies, as discussed in the article below.

A major lure for Black musical talent was the Music Inn, founded in Stockbridge in 1950 by Philip and Stephanie Barber.

"To be sure, we in Berkshire were not perhaps as stiff and formal as they in Suffolk of olden time; yet we were very quiet and subdued, and I know not what would have happened those clear Sabbath mornings had someone punctuated the sermon with a wild scream, or interrupted the long prayer with a loud Amen!"
W. E. B. Du Bois, *The Souls of Black Folk,* 1903.

Blues musician John Lee Hooker at the Music Inn (School of Jazz) in Stockbridge in the early 1950s. Photograph by Clemens Kalischer, Image Photos, copyright 2002.

The couple established it as a center for jazz, and for ten years it was a premier center for jazz education and performance in the nation, attracting many of the jazz greats, who studied, taught, played, and recorded there. At first the Music Inn was not generally accepted. Stephanie Barber noted: "Black people were not popular in New England. In the early days, we had problems finding beds in local inns for artists who happened to be Black when we overflowed our own capacity. People in the village did not approve of what we were doing. But in good New England fashion, they believed we had the right to do it" (Rogovoy 1998). The Barbers sold the inn in 1960, and while it remained open for two more decades, the focus shifted first to folk music and then to rock and roll.

David Levinson

African American Literary Societies

In May 1883 the Sewing Society of the African Methodist Episcopal Zion Church in Great Bar- rington formed a literary society. As Elizabeth McHenry has pointed out in *Forgotten Readers*, literary societies were a significant component of Black life beginning in the early nineteenth century and continuing well into the twentieth century. As elsewhere, the formation of the literary society by the small Black community in Great Barrington shows clearly the importance these individuals placed on reading, learning, and the discussion of ideas. The society and other church groups remained active well into the twentieth century, organizing public readings, plays, musicals, debates, and concerts and arranging for guest speakers (including W. E. B. Du Bois). Most of these events were public ones, staged in larger venues than that of the church, such as the second-floor meeting room of the town hall. (At the time, the whole second floor of Great Barrington's town hall was open for meetings.) By offering these events to the paying public, the church secured additional funds.

David Levinson

Robert A. Gilbert, Photographer and Ornithologist

Robert Gilbert (standing far right) with a group at the Umbago cabin, Pine Point. Photo courtesy of William Brewster Photographic Collection, Massachusetts Audubon Society.

Robert Gilbert (1869–1942) is an example of a Black man whose contributions went unnoticed or were credited to someone else. In the 1970s, two thousand antique photographic glass plate negatives dating to the late 1800s were found in an attic in Lincoln, Massachusetts. They were at first assumed to be the work of William Brewster of Cambridge and Concord, Massachusetts, the first president of the Audubon Society and a prominent ornithologist. John Hanson Mitchell, author of *Looking for Mr. Gilbert: The Reimagined Life of An African*, came to believe that the majority of these photographs were actually taken by Robert Alexander Gilbert, a little-known but talented Black man who worked for and was a close friend and companion of Brewster. The evidence that Mitchell unfolds in his book suggests that Gilbert was well traveled, a skilled taxidermist, a naturalist, a musician, an inventor, a chef, a devoted father and husband, and a church deacon.

Robert Gilbert was born in Natural Bridge, Virginia, in 1869 and attended high school in Lynchburg, Virginia. He became a trained classical pianist. At seventeen, Robert joined his older brother, William, who was living in Boston with his aunt, Elizabeth. Robert married Anna Scott in 1896. The couple had three daughters—Mary, Emma, and Edyth. Robert died in Cambridge on 7 December 1942.

Mitchell writes, "You can find sorted and displayed [animal] skins prepared by Gilbert, but credited to William Brewster in little natural history museums all over New England, everywhere from the Berkshires to the Harvard Museum of Natural History" (Mitchell 2005). Pleasant Valley Audubon Center in Lenox has numerous birds that fall into this category, having been credited to Brewster but which were, according to Mitchell, most likely shot and stuffed by Gilbert.

Brewster was a lifelong friend of Stockbridge resident Daniel Chester French (sculptor of *The Lincoln Memorial* and *The Concord Minuteman*). In June of 1883 Gilbert, Brewster, and French spent nine days on Mount Greylock collecting ornithological data and noting sixty-six species of birds sighted. Reference is made of Brewster being one of the first scientists to climb Massachusetts's highest peak and likely the first ornithologist to make the climb. Gilbert should have shared this honor, though he was not acknowledged. He and Brewster were again in the Berkshires in 1892, 1893, and 1894, and noted unusual sightings of birds. Brewster (1884, 5–16) wrote, "Probably no other area of similar extent in Massachusetts has held out as inviting a field to the ornithologist as Berkshire County." He wrote of coming to the Berkshires annually to observe birds, and of "waiting for a train in the railroad station in Glendale, Berkshire County, Massachusetts[,]" observing particular birds and nests. Mitchell wrote in 2005: "If Brewster was here, Gilbert was with him."

Ellen Broderick

"Massachusetts Landscape, Elm," photo by Robert A. Gilbert. According to John Mitchell it "bears all the hallmarks of Gilbert. He seems to have favored perspective, and he often positioned his camera in such a way as to favor angles. Notice how the hedge curves toward the trees on the right, and the wall matches the hedge line, and both the hill above and the hedge flow toward the empty sky framed by the apple trees on the right." Photo courtesy of William Brewster Photographic Collection, Massachusetts Audubon Society.

The Harlem Renaissance

Between 1920 and 1930 there was an unprecedented outburst of creativity in New York City's Black community in the fields of art, music, literature, and social commentary. This cultural movement, first known as the New Negro Movement and later as the Harlem Renaissance, exalted the unique culture of African Americans, who were encouraged to celebrate their heritage. Never before had so many white Americans read the poetry, novels, essays, criticism, and plays and embraced the music, community productions, expressions, and style of Black Americans. "It was a time," recalled the poet Langston Hughes, "when the Negro was in Vogue. I was there. I had a swell time while it lasted. But I thought it wouldn't last long."

Hughes was correct in this; the movement's demise came quickly with the Great Depression.

But while it lasted, it was an optimistic time, when many Harlemites thought that the race problem could be solved through art—"civil rights through copyright" was the popular slogan. This turned out to be an incorrect assumption.

Contributing to the rise of the Harlem Renaissance were the great out-migration of African Americans from the South to northern cities such as New York, Chicago, and Washington, D.C., and trends in American society as a whole toward experimentation. The 1920s saw the rise of radical Black intellectuals, including the critic and sociologist Alain Locke; Marcus Garvey, founder of the Universal Negro Improvement Association; and W. E. B. Du Bois, editor of *The Crisis* magazine. Several of the important participants in the Harlem Renaissance had strong ties to Berkshire County. One was Du Bois himself, whose intellectual and civil rights work was seen as laying the groundwork for the Harlem Renaissance. He was also personally involved, since his daughter, Yolande, was married for a brief time to Black poet Countee Cullen. Another was James VanDerZee, photographer of the movement, who was born and grew up in Lenox. A third was the poet, writer, diplomat, and civil rights leader James Weldon Johnson, who summered and wrote for many years in Great Barrington. Finally, there was National Association for the Advancement of Colored People (NAACP) pioneer and novelist Walter White, who wrote his 1923 novel, *The Fire in the Flint*, in twelve days while staying at the "Riverbank," NAACP official Mary White Ovington's cottage in Alford.

Barbara Bartle

James VanDerZee, self portrait, 1922. Photograph by James VanDerZee. Copyright Donna Mussenden VanDerZee.

The Dilemma of the Negro Author

. . . the Aframerican author faces a special problem which the plain American author knows nothing about—the problem of the double audience. It is more than a double audience; it is a divided audience, an audience made up of two elements with differing and often opposite and antagonistic points of view. His audience is often both white America and black America. The moment a Negro writer takes up his pen or sits down to his typewriter he is immediately called upon to solve, consciously or unconsciously, this problem of the double audience. To whom should he address himself, to his own black group or white America? Many a Negro writer has fallen down, as it were, between these two stools. Johnson, James Weldon.

"The Dilemma of the Negro Author." *American Mercury*, XV (Dec. 1928), 477. Quoted in Henderson, Bill (Ed.). *The Pushcart Prize, III: Best of the Small Presses.* 1978-79 ed. NY: The Pushcart Press, 1978. p. 284.

James VanDerZee, Photographer

For the thousands of pictures he took during the Harlem Renaissance of the 1920s and early 1930s, James VanDerZee (1886–1983) is widely acknowledged as the first great African American photographer of the twentieth century. He ran a commercial photographic studio with his second wife, Gaynella, in Harlem, where he recorded the people and life of this vibrant era—pictures that show with great pride and clarity the achievements in the fields of literature, art, and music.

VanDerZee was discovered by the world at the age of eighty-three, when several of his photographs were used by the Metropolitan Museum of Art in its show "Harlem on My Mind" in 1969. In 1993 the National Portrait Gallery in Washington, D.C., had a retrospective of this work, and his innovations

James VanDerZee, self portrait at age 14 in Lenox. Photograph by James VanDerZee. Copyright Donna Mussenden VanDerZee.

and work in this medium have since come regarded as masterful, both from the artistic and documentary points of view.

Born in Lenox on 29 June 1886, VanDerZee enjoyed a career spanning a remarkable eighty years, from the first photographs taken in Lenox of his family and friends to the late portraits he made when he was in his nineties of Bill Cosby, Eubie Blake, Jean-Michel Basquiat, Muhammad Ali, Cicely Tyson, Miles Davis, and others. His family had come from New Baltimore, New York. For a time his parents worked as servants for Ulysses S. Grant before settling in Lenox to await the birth of their first child. There VanDerZee's father became sexton of Trinity Church.

Later in life VanDerZee recalled that he had a happy and comfortable childhood living on Taconic Street surrounded by relatives. On one side were the Osterhouts, who ran a laundry from their home, and on the other were the Egberts, who operated a bakery. VanDerZee did not recall any hardship, there having always been plenty of food and firewood in winter. He also did not recall any family quarrels or sibling rivalry; they were a close family. Family prayer meetings were held at this grandfather's house, and family outings were common.

The children were encouraged to excel in school. Because there were only six or seven Black families in Lenox during those years, the VanDerZee children were often the only Black children in class. VanDerZee was not aware of any prejudice, but he mingled with whites only in church and school. He did mention one incident that he was never able to forget. When a geography lesson on Africa had been assigned, he had stayed home. The book had said that the Black race was known for its thick lips and kinky hair, and he did not want to be present when that came up, so he took a walk with his brother Walter to Pittsfield. But it turned out that it was the lesson for the next class session, and he had to endure the comments of his classmates. At school VanDerZee showed a talent for art and music. In 1906 when he left for Harlem, he was an aspiring

violinist and equally skilled at the piano. It is possible that Joseph Le Maire of Aspinwall was his music teacher. VanDerZee studied music at the Carlton Conservatory in New York City. In 1907 he married Kate, who became the mother of their two children. He returned to Lenox for the summers.

After landing a job in Newark, New Jersey, in 1915 as a darkroom technician, his career as a photographer superseded that of musician. Just two years later, in Harlem, he opened his own studio at 135th Street with his second wife, Gaynella Greenlee, and then, as he prospered, opened a larger shop at 272 Lenox Avenue. All the important people and organizations of Harlem flocked to his studio to have their pictures taken, VanDerZee's reputation having grown. He was chosen the official photographer for Marcus Garvey, founder of the UNIA (Universal Negro Improvement Association), known as "The Back to Africa" movement.

Around 1930 VanDerZee visited Lenox, and there was much in his birthplace that he remembered—the three houses in a row, the stable, and the old abandoned sawmill. The Osterhout aunts and his great aunt Egbert were still taking in laundry and baking. But within ten years everything changed. A highway was put through the property. Although the state had paid the family for the property, VanDerZee had objected to the sale. He had wanted the family enclave to stay intact, but other members of the family had favored selling and eventually persuaded him to agree.

VanDerZee's fortunes as a photographer declined after World War II owing to the advent of the Brownie camera. In 1969 his work was rediscovered, thanks to its inclusion in the Metropolitan Museum of Arts "Harlem on My Mind" exhibition. VanDerZee returned in 1970 to Lenox for the opening of an exhibition of his pictures at the Welles Gallery. He had been in correspondence with David Dana, president of the Lenox Library, and Dana arranged for this exhibition. By the 1970s, however—specifically after the death of Gaynella in 1976—he was living in poverty on West 94th Street and was receiving little or no compensation for the republication of his works.

In 1978 VanDerZee married his third wife, Donna Mussenden, and through her efforts his pictures again gained the attention of the public, and he took his place as one of the greatest photographers in American history. With many honors, including four honorary degrees, one an honorary doctorate from Howard University, he died in Washington, D.C., at the age of ninety-six, on 15 May 1983. At his death it was said that he was a man who saw beauty in people and was willing to work hard to get his camera to see it. He recorded a time, place, and culture—Harlem during its renaissance—that we can recapture as vividly as any decade in our history.

Barbara Bartle

W. E. B. Du Bois, Native Son

The Housatonic River, Du Bois's "golden river," flows through downtown Great Barrington in 2000. Photo by Rachel Fletcher.

W. E. B. Du Bois (1868–1963) is best known for his stance on civil rights, innovative social research skills, literary talent, and historical analysis. Yet it is not surprising that his interests extended to an understanding and an appreciation of the natural world. In 1920 in his first autobiography, *Darkwater*, Du Bois described his birth, on 23 February 1868, in Great Barrington, Massachusetts, when he wrote: "I was born by a golden river and in the shadow of two great hills." On a return visit in 1930 he admonished the town fathers to "rescue the Housatonic and clean it as we have never in all years thought before of cleaning it." This concern for the natural world in which he was born remained a constant with Du Bois throughout his adult life. He was primarily a New England puritan, but he never lost the interest he had in the natural world, from his boyhood in Great Barrington to his adopted home of Accra, Ghana. This interest did not escape his fellow citizens, who in a tribute in the 1961 Bicentennial collection noted, "It has long been a habit of his each fall to drive through Great Barrington, for he says no where in the world is such a beautiful fall as in his home town."

Du Bois became interested in the environment at a young age. He was born in a time and place

W. E. B. Du Bois, son Burghardt, and wife Nina in 1898 or 1899. The photo was made in Xenia, Ohio, locale of Wilberforce University, where Du Bois was then teaching. The second photo of just wife and son was carried by Du Bois for several years. Photo left courtesy of Special Collections and Archives, W. E. B. Du Bois Library, University of Massachusetts, Amherst. Photo right from Ruth D. Jones Collection, W. E. B. Du Bois Memorial Committee.

where he was free to explore his natural surroundings unfettered by the obligations of the majority of the other youth of his race in the United States. It was this freedom that molded him into the consummate thinker, writer, and activist that he became in later life.

Early in life he and his mother lived with his grandfather on the Egremont Plain. He described his grandfather's house as a delectable place—simple, square, and low, with the large room of the fireplace, the flagged kitchen, half a step below, and the lower woodshed beyond. Steep, strong stairs led up to the sleeping quarters, while without was a brook, a well, and a mighty elm.

Most of the research and writing about Du Bois has centered on race, politics, or history. That is how he is known, and it is only fitting and right that he should be remembered for the great work of his life and the legacy that he left for all Americans. Yet his writings reveal how much he appreciated the place of

his birth and the natural world wherever he traveled. David Levering Lewis noted, "The importance of the Great Barrington Period, its imprint upon all that Willie Du Bois grew to be, was deep, and certainly singular" (Lewis 1993). Du Bois wrote in one his three autobiographies, *Dusk of Dawn* (1940, 2), "As I have written elsewhere, I was born by a golden river and in the shadow of two great hills. My birthplace was Great Barrington, a little town in western Massachusetts in the valley of the Housatonic, flanked by the Berkshire Hills. Physically and socially our community belonged to the Dutch valley of the Hudson rather than to Puritan New England, and travel went south to New York often more easily than east to Boston. But my birthplace was less important than my birth-time." Du Bois emphasized the political background of his birth inasmuch as he was born during the midst of one of the greatest social experiments in United State history—the Reconstruction—but placed far too little value on the place of his birth. Politics surely would be

133

the important focus of his life, yet a careful reading of his writings reveals the impact the Berkshires had on his long life. He continues in *Dusk of Dawn* (1940, 9): "My town was shut in by its mountains and provincialism; but it was a beautiful place, a little New England town nestled shyly in its valleys with something of Dutch cleanliness and English reticence. . . . The Housatonic yellowed by the paper mills, rolled slowly through its center; while Green River, clear and beautiful, joined it in the south. Main Street was lined with ancient elms; the hills held white pines and orchards and then fade up to magnificent rocks and caves which shut out the neighboring world."

Du Bois escaped this provincial town, at the age of seventeen, when, in his words, he "stepped beyond the shadow of the hills which hemmed in my little valley" (1940, 19). Yet he would remember in each succession of his autobiography the uniqueness and the beauty of the place. He would remember its freedom—"the town and its surroundings were a boy's paradise: there were mountains to climb and rivers to wade and swim; lakes to freeze and hills for coasting. There were orchards and caves and wide green fields" (1940, 13). He went skinny-dipping in the Green River and hiked Monument Mountain, which he called the Mountain of the Moon (Lewis 1993, 37).

Even when Du Bois found that the social relations between the races, especially his own relationships, failed to live up to his expectations, he turned to the natural world. Indeed, when he remembered his greatest pleasure and his greatest pain of boyhood, the Berkshires played an intimate role. Du Bois left the Berkshires to study at Fisk University in Nashville, Tennessee, but he did not forget his Berkshire Hills. In a letter home in 1886 to the pastor of the Congregational Church, who had helped finance his education, he wrote: "Although this sunny land is very pleasant, notwithstanding its squalor misery and ignorance spread broadcast; and although it is a bracing thought to know that I stand among those who do not despise my color, yet I have not forgotten to love my New

England hills, and I often wish I could join some of your pleasant meetings in person as I do in spirit" (Du Bois 1973–1978, vol. 1).

One of the most important passages in his writing illustrating Du Bois's attachment to the place of his birth is that dealing with the death of his son, Burghardt, in Atlanta, Georgia. In his recounting of this Du Bois remembered the day his son was born in Great Barrington. His wife, Nina Gomer, had gone back to Du Bois's hometown to give birth. A note told him of his son's birth. He wrote: "Wife and child fled fast and faster than boat and steamcar, and yet [I] must ever impatiently await them; away from the hard-voiced city, away from the flickering sea into my own Berkshire Hills that sit sadly guarding the gates of Massachusetts." And of his child's death he wrote: "Blithe was the morning of his burial, with bird and song and sweet-smelling flowers. The trees whispered to the grass. . . . We could not lay him in the ground there in Georgia, for the earth there is strangely red; so we bore him away to the northward, with his flowers and his little folded hands. In vain, in vain—for where, O God! Beneath thy broad blue sky shall my dark baby rest in peace—where Reverence dwells, and Goodness, and a Freedom that is free?" (Du Bois 1990, 103–104).

When his wife, Nina Gomer, died, he wrote: "I have just returned from the town where I was born, Great Barrington, Massachusetts. There I laid to rest, in the sunshine and under great and beautiful elms, the wife to whom I have been married for 55 years. . . . [I]t seemed fitting at the end of her life, she should go back to the hills of the Berkshires, where the boy had been born and be buried beside him, in soil where my fathers for more than two centuries lived and died" (Du Bois 1950, 52).

Du Bois not only loved his home place but was also very attached to the Housatonic River. His best memories, after living on his grandfather's land on the Egremont Plains in what Du Bois called the House of the Black Burghardts, was living with his mother in small rented quarters, sometimes in the

Du Bois, Naturalist

"Rescue the Housatonic and clean it as we have never in all the years thought before of cleaning it. . . restore its ancient beauty: making it the center of a town, of a valley, and perhaps—who knows? of a new measure of civilized life."

"For this valley, the river must be center. Certainly it is the physical center; perhaps, in a sense, the spiritual center. Perhaps from that very freeing of spirit will come other freedoms and inspirations and aspirations which may be steps toward the diffusion and diversification and enriching of culture throughout this land."

Speech of W. E. B. Du Bois '84, at the Annual Meeting of the Alumni of Searles High School, 21 July 1930. Reprinted from *The Berkshire Courier*, 31 July 1930.

back of other's homes. But always there was the Housatonic River. A group of his friends purchased the House of the Black Burghardt's property for his sixtieth birthday in 1928. Two years after receiving the deed to his family homestead, he was invited to give the keynote speech at his high school reunion. He chose as his title "The Housatonic River." In this speech Du Bois set the stage for his philosophy of nature in general and extolled the preservation of a natural resource. He used knowledge based on his many travels to talk about how citizens of Great Barrington needed to preserve this essential resource.

Du Bois decided in his final years to settle in Ghana on the west coast of Africa. It must have been a difficult decision, because no one can doubt that W. E. B. Du Bois loved the House of the Black Burghardts on Egremont Plain, the Housatonic River in the Great Barrington of his youth, New England, and the whole of the vast United States of America. His beloved Burghardts and his wife Nina, all the generations of fathers and mothers, were buried in Berkshire soil. If circumstances had been different, his final resting place would have been there, too.

The year of Du Bois's death was as his birth—historic. He died on the day of the 1963 March on

Washington, D.C. They announced his death just before the speakers came to the podium, and one of those speakers, Martin Luther King Jr., said of him: "History cannot ignore W. E. B. Du Bois because history has to reflect truth and Dr. Du Bois was a tireless explorer and a gifted discoverer of social truths." Instead of being interred in his birthplace, he is buried by another great body of water, the wide Atlantic Ocean, where his African ancestors had boarded the first slave ships to the New World. In birth as in death his life and contributions to race and ecology are significant. He was a keen observer of his surroundings, of people, of times. He was a great thinker and activist, and he was renewed by the natural world, since it was from the natural world that sprang his African ancestors. From a small child growing up against the backdrop of a golden river in the green hills of the Berkshires, he became a keen observer of place in relation to nature and to humans. So, Du Bois's analysis of humankind, place, or nature was not far removed from his early understanding of the place that made him who he was.

Frances Jones-Sneed

Du Bois Williams,
Professor and Sole Grandaughter
of W. E. B. Du Bois

Yolande Du Bois Williams (b. 1932) is the sole grandchild of William Edward Burghardt Du Bois. Du Bois, as she is known to her family and close friends, has a somewhat brief history with her grandpa's birthplace. Yet as the direct descendant of W. E. B. Du Bois, her story makes an important contribution to demonstrating how his legacy continues into the twenty-first century and beyond Great Barrington.

Yolande Du Bois Williams was born on 11 October 1932 in Philadelphia to Nina Yolande Du Bois and Arnette Franklyn Williams. Her mother was known as Yolande (pronounced *yo-lawnd*), so she prefers to be known as Du Bois (*doo-boyce, boyce* rhyming with *Joyce*) in keeping with the family's pattern of using the middle name.

Du Bois's connection to Great Barrington and the upper Housatonic Valley is deep and strong. Her maternal ancestors had a long history in this area. Du Bois's world-renowned grandpa was born and raised in Great Barrington. Also born in Great Barrington, her mother is buried there, in the Mahaiwe Cemetery. Despite the depth and strength of her connection to it, in her seventy-three years of life, Du Bois recalls only two visits she has made to the town. The first time she remembers visiting Great Barrington was in March 1961 to bury her mother. (According to David Levering Lewis, Yolande's funeral services were held in Baltimore; no burial place is mentioned.) The second time she remembers traveling to the town was in 1969, when Julian Bond and numerous other leaders and activists celebrated the official dedication of the W. E. B. Du Bois Memorial Park at his boyhood home site on Route 23.

Du Bois started preschool, as a precocious, two-year-old toddler, at the Modern School in Manhattan, New York. This school was founded by Mildred Johnson and still existed in 2006. (Johnson was the daughter of Rosamond Johnson and the niece of James Weldon Johnson, noted writer and human rights activist and a summer homeowner in Great Barrington.) In 1941 Du Bois joined her grandma Nina and mother, Yolande, in her grandpa's newly constructed family home in Baltimore. She graduated from high school in 1950 and, at her grandpa's urging and her own personal longing, went to the International Union of Students, held in Prague, Czechoslovakia. Then, in the fall of 1950, she entered Fisk University, in Nashville, a family legacy started by her grandfather (class of 1888) and continued by her mother (class of 1924). Du Bois completed her bachelor's of science degree in 1959 at New York University (NYU).

Immediately on leaving NYU, Du Bois started working at the Youth House for Girls in the Bronx, New York. To some extent this marked the beginning of her career as an educator, also a family legacy. Her mother had taught school in Baltimore, mainly as her life's professional work. Her grandpa had led a varied professional life as a scholar and activist. Of the many "professional hats" that he wore, W. E. B. Du Bois considered his work as a teacher or educator to be his most important work. Between 1976 and 1979

Du Bois Williams and grandmother (Grandma) Nina taken in Washington D.C. when she was 11 years old. Photo courtesy of Special Collections and Archives, W. E. B. Du Bois Library, University of Massachusetts, Amherst.

Du Bois Williams completed a doctor of philosophy in psychology, with a major and minor in social psychology and community psychology, respectively. She was the first African American woman to receive a PhD in psychology from the University of Colorado at Boulder.

Between 1979 and 1980 Du Bois "roamed," in search of work. Then during 1981 and 1988 she worked in the fields of mental health and mental retardation in Galveston and, later, in Houston. In 1988, after five years in a clinical psychology practice in Houston, she accepted a position as a visiting professor of psychology at Xavier University of Louisiana, in New Orleans, receiving the "Best Teacher" award at the end of her first year. She was awarded tenure in 1995 and remained an active professor, now ten years later as of this writing, despite a current forced leave of absence due to Hurricane Katrina.

Married four times, Du Bois is the biological mother of four children, one female and three males, and the stepmother of one male (deceased). She also has five grandchildren.

Mary Nell Morgan

The Jolly Club #12

The Jolly Club #12 was founded on 6 November 1948 in Great Barrington as a "social entertainment club to have social interaction on Saturday nights," according to the group's minute book. The book later reported that on 5 November 1949:

> Club dinner held at Mrs. Juliane Hamilton house 118 Main St. The menu consist of broiled chicken, peas, escalloped potatoes, pork chops, rolls, butter, peanuts, candy, ice cream, apple pie, tea, coffee, soda. Favors were given to each one. Games played. There 11 members present. It was an enjoyable evening. Next meeting be at Mrs. Gunn.

Jacob's Pillow

Jacob's Pillow is one of the world's preeminent dance festivals, operating a school and performing festival, archival, and community programs from its National Historic Landmark site in Becket, Massachusetts. It was founded on the old Carter farm in 1933 by modern dance pioneer Ted Shawn, who once wrote, "The dance includes every way that men of all races in every period of the world's history have moved rhythmically to express themselves." This all-inclusive philosophy has brought a wide range of artists to the Berkshires in the intervening decades. The Jacob's Pillow Archives holds evidence, documented in photographs, videos, programs, and other materials available for viewing, of numerous African American artists who have performed on the Pillow's stages and taught in its studios from 1942 to the present, a record that is unparalleled in both longevity and scope.

This activity began auspiciously in the Ted Shawn Theatre's inaugural season, when a week was devoted to "Primitive Dance and its Adaptations" in a festival exploring the many influences on American dance. Asadata Dafora, a pioneer in presenting African dance on the concert stage, headlined this program, and there is some remarkable color film footage documenting the occasion. The theater itself, still in use as of this writing and known as the first to be built especially for dance in this country, is distinguished by seven immense timber beams that were hand-hewn by Great Barrington's Warren H. Davis. Other trailblazing African American dancer-choreographers, such as Pearl Primus and Talley Beatty, also came to the Pillow in the 1940s, along with Janet Collins, who would later become the first Black artist to appear on the stage of the Metropolitan Opera. Before his death in 1972, Shawn helped foster the careers of Alvin Ailey, Geoffrey Holder, Donald McKayle, and others, and he sponsored the first professional appearance by Dance Theatre of Harlem in 1970.

Asadata Dafora in a studio portrait by Eileen Darby, taken around 1942 when he was preparing for his Jacob's Pillow debut as part of the first season in the Ted Shawn Theatre. Photo courtesy of Jacob's Pillow Dance Festival Archives.

During the 1980s there was a marked increase in the number of African American companies appearing at the Pillow, from a high of four per season in previous years to a new average of ten or eleven each festival. This coincided with a general profusion of activity as two more stages were added to the facilities, and it was accompanied by an increased emphasis on archival documentation, since each performance was captured on videotape. Highlights included engagements by stellar "tappers" such as Savion Glover, Gregory Hines, and Jimmy Slyde, and world premiere dances by Bill T. Jones, Ronald K. Brown, and Garth Fagan, as well as a Jazz Series featuring Sonny Rollins, Wynton Marsalis, and Odetta. Another high point was reached in 2002 when Katherine Dunham made her first Pillow appearance at age ninety-three, teaching in the Pillow's school and presiding over a

Alvin Ailey in costume for his "Blues Suite" at Jacob's Pillow, c. 1961. Photo by John Lindquist, Harvard Theatre Collection. Courtesy of Jacob's Pillow Dance Festival Archives.

An even more obscure chapter in the Pillow's African American heritage was written by an early feminist and labor leader, Helen Marot. In 1909, when she signed the document that gave birth to the NAACP, Marot owned a farm on Becket's George Carter Road that would later become part of the Pillow. These broader associations, along with an incomparable roster of Black artists, distinguish Jacob's Pillow as a primary home to the African American experience in Berkshire County, and the abundant information available on-site makes it an important point of pilgrimage.

Norton Owen

tribute performance that included celebrities such as Harry Belafonte and Danny Glover.

In 1998 Joanna Haigood's Zaccho Dance Theatre mounted an elaborate site-specific work entitled "Invisible Wings," underlining the Pillow's status as a station on the Underground Railroad. Audiences were invited to explore the site's history in a comprehensive experience, with a simulated slave auction and the unsettling sight of a young African American being chased through the woods by bounty hunters. A documentary film on this production provides a glimpse of the site's rich historical background reaching far beyond its performance credentials.

Robert Henry Johnson of Zaccho Dance Theatre in Joanna Haigood's "Invisible Wings," 1998. Photo by Liz Zivic. Courtesy of Jacob's Pillow Dance Festival Archives.

Local Black Children as
Norman Rockwell Models

The Problem We All Live With by Norman Rockwell. Published in the 14 January 1964 issue of *Look* magazine. Reproduced by permission of the Norman Rockwell Family Agency, Inc. Collection of the Norman Rockwell Museum at Stockbridge, Massachusetts.

merican artist and illustrator Norman Rockwell worked forty-seven years for The Saturday Evening Post *and ten years for* Look, *depicting distinctly American themes and issues, including the 1943 series* Four Freedoms. *Among his portrayals of landmark civil rights events are* The Problem We All Live With *and* Murder in Mississippi, *the latter addressing the murder of civil rights workers James Chaney, Michael Schwerner, and Andrew Goodman, who were found dead in Philadelphia, Mississippi, in 1964. A Stockbridge resident, Rockwell was an original sponsor of the 1968 Du Bois Memorial Committee to create a fitting memorial to W. E. B. Du Bois in his native town of Great Barrington. In this essay Elaine Gunn, who relates her own experiences in "Life in the Invisible Community" elsewhere in this book, here recalls when various Gunn children served as models for Norman Rockwell's paintings.*

Mr. Rockwell was looking for a model to portray the little girl who had integrated the William Frantz School in New Orleans in 1960, under a federal mandate. The Supreme Court decision had been handed down in 1954, but many schools in the south, including the William Frantz School, had not complied. In 1960 a federal judge mandated that those schools be desegregated by November of 1960.

Little Ruby Bridges was about six years old. We did hear that there was another school across town in New Orleans that was being integrated the same day with a few children, but Ruby was the only Black child who would be going to William Frantz. We heard that Ruby was told not to speak to anyone and that there would be some officers coming to take her to school. They happened to be federal officers as Rockwell portrayed in his piece [*The Problem We All Live With*]. We saw this unfold on black and white

TV, a little Black girl being escorted from the car to the school and up the steps with hecklers in the background. I remember how small she seemed with those officers escorting her.

I remember the little dress she was wearing and how it seemed to billow up and down as she went up the steps, and all I could think of was a little crinoline petticoat that many of us mothers dressed our little girls in, in those days. I remember hearing that a reporter asked her what she was mumbling as she walked up the steps, and she replied that she was praying for those folks who were heckling.

Mr. Rockwell had left the *Post* in 1963, and began working for *Look* magazine. One day in the fall of 1963, he knocked on my door. What a surprise! He introduced himself, though I knew who he was. He told me why he was there and said he understood that I had a daughter about so-and-so age. I told him about Anita, but said she wasn't home from school yet. He asked if he could wait for her. I did invite him in. We sat at our dining room table until Anita came home from school. I introduced her. He took her little hands and asked her if she would like to model for him. She answered yes. Then he asked her about her violin lessons as she was carrying her case. He then turned to me and said, "Mrs. Gunn, I like the little dress Anita is wearing. Can you have two made like that for me in white?"

It happened that the wife of Reverend Durant, the pastor of Clinton A. M. E. Zion, was a dressmaker, and she made the two white dresses, one for Anita and one for Lynda, who lived in Stockbridge, and was Aunt Sin's and Uncle David [Gunn's] granddaughter. Mr. Rockwell usually chose more than one model and then decided which one to use, or sometimes he would use composites of a few models. Our family was invited to Rockwell's studio one Sunday morning. He was waiting for all of us. He had arranged the chairs to accommodate us. He served us bottles of coke and went to work with his photographer taking photos of Anita. Sometimes he would take as many as forty or fifty, using bits and pieces of each. Later we were told that he used Lynda with touches of Anita, but Lynda comes through loud and clear.

The Problem We All Live With was his first illustration for *Look* magazine and came out in 1964 with no text. We heard that it did anger some folks in the South. He did receive a few disparaging letters.

Three years later Mr. Rockwell called to ask if my younger daughter Tracey could pose. I told him that she would, whereupon he asked the family to once again come to his studio on a Sunday morning. Deja vu! We did the whole thing again with a couple of changes. I decided to use the white dress that her sister had worn three years earlier. This was in 1967. Tracey was just six years old. When we arrived at the Rockwell Studio, we were again greeted warmly and offered bottles of Coke. A huge white cat was brought in, and Tracey was asked to pick up the cat the way she normally would. The cat had been tranquilized, we were told. So we sipped our Cokes as Mr. Rockwell posed Tracey and the photographer took the pictures. At some point Wray Jr. [son of Wray Gunn] posed as well, at a different time. That image came out in *Look* in 1967. He had painted the dress pink. The title was *Moving Day*. That image was supposedly based on a suburb of Chicago, during the time when a few areas were being integrated.

Once I asked Tom Rockwell about his father's painting *Murder in Mississippi*. He told me that his father was so angry about what had happened to those three young men that he had to put something on canvas. That happened in 1964. So you see it doesn't surprise me that Walter [Wilson] asked Rockwell if he could use his name to support his efforts to honor Du Bois in his hometown. I remember him as being warm, friendly, and gentle, especially with the children.

Elaine S. Gunn

Introductory material about Rockwell comes from the Norman Rockwell Museum, www.nrm.org.

Sports

Integration in sports was slow to come to the region. In the early 1900s the Sheffield Black community formed the Sheffield Feathertales baseball team, which played the Lee all-Black Long Hills. Two decades later, Blacks formed the Colored Giants baseball team in southern Berkshire County and the W. A. C. team in Pittsfield. These teams played white teams, but integrated teams did not yet exist. That changed in the 1930s and especially the 1940s as school integration and more Black children in the schools led to integrated teams in basketball, baseball, football, and track and field. The first Black coach of a white team was David Gunn Sr., who coached the Lenox School and Lenox High School basketball and baseball teams in the 1940s and, later, in Great Barrington, the Cornwall Academy's basketball and soccer teams.

Much Black sports activity took placed outside of the public eye. An exception was James M. Harrison, a standout football and baseball player at Columbia and Howard universities, who in 1923 related how, as a summer employee of the elegant 1903 Aspinwall Hotel in Lenox, he organized a baseball game between the bellhops and the dining room staff. The bellmen dominated. Harrison sent for a university friend, Thomas, and exacted revenge in a rematch. Interest was high, so Harrison culled the best of the bellmen and the waiters and formed the Aspinwall Giants. The hotel's management being agreeable, Harrison solicited donations for uniforms. "In two days I had more than enough money to get an outfit consisting of uniforms, bats, shoes, gloves, and balls," he recalled. "It was the first time in the history of the Berkshires that a uniformed team of colored players played in that section. Our fame descended from the hills to the village below and we were matched against the Lenox High School (white). It was a beautiful game and resulted 3 to 2 in our favor. President Taylor, formerly of the Boston Red Sox, witnessed it from a tally ho" (Harrison 1923).

Perhaps the greatest Black athlete in Berkshire County history was Billy Hart of Williamstown, who played three sports at the professional level. Hart graduated from the old Williamstown High School in 1948, played football at St. Michael's College in Vermont, and then got into semipro football, during which time he was drafted by the

The Lenox Merchants in 1953–1954 with Billy Hart and Bill Harrell in the front row (third and fourth from right). Team: (front left) Billy Dearstyne, Francis Mahoney, Vernon Cox, Billy Hart, Bill Harrell, Jerry Calabrese, and Glen Bissell; (rear left) William "Butch" Gregory, Fred Connor, Ken Goodwin, Joe Kubachka, Billy Hogan, and Al Roux. Photo courtesy of Barbara Bartle Collection.

David Gunn Sr., physical instructor and coach, Lenox School, 1945. Photo courtesy of Wray Gunn Collection.

Chicago Cubs and played for a while in their minor league system. In the 1950s he signed on with the Lenox Merchants, a semipro basketball team. After returning to the Berkshires, he proved himself an outstanding tennis player and won several regional championships.

The athlete who enjoyed the most success outside the area was baseball player Frank Grant of Pittsfield, who played for the Buffalo Bisons of the International League from 1886 to 1888. One of the best players in all organized baseball, his career was cut short by the owners' ban on Black players.

The most famous team in Berkshire history was the Lenox Merchants, an integrated semipro basketball team that competed from 1949 to 1960. Founded and managed by Butch Gregory of Lenox, it played in a league of eastern semipro teams. The team had several regular Black players, unlike most other teams, which refused to sign them. Billy Harrell from Siena College later crossed over to play professional baseball for the Cleveland Indians and the Boston Red Sox. Bobby Knight came from the Harlem Globetrotters (whom the Merchants also played), and the third and fourth players were Williamstown's Billy Hart and Stockbridge's St. Clair Gunn. The Merchants team's fame came from exhibition games in the 1950s against professional teams. The high point was the 1954–1955 season, when the Merchants defeated both the Boston Celtics and the Minneapolis Lakers. Victory over the Celtics was aided by the presence of Ray Felix, a Black center who had signed to play with the New York Knicks. Overall, the team had won seven of eleven games against the professional teams. The main motivation for the exhibitions was money, since the Merchants could pack the house (Lenox High School and the Pittsfield Armory) and the visiting pro team received about $1,000 per game.

Numerous African American athletes played for Pittsfield minor league teams, and in the 2001 and 2002 seasons former Boston Red Sox first baseman George "Boomer" Scott managed the Pittsfield Bears. Another notable outsider was heavyweight boxer Archie Moore, who trained in North Adams for his unsuccessful 1955 title fight against Rocky Marciano.

Derek Gentile and David Levinson

Frank Grant, Baseball Player

Frank Grant, second baseman for Buffalo International League team. Source: *Sol White's Official Base Ball Guide*. (1984 reprint of 1907 edition.) Columbia, South Carolina: Camden House Library of Baseball Classics.

One of the best players in organized baseball during the late nineteenth century, Frank Grant (1865–1937) was born on 1 August 1865 in Pittsfield and grew up in Williamstown. He was the youngest of seven children born to Franklin and Frances Hoose Grant. Given the name Ulysses F. Grant at birth, he began being called Frank by his family after his father, Franklin, died when he was four months old.

By age eighteen Grant made a name for himself as a pitcher on a local team called the Greylocks. A Williamstown native recalled that Grant "could do more tricks with a baseball than anyone I ever saw." His quickness in the field, combined with his strong arm, earned him the title of "the Black Dunlap," after Fred Dunlap, the best second baseman in the 1880s. Within a year Grant moved to Plattsburgh, New York, and started playing for a semipro team called the Nameless while working as a waiter in a Lake Champlain resort hotel.

Grant entered organized baseball in 1886, playing for the Eastern League in Meriden, Connecticut. When the league folded, midway through the season, he signed on with the Buffalo Bisons, of the International League. Playing for Buffalo through 1888, Grant was the only Black player to play three consecutive seasons for the same predominantly white team. He played second base and had a .340 batting average, which was the third highest in the league. In 1979, almost a half-century after his death, Grant was named to the Buffalo Bisons team's Hall of Fame and was honored with a plaque displayed in the stadium.

By 1887, however, "Jim Crow had reserved a box seat in nearly all major and minor league parks." Ability did not matter; Grant was slowly squeezed out of organized baseball. His teammates refused to have their team photo taken with him, and other teams refused to take the field if he played. He and other Black players had to make wooden shin guards to protect themselves from other players' deliberate attempts to spike them. The league directors decided that year "to approve no more contracts with colored men." After 1890 Grant joined the Negro league Cuban Giants and, later, the New York Gorhams as well as several other teams.

Grant's professional career ended in 1903, and he faded into obscurity, spending the remainder of his life as a waiter in New York City. He died on 27 May 1937 and was buried in Ridgelawn Cemetery in Clifton, New Jersey. In February 2006 Grant was elected to the Baseball Hall of Fame.

Frances Jones-Sneed and Suzette Naylor

Billy Hart, Athlete

There is little argument that William F. "Billy" Hart (1927–1995) was the greatest African American athlete in the Berkshires in the twentieth century. Born in 1927, he attended Williamstown High School and was a three-sport athlete there, captaining the football, basketball, and baseball teams in his senior year. Hart matriculated to St. Michael's College in 1946 and played all three sports in college, as well. He was the team's leading scorer in football in his sophomore and junior years as a halfback, was an all–New England basketball player, and in baseball was considered the greatest leadoff man in the history of the team's program, hitting .355 in 1949. He was elected to the St. Michael's Athletic Hall of Fame in 1990.

Hart was signed by the Chicago Cubs baseball team in 1949, and left school to play in the Cubs's minor league system. He was clearly one of the team's best young prospects, but he was also Black. The Cubs in the late 1940s were not one of major league baseball's more enlightened teams. Hart quit the organization two years later, frustrated by the organization's failure to promote him, despite two solid seasons.

In south Berkshire, Hart is best known as a starting guard on the semipro Lenox Merchants basketball team. The Merchants were composed of college and pro ballplayers, including the former New York Knickerbockers Al McGuire and briefly, Ray ("the Count") Felix. The squad regularly played (and defeated) professional teams in the mid-1950s, and Hart averaged eleven points per game against these teams in the 1952 season. His best game for the Merchants was a seventeen-point effort that year against the Boston Celtics, in an 88–71 loss.

After his playing days with the Merchants were over in 1954, Hart continued his athletic career, and was a nationally ranked tennis and paddleball player in his age group until well into his 60s. He died in 1995.

Derek Gentile

William F. Hart, St. Michael's College Class of 1951. Inducted in the St Michael's Athletic Hall of Fame, September 29, 1990. Photo courtesy of Saint Michael's Sports Information.

Larry King, Athlete

One of the best all-around athletes in Berkshire County history is Larry King of Pittsfield. A three-sport athlete at Taconic High School, he played football, basketball and track. King also played baseball as a youngster. Born in Lexington, Virginia, he moved to the Berkshires with his family as a twelve-year-old, when his father took a job in Dalton.

King, a 1974 graduate of Taconic High School, was the leading scorer in Berkshire County his senior year, with sixteen touchdowns and three extra point conversions. In basketball he was a three-year starter, and in track he helped Taconic win the sectional championship his junior year. At various times in his track career, King was a long jumper, triple jumper, low hurdler, 100-yard-dash man, and a member of the relay team. He earned a scholarship to Syracuse University, he was a four-year starter for the Orangemen as a defensive back. He also punted and returned kicks. King's longest punt was a 61-yarder his senior year.

In his senior year King became the first Berkshire County football player to be named to a football all-star team, playing for the East in the East-West Shrine game. He played defensive back in the contest, won by the West, 23–3. In 1978 King was signed by Winnipeg of the Canadian Football League (CFL), and he played several years in the CFL.

Derek Gentile

Sources

Kinship

Elliot, Clint. Personal communications with Rachel Fletcher, January 2006.

Gunn, Wray. Personal communication with David Levinson, 2004.

Muller, Nancy. "W. E. B. Du Bois and the House of the Black Burghardts: Land, Family, and African Americans in New England." Diss., University of Massachusetts, Amherst, 2001.

Neizer, Roberta M. Personal communications with George Darcy, March, 2000.

Neizer, Roberta M. Personal communications with Rachel Fletcher, February–March 2006.

Smith, Alene Jackson, and Adeline Jackson Tucker. *Live, Labor, Love: The History of a Northern Family 1700–1900.* Westminster, MD: Heritage Books, Inc., 2004.

Guest Homes for African Americans

Crawford Jr., Isaac. Personal communication with author, 1998.

Drew, Bernard A. "Willoughby's Sunset Inn." *Berkshire Eagle,* 22 May 2004.

"Great Barrington News." *Berkshire Courier,* 2 Dec. 1897.

Humphrey, Jo. Personal communication with Norton Owen, 2005.

Obituary. *Berkshire Courier,* 4 March 1932.

Obituary. *Berkshire Courier,* 4 Feb. 1954.

Obituary of Jason Cooley. *Berkshire Courier,* 19 Jan. 1911.

Obituary of Martha Crawford. *Berkshire Courier,* 6 April 1989.

"Charles Allen, Owner of Inn, Dies Suddenly." *Berkshire Eagle,* 16 Jan. 1946.

Untitled article. *Springfield Republican,* 28 Jan. 1945. [Located in the Black History file, Local History Room, Berkshire Athenaeum. Pittsfield, MA.]

Entertainment and Social Life

Berkshire Eagle, 4 Sept. 1901.

Bicentennial Book Committee. *Great Barrington Bicentennial 1761–1961.* Great Barrington, MA: 1961.

"Catherine Van Buren: Lyric Soprano, Musical Theatre, Teacher." *Berkshire Eagle,* 19 May 1944.

Clinton African Methodist Episcopal Zion Church. Minute books and ledgers, 1940–1960. Great Barrington, MA.

Fitzgerald, Michael. *The Lenox School of Jazz,* 1993.

Grieve, Alan. *Berkshire Band: A Pictorial Review from 1888 to 1984.* Pittsfield, MA: Peter Drozd Graphic Arts, 1992.

Gunn, Elaine. Personal communication with the author, 2004.

Gunn, Wray. Personal communication with the author, 2004.

Jacob's Pillow. "Jacob's Pillow Archives: Past Performers: 1933–1949." http://www.jacobs pillow.org/archives/ past-performers-30-40s.asp (accessed 11 Oct. 2004).

Jacob's Pillow. "Jacob's Pillow Archives: Past Performers: 1970–1979." http://www.jacobs pillow.org/archives/ past-performers-30-40s.asp (accessed 11 Oct. 2004).

National Park Service. "Places Where Women Made History: Colonial Theater." http://www.cr.nps.gov/nr/ travel/pwwmh/ma37.htm (accessed 9 Sept. 2004).

Rogovoy, Seth. "Music Foundation to Honor Music Inn Legacy and Founder Stephanie Barber." *Berkshire Eagle,* 21 Aug. 1998.

Rogovoy, Seth. "The Rogovoy Report." *Berkshire Eagle,* 30 Aug. 2003.

St. John's Lodge No. 10 F. & A. M. Pittsfield, Massachusetts. 100 Years Anniversary Celebration. Honoring – All Past Masters. "Program and Dedication Book, Pittsfield, MA, 20 Dec. 1998.

African American Literary Societies

Du Bois, W. E. B. "Early Writings: Columns from the New York Independent." Reprinted in *The Seventh Son: The Thought and Writings of W. E. B. Du Bois.* Vol. 1, 1883–1885, ed. by Julius Lester, 154–69. New York: Vintage Books, 1971.

McHenry, Elizabeth. *Forgotten Readers: Recovering the Lost History of African American Literary Societies.* Durham, NC: Duke University Press, 2002.

Robert A. Gilbert, Photographer and Ornithologist

Brewster, William. "Breeding of the Louisiana Water Thrush (*Seiurus motacilla*) in Berkshire County". *The Auk* 26 (July 1909): 310–11.

Brewster, William. "Breeding of the Prairie Horned Lark (*Otocorys, alpestris practicola*) near Pittsfield, MA" *The Auk* 11 (1894): 326–27.

Brewster, William. "Breeding of the Rough Winged Swallow in Berkshire County, Massachusetts." *The Auk* 24 (April 1907): 221–22.

Brewster, William. Letter printed in Allen's "Revised List of the Birds of Massachusetts." Bulletin of the American Museum of Natural History 1 (1886): 269–70

Brewster, William. "Notes on the Summer Birds of Berkshire County, Massachusetts." *The Auk* 1 (1884): 5–16.

Du Bois, W. E. Burghardt. "Opinion of W. E. B. Du Bois." *The Crisis* 18, no.1 (1919): 7–14.

Laubach, Rene. "Birding with Mr. Brewster." *Sanctuary* 31, no. 7 (May–June 1991): 12–13.

Laubach, Rene. Interview by Ellen Broderick, 3 Jan. 2006.

Mitchell, John. Telephone interview by Ellen Broderick, 8 Dec. 2006, Littleton, MA.

Mitchell, John Hanson. *Looking for Mr. Gilbert: The Reimagined Life of an African American.* Emeryville, CA: Shoemaker & Hoard, 2005.

The Harlem Renaissance

Huggins, Nathan I. *Harlem Renaissance.* New York: Oxford University Press, 1971.

Lewis, David Levering. *Harlem Renaissance Reader.* New York: Viking, 1994.

Lewis, David Levering. *When Harlem Was in Vogue.* New York: Oxford University Press, 1981.

James VanDerZee, Photographer

De Cock, Liliane, and Regnald McGhee, eds. *James VanDerZee.* Dobbs Ferry, NY: Morgan & Morgan, 1973.

Haskins, James. *James VanDerZee: The Picture Takin' Man.* New York: Dodd, Mead & Co., 1979.

McGhee, Reginald. *The World of James VanDerZee.* New York: Grove Press, 1969.

Mercer, Kobena. *James VanDerZee.* New York: Phaidon, 2003.

Uncommon Images. A film by Evelyn Barrow. New York: Filmakers Library.

VanDerZee, Donna Mussenden. Interview with Rachel Fletcher, 10 Nov 2005.

VanDerZee, James, et. al. *The Harlem Book of the Dead*, 1978.

Willis-Braithwaite, Deborah. *VanDerZee, Photographer.* New York: Harry N. Abrams, 1993.

W. E. B. Du Bois, Native Son

Du Bois, W. E. B. *The Correspondence of W. E. B. Du Bois.* Ed. by Herbert Aptheker. 3 vols. Amherst: University of Massachusetts Press, 1973–1978.

Du Bois, W. E. B. *Dusk of Dawn: An Essay toward an Autobiography of a Race Concept.* New York: Harcourt, Brace and Co., 1940.

Du Bois, W. E. B. "The Housatonic River Speech." Annual Meeting of the Alumni of Searles High School, 21 July 1930. *Berkshire Courier*, 31 July 1930.

Du Bois, W. E. B. "I Bury My Wife." *Chicago Globe*, 15 July 1950, 52.

Du Bois, W. E. B. *The Souls of Black Folk.* New York: Vintage Books, 1990. [First pub. in 1903.]

Lewis, David Levering. *W. E. B. Du Bois: Biography of a Race, 1868–1919.* New York: Henry Holt, 1993.

Du Bois Williams, Professor and Sole Grandaughter of the W. E. B. Du Bois

Lewis, David Levering. *W. E. B. Du Bois: Biography of a Race, 1868–1919.* New York: Henry Holt & Company, 1994.

Lewis, David Levering. *W. E. B. Du Bois: The Fight for Equality and the American Century, 1919-1963.* New York: Henry Holt & Company, 2001.

Williams, Du Bois. Personal communications and interviews with MaryNell Morgan, 1986–2006.

Jacob's Pillow

The Founding of the NAACP. http://www.glencoe.com/sec/socialstudies/btt/celebrating freedom/pdfs/181.PDF (accessed 3 April 2006),

Owen, Norton. *A Certain Place.* Becket, MA: Jacob's Pillow Dance Festival 2002.

Shawn, Ted. *How Beautiful upon the Mountain.* 1943. Becket, MA: Jacob's Pillow Dance Festival.

Shawn, Ted. *The Story of Jacob's Pillow, 1969.* Becket, MA: Jacob's Pillow Dance Festival.

Sports

Harrison, J. M. "Unpublished History of Football and Baseball." *Norfolk Journal and Guide*, 27 Jan. 1923–29 April 1923. Transcription by John T. Kneebone.

Moore, Steve. "The Lenox Merchants." *Berkshire Sampler*, 3 Feb. 1985.

Riley, James A. T*he Biographical Encyclopedia of the Negro Baseball Leagues.* New York: Carroll & Graf, 1994.

Frank Grant, Baseball Player

Gentile, Derek. "Hometown Ballplayer a Hall of Fame Finalist." *Berkshire Eagle*, 29 Nov. 2005, 1, 4.

Naylor, Suzette. "Frank Grant: A Life." Senior seminar paper. Massachusetts College of Liberal Arts, North Adams, MA. [Located in the Special Collections of the Eugene Free Library at the Massachusetts College of Liberal Arts.]

Overfield, Joseph. *The 100 Seasons of Buffalo Baseball.* Kenmore, New York: Partner's Press, 1985.

Ribowsky, Mark. *The Negro Leagues, 1884 to 1955.* Secaucus, NJ: Carol Publishing Group, 1995.

Riley, James A. *The Biographical Encyclopedia of the Negro Baseball Leagues.* New York: Carroll & Graf, 1994.

Ward, Geoffrey, and Ken Burns. *Baseball: An Illustrated History.* New York: Alfred A. Knopf, 1994.

White, Sol. *Sol White's Official Baseball Guide.* Columbia, SC: Camden House, 1984. [First published 1907 by Walter Schlichter, Philadelphia.]

Personal Essays

The essays that follow, written especially for this book, move beyond history and what documents tell us, to give voice to the experiences and perceptions of African American women who lived and worked in the region for many years.

Elaine Gunn's Reflections:
Life in the Invisible Community

It is an irony of our history that W. E. B. Du Bois and James Weldon Johnson, two intellectual and academic world-renowned giants, walked the streets of Great Barrington, yet for years there was little physical evidence or ceremonial recognition in the town showing they were ever here at all. These two men were at the forefront of resistance to racial subordination at the turn of the twentieth century when segregation was being consolidated. Through the years just a few were aware of a small plot of land on Route 23 where native-born Du Bois's grandparents lived, and only a few also knew about a house hidden from view on Alford Road, where Johnson spent his summers. A few others knew that Johnson would frequent the public library on Main Street. This omission is part of the larger invisibility of the Black community in the Berkshires and may be corrected with the publication of this volume and the larger work of the sponsoring Upper Housatonic Valley Heritage National Area committee.

The omission is also one indication of ongoing subtle and pervasive forms of discrimination, segregation, and racism at work sixty-plus years ago when I arrived in the Berkshires to take up residence in the town of Stockbridge. Indeed as a young person from a Middle Atlantic state, it was a revelation that forms of discrimination I had been used to in Maryland would meet me here in my new home in Massachusetts. With the exception of integrated schools and movie theatres, very little was different. I shall never forget seeing conditions on the west side of Pittsfield, where most of the Black people lived near the railroad tracks in rundown houses on unpaved roads.

But it was not just physical conditions. One restaurant on West Street had two doors, one on the right and one on the left. Blacks always went in on the left and were seated on the left. A solid wall separated the two dining areas. If one happened to go into the right side of the restaurant, you would notice that all of the tables had reserved signs on them. It wasn't until years later that I understood the subtle racism of this practice.

At Williams High School in Stockbridge, there were a total of six Black students, three in elementary and three in high school. I was the only Black girl in high school at that time, and I was a member of the girl's basketball team. We girls enjoyed a friendly relationship during practice sessions and during games. However, the friendliness ended there. I was never invited to a party or to anyone's home, even on graduation day.

After completing school, I left the area to attend college in New York. Upon returning to the Berkshires, I married and settled in Great Barrington. In the early 1950s when we were looking for a home to purchase, we were confronted with overt acts of racism. Three in particular stand out in my memory. One man refused to sell his house to us simply because we were Black. The president of the Great Barrington Savings Bank offered us a home on the railroad tracks that had been repossessed. A realtor at Wheeler and Taylor would only show us a Quonset hut on Route 71 towards North Egremont. These were not isolated incidents, but signs of the time and the attitudes towards people of color. Since then we have dealt with both institutions cordially without incident on a business level. But the experience, which was personally painful, was a dramatic reminder to the presence of racial prejudice at the core of the town's commerce at that time.

We finally purchased the Sunset Inn on Rosseter Street in Great Barrington. The inn had been a guesthouse predominantly used by Blacks from the New York area, during the 1920s and 1930s. Recently, I learned that W. E. B. Du Bois had been a guest there when he returned to visit his home town. My husband's aunt and uncle had operated the Inn and our children were raised there.

A Call to Improve Housing

In February 1943, Clinton A. M. E. Zion pastor, Rev. H. W. Morrison went before the Great Barrington selectmen to complain about inadequate housing for many African Americans in town. Below is the story from *The Berkshire Courier*.

Housing conditions for colored people in Great Barrington, the board of selectmen as told Monday night by Rev. Henry W. Morrison, are for the most part unfit for human habitation. Mr. Morrison, pastor of the A.M.E. Zion church for the past few years, and well known locally for his efforts on behalf of his parishioners, gave the board a plea for improvement in available housing facilities for his people.

Mr. Morrison told the board that when the present war is over, America faces a new problem, which is involved with the general improvement in the national attitude towards people of different races and creeds.

He lauded the board for its past attitude of justice towards all and the townspeople of Great Barrington in general, but brought out that many of the "shacks" in which colored families are forced to live here are breeding places of crime and disease.

The immediate cause for his appearance, he said, is the fact that a local cleaning and pressing establishment has an exhaust that sends constant noise and cleaning fluid odors into the adjacent home of an elderly colored woman. He asked that the condition be remedied, and while on the subject, asked that the board investigate the conditions under which several other colored families are forced to live. He described two localities in town, the houses of which are poorly equipped, some having constantly wet walls, while others lack the facilities for decent, ordinary existence.

The board discussed Mr. Morrison's request, and decided that either the board of health or the building inspector should be notified of the conditions he reported.

Source: *The Berkshire Courier*, "Charges Negroes Are Ill-Housed Here," 15 February 1943.

Elaine Gunn with her class at Bryant School in the 1980s. Photo courtesy of Elaine Gunn Collection.

Another real estate deal years later would turn out much worse. This was a controversy that took place in Great Barrington in 1980–1981 when an older Black couple moved into a previously all-white neighborhood. A white woman in the neighborhood harassed the couple to the point of throwing a stink bomb through the couple's window and then setting their garage on fire. The woman was tried in Springfield District Court, sentenced to two years, and served time in federal prison in Lexington, Kentucky. The Black couple continued to live in the house for another five years. This incident created quite a stir in the town for quite a while.

One outcome of this particular racist episode was the start of an ethnic fair celebration that was held for a number of years at St. Peter's Community Center at the corner of Cottage and East Streets. The community and the churches in particular made a concerted effort to come together following this episode. There have been other efforts to address race relations. Notable among these was the work of the civil rights activist Reverend Nehemiah Boynton of the First Congregational Church in Stockbridge in the 1950s and 1960s. Also, attempts to address human relations were made under the influence of the Great Society antipoverty programs of the late 1960s, including efforts to facilitate community association through Construct—a housing construction program—and Head Start, and realistic assessments of poverty in the area. There was also a series of annual Brotherhood Dinners in Pittsfield, and all of these served to bring different sectors of the community together at least on a limited basis.

During the early 1950s when I was a stay-at-home mom, I became interested in learning more about Du Bois beyond the fact that he had been born here. According to my husband and his relatives, there was no mention of either Du Bois or Johnson in social studies or history classes in the schools they had come through. So I went to the Mason Library hoping to borrow *The Souls of Black Folk*. The librarian informed me that she knew they had a copy somewhere, "probably in a box," but that she would have to look for it. I was told to come back in a few days to allow her time to find it. When I returned, I was handed a very old, worn, and fragile copy of Du Bois's book of essays that detailed the mistreatment of Black people at the dawn of the twentieth century and widely recognized as so very important in helping all who read it. Even early in the twenty-first century, one hundred years after the publication, one can certainly see the relevance, similarities, and parallels of some attitudes and behaviors towards people of color that Du Bois wrote about.

By 1971, three students at Monument Mountain High School, one of whom was my daughter, met to discuss meeting with the Superintendent of Schools to ask about the possibility of including a Black Studies program in the curriculum. This occurred at a historic moment. We had approached the end of the civil rights decade. Dr. Martin Luther King Jr., the most charismatic civil rights leader of the twentieth century, had been assassinated. We had just celebrated and memorialized both King and the intellect, philosophy, and wisdom of Dr. W. E. B. Du Bois. Yet the students in the Berkshire Hills Regional School District only knew of and studied these and other important Black Americans on their own. There was no curriculum in place within the district. Young Blacks in the area felt left out, as if the movement had passed them over except for the TV news and images they saw depicting Blacks being denied their basic rights, and having hoses aimed at them, or dogs barking and snarling at them, or being beaten by police officers.

They did meet with the Superintendent, who was receptive to the idea. He asked the three to write an acceptable proposal that he could then submit to the school committee. They wrote a short proposal, my daughter informed me. The Superintendent did submit it, the committee approved it, and a young Mr. Homer Meade, fairly new out of Cornell University, was hired to teach English and an elective Black Studies Program at Monument Mountain, beginning in September of 1971. I believe Mr. Meade, now Dr. Meade, taught at Monument Mountain for about seven years. I do not know the status of the program at this time.

I was a teacher for twenty-one years in the Berkshire Hills Regional School District at Bryant Elementary in Great Barrington. During that time there was an occasional Black substitute teacher at the high school level, but only one other fulltime Black teacher at the high school. That was Dr Meade. In the middle to late 1950s, three Black teachers were hired at Searles High School. George Taylor taught social studies, Earl Bean taught science, and Martha Pierce taught business subjects. The Southern Berkshire Regional School District (Sheffield and surrounding towns) has hired Black substitute teachers.

At that time I knew of no other Black persons employed in white-collar positions as salespersons, bank tellers, office personnel, or telephone operators in all of South Berkshire. Later in the 1960s two Black telephone operators were hired. England's Department Store in Pittsfield did have a Black saleswoman and one Black woman in the personnel office in the middle to late 1950s. Pittsfield also had one Black dentist during this time. Several white dentists would welcome Black patients, although one of these in Great Barrington would only allow his Black patients to come after dark! A few years ago one local bank hired a Black female bank teller. She left after two years. When I asked her why she left, she informed me that others with less education had been promoted over her. One Black police officer was hired by Great Barrington, in 1974. He left after a few years. My husband and Darius Petty were hired as special police officers for a while during the 1960s to police the Barrington Fair, and then to walk the beat in downtown Great Barrington.

This pattern continued and continues. I have seen one other person of color as a bank teller within the past year. I am not aware of any Black office personnel in the town currently. One young Black woman was one of the personnel pool at a local real estate office in the 1980s for a period of time. One retailer hired a local Black man for a short period of time in the 1970s and another retailer hired a local young Black man for a period of time in the middle 1980s, I believe. Brooks Pharmacy has hired an occasional clerk, and there is one man who was hired by the pharmacist, Melvin Katsh, and who stayed with the pharmacy for many years, later continuing to work for Brooks, and now for Bill's Pharmacy. Great Barrington Price Chopper has employed a Black cashier for the past few years. I suppose one could say that these were/are attempts to bridge the racial harmony gap. However, the lack of a Black presence in these areas of employment continues.

Most of the Black community moved here from the southern states, and when they arrived in South Berkshire in the early to middle part of the twentieth century, they accepted jobs as maids, cooks, butlers, and nannies for private families and as waiters and chefs at inns. One or two men were hired as day laborers in the cotton mills; one or two in the 1950s were hired at GE in Pittsfield, and at the Plastics plant in Sheffield. A few were recruited from New York City to work at the dry cleaning establishments in town, and Wray Gunn, a chemist from Stockbridge, was hired at a chemical plant in Canaan, Connecticut, following graduation from the University of Massachusetts.

Two black women entrepreneurs were pioneers in Great Barrington before the civil rights movement of the 1950s. Mrs. Susie Brinson, originally from Georgia, along with her husband, Albert, opened and operated the first dry cleaning business in Great Barrington, arriving here in the mid-1920s and finally closing her business in the 1970s after fifty years of service.

Isaac Crawford Sr., and Martha Wright Crawford moved their family here from Indiana in the early 1940s. Mrs. Crawford owned and operated four businesses in town before the civil rights movement. She began with a tea room located in the Caligari block on Main Street next to Brinson Cleaners, and then opened Crawford's Inn and Snack Bar on Elm Court next to her home. The inn and snack bar catered to vacationing Black folk and local youth. Later she added an employment agency and a catering business to her enterprises. All of these businesses competed with the white establishment.

There are still no Black real estate offices, or doctor's offices, to my knowledge. I do not know why, but the lack of Black presence in the business community is glaring. John James, an architect in Sheffield, has been operating a practice for several years and is an exception to the rule.

The area is blessed with several highly regarded colleges including private liberal arts schools, and public institutions offering BA and associate degrees. There have been few Black professors at these institutions over the years. There weren't any at Massachusetts College of Liberal Arts when I was there. There was one at Berkshire Community College in the middle 1970s, Bernice Morehead. Simon's Rock has had a few, off and on, probably beginning with Meade in the late 1970s, then at least two black women, Cecelia Gross in the 1970s and Audrey Kerr in the 1990s. Professor Kerr conducted a study on African Americans from the area.

A key person at Simon's Rock was Ruth Jones, who served as secretary/treasurer of the first Du Bois Memorial Committee and the right arm of Walter Wilson, who headed that effort. Ruth was very active in the civil rights movement, and the very first cataloguer hired by Mrs. Betty Hall, the school's founder, just as Simon's Rock was opening in the mid-1960s. She was just the right person, having all of the secretarial skills that the memorial committee needed at that time. Mrs. Hall allowed the committee to meet in a room at Simon's Rock College. Ruth stayed there for over twenty years and then lived in California, Tennessee, and Colorado. She passed away in May 2005.

In the larger areas around Pittsfield, a lack of participation in higher education and training suggests the need both for better community attention and for outreach by education and training institutions. This is a response, no doubt, to the sense of limited options even in mid-range employment and isolation from a larger Black community in the nation. The employment, education, and business conditions here may account for the tendency of so many young Blacks to move away from the area to seek education and career opportunities.

Elaine Gunn in Great Barrington in 2006, viewing film footage of the 1969 W. E. B. Du Bois Memorial dedication. Photo by Rachel Fletcher.

When I look around now, I see much more positive activity. There is the work of the Heritage Trail Committee devoted to awareness of a community many refuse to see. It is a major step forward from my days working, often alone, to get up exhibits for my fourth graders in Black History Month and to write a curriculum for wider use in the schools. It has been a learning experience and there is still a lot to learn.

There has been no great change in the intervening years with a few exceptions. Town folk and others now know who W. E. B. Du Bois was. There are plaques, a mural, and a river garden to honor him and regular memorial celebrations to remind us that he was our first civil rights activist. It has been thirty-five years since the active decade of the civil rights movement. It's time that we fill in the gaps. Let's begin with erecting signs at the intersection of Maple Avenue and Route 23 announcing Great Barrington as the home of W. E. B. Du Bois, with arrows pointing to his homestead, to the wall mural, and to the river garden named for him. [Editor's note: Signs noting that Great Barrington was Du Bois's birthplace were erected in 2006.] We owe it to our young people to include the study of Du Bois and Johnson and other local Black leaders, such as Dorothy Amos and Margaret Hart, in the social studies/history curriculum throughout the schools in Berkshire County.

Elaine S. Gunn

P. S. One of my sons, Clarence S. Gunn III (Clay) was a star basketball and football player at Monument Mountain Regional High School in the 1970s. He was named to the Monument Mountain Basketball Hall of Fame in the 1990s.

Elaine S. Gunn lives with her husband, Clarence S. Gunn Jr., in Great Barrington, where they raised five children. She is a retired teacher from the Bryant School and a participant in the movement to construct a memorial for W. E. B. Du Bois. She was active in the 1969 commemoration and continues to speak and organize on behalf of a fitting memorial. In 2006 she was the first recipient of the Du Bois Center of American History Pioneer Award. The essay was written by Elaine S. Gunn and includes material gathered during an interview with Alex Willingham.

Sources

Bahlman, D. R. "Eloise B. Woods, 79, Civil Rights Advocate." *Berkshire Eagle*, 31 March 2005, B2.

Consolati, Florence. "Walkabout Slowly." *Berkshire Record*, 31 March 2005.

McNiff, Alice. "Profile of a Negro Community: Southern Berkshire County." 1964. Unpublished manuscript.

Nichols, Pat. "Reclaiming a Hidden Past and Taking It to Schools." *Berkshire Eagle*, 2005, E1.

Woods, Mark. "Eloise Brinson Woods, 79, Barrington Pioneer, Dies." *Berkshire Record*, 7 April 2005.

Mae E. Brown: An Educator's Reflections

I was born in Cason, Texas, 23 October 1914. That's where my grandparents also lived. They had several hundred acres of land, so they were self-sufficient They had huge peach orchards on one side of the house, and pear and plum orchards on the other side. We always had something to sell. Having fruit trees, of course they had to have bees. The honey that my grandfather would sell—one was honey in the comb, another was honey that you get from the containers, and a third was the squeezed honey. They also raised geese and ducks, and they sold the feathers and the downs. My grandfather was able to sell downs for one price, and another price for the feathers. He also had a blacksmith shop where he shoed mules and horses. They had double barns. They had farming land where they grew sugarcane, sorghum, cotton, and corn. At that time, my joy was feeding an ear of corn into a machine and hearing it go "pop-pop-pop-pop-pop." To me it was fun. I shucked the ear of corn; then the machine shelled it from the cob. It was a wonderful family, because all the family always helped everybody. Whatever you needed, there was always someone to help you out.

In the fall that I turned ten, we moved to Hawkins, Texas. My mother took ill. She sent my brother to get one of my cousins, to get her sister, Aunt Mintie. My mother asked Aunt Mintie to take my brother and me and make a home for us, and that's what she did. We moved from Cason to Mount Vernon, then to Uncle James's house. Leaving there, we moved to another one of Uncle Steve's houses. Leaving there, we moved to Mr. Pitts's place and made a crop. Then we moved to Hawkins, Texas, where my mother died. Then we moved to Big Sandy, Texas, at Aunt Mintie and Bro Rodgers, and this was always home. Even when I went through a divorce, and when the four walls seemed to close in on me, I'd make a reservation, go upstairs and pack my bag, leave my car in long-term parking, and fly home. They never asked me one time, "Why can't you get along? What's going on?" I was always welcome.

My mother told my brother and I that she would not live until we were grown. She demanded obedience. If we told the truth, we did not get punished, but if you told a lie, you'd think the heavens—in those days they used switches; she'd go out and get the switch.

I finished two years of college in 1935 at Jarvis [Christian College]. I came back to Jarvis in 1941 and got my bachelor's degree in home economics. Then I went to Kansas State, in Manhattan, Kansas, and got a degree in institutional management. After completing the year with institutional management, I came back to Jarvis and took charge of the food. This was during World War II. In 1943 I was married. He was in the service. He had not completed his education. He wanted to do it in Boston, so in 1944 I moved to Boston. But he was still in the service, and he was shipped out to the Southwest Pacific, so that left me in Boston all by myself. But it didn't matter, because I knew as long as Aunt Mintie lived, whatever I needed, I would have it. That's one thing I've wanted all the kids that I've had anything to do with, to be able to stand up on your own feet and look someone dead in the eye and let them know exactly how you feel about what's going on, but most of all, be prepared for the job you're looking for and demand it if it's necessary. I taught three years at Wiley College starting in 1948. I was in the home economics department there. It was only sixty miles from where I grew up. It was a wonderful experience because there were a lot of young people there. Men who had been in the service were there, and their wives because they wanted to take this opportunity to be with their husbands and also to get an education. It was a wonderful, wonderful experience, and Miss Williams was the person who was my assistant. She did nutrition and all foods. I did clothing, from babies' to wedding gowns. She was a person who if you were working on a project and you had to turn in information to the office, if you needed it on the tenth, she was going to give it to you on the ninth. I lived in a home management house with six girls. It was a wonderful experience. I thought all Negroes knew how to cook. I found out that people are people wherever they are. The girls were so marvelous to work with. My husband came down the second year. He was a journalist and started a newspaper. We got a lot of publicity. At the end of the school year, we had a fashion show.

In Boston I worked at Mass. General Hospital. I thought if I could help someone in need that maybe someone would help him [my husband] if he needed it. When I left there, I worked at Filene's, the big store there. They had not begun to branch out at that time. Jordan Marsh and Filene's were big stores in Boston. I would walk right through the statehouse. In 1951 I received an MS degree from Simmons College and completed my education courses at Boston University.

I was looking for a job. I went into the office of someone on Beacon Hill. I applied for a job. She looked me dead in the eye and said, "We have to give our girls a job first."

I looked her dead in the eye and said, "I am one of your girls. I just completed my studies at Simmons College." If you know New England, and you know New Englanders, you know how New Englanders can turn on their heels. She turned on her heels and went back in her office. I turned on my heels, I went down to the library, and I filled out three applications: one for the Cape, where I really wanted to go; one for Lenox; and one for Winchendon. I didn't

Mae Brown in her home in Housatonic c. 1999. Photo by Erik Callahan.

hear from Winchendon, and I wasn't accepted for the Cape. I did get accepted at Lenox. I stayed there for twenty-three years. I taught home economics and supervised the cafeteria for fourteen years.

Every year we had a fashion show. John Lewarn Jr. was an artist, and he was the head of the art department. The kids would do all of their drawing and painting and whatnot, and they would be displayed on the gymnasium walls. I had both boys and girls—we both did—and at the end of the year we would have this fashion show starting from the youngest and on up. Miss Prindergast, she and her husband owned the drug store there, and she was a model down in New York. All I had to do was get the kids ready. She helped out with the choreography. It was fascinating. I love kids. Well, not just kids but everybody. But I especially like working with kids because they are so open and so generous and so loving and they want to succeed, and you want to give them everything you've got. It was a marvelous experience for me.

I lived in this house from 1955; I bought it in 1954. When I first came to Lenox, I lived with Bob Smith and his wife. Bob was a writer with a home on West Avenue. When I came from Boston, I came to the hotel [Curtis Hotel]. They've made a living quarters out of it now, but when I first came, it was a hotel. Bob's wife came, and they rented me a room with a private bath. I could take my meals with them, and they would even make sandwiches for me to take to school. From there, they decided that they wanted to set up their office in New York City, so Mrs. Aiba who lived up on the hill—near the Church on the Hill—she rented a room to me. She was so wonderful. Mrs. Aiba was of German descent. She came to this country several years before

When I was in Boston and all alone and my husband was coming home from overseas, I wanted to get a place for my husband and I, so the people at the hospital would say, "Now, Mae, don't go below such and such a street," because they knew the town. I didn't know the town. There was a vacant apartment that Mr. King owned, and I talked to Mr.

King. Mr. King said to me: "I will have to talk to my wife and my daughter and see if they are willing to bear the brunt if other customers move out. I will call you at eight o'clock tonight." At eight o'clock that night, the telephone rang, and he said, "Mrs. Brown, this is Mr. King." I held my breath. I said, "Mr. King?" He said: "Yes. I didn't bother to talk to my wife or my daughter. I've dealt with people all my life and I know honest people when I see them. I've decided to let you have the apartment."

I felt as if the world had lifted off my shoulders. Because I had gone looking for apartments, and sometimes people would be at the head of the stairway, and they'd see me look at the plaque that they had in the window—"Room for rent," or whatever—and sometimes they'd pull it in. But, you know, you don't let those kind of things deter you. Whatever you want, you go after it. And if one doesn't do it, try another. Like the book says, "If they close the door, go in the window." So, remember that.

I've heard stories that if you are Black in the fifties and driving through Housatonic, you didn't stop. But I don't think it was only Black, because Alice Bubriski, who was Polish, was discriminated against. But you see, I bought this house in Boston. Number One Beacon Street. In 1954 when we were on vacation. It was sight unseen because the next-door neighbor there had a garage, and the way they [the realtors] took the picture, I thought the house had a garage.

I had been denied houses and so forth, so when I bought this house, it had no heating system in it. It had space heaters. My husband was getting transferred from Boston to the Pittsfield post office. I bought the house, and then I had to get an opportunity to get a heating system put in, and that's why I bought it in 1954 and didn't move in till 1955. But it was even hard. If Bob Smith and his wife didn't come up when they came up, I don't know where I'd have ended up, but they came up. In 1955, I was able to come here [to Housatonic]. Then, for twenty years I commuted back and forth to Lenox, even with a broken wrist at one time.

There's discrimination everywhere. One day I was crossing the street, and kids were in a car parked at the Corner Store. They were chanting, "Nigger, nigger, nigger, nigger, nigger." I asked who their parents were. I told their parents, "You must instruct them not to say this sort of thing because they may end up saying this to the wrong person, someone who thinks they are looking for a fight."

You see a lot of people make a mistake and think that discrimination is just down South. Discrimination is everywhere, but you just don't cave into it. And that is why it is important to be fully aware of who you are, what your goal is; you just be able to look a person square in the eye and stand up for yourself, and that way you always feel good about yourself and you got fight in you. I'm not saying you go out fighting and looking for something to disagree or to make trouble. No. I'm not saying that at all. But to be able to stand on your own two feet, knowing you are educated to that degree that you are seeking this employment. Now, for instance, take the type of communication that we've got today. I wasn't privileged to that. So I am ignorant of that. So, what I know I know, and I feel that at ninety-one I am blessed that I got eyesight—twenty/twenty eyesight— and I can even still sew and make all the garments, and things like that. Not just for the money, but the fact that it gets people coming in and out and it's company.

I'm up and going. I go to church, I go to the Thursday Morning Club, a group of us go out. The Thursday Morning Club is a Federated Club. They give scholarships for serious students. Depending on the amount of money that they have, as to how many scholarships they give. We meet the second Thursday of every month. It's not just a club for having fun, but it's a club that helps youngsters.

I'm a member of the First Congregational Church in Great Barrington. I've been a member since 1960. I was going to the A. M. E. Zion Church, and at that particular time, the minister lived somewhere in Connecticut. I don't even remember his name. They were supposed to have service at eleven o'clock, and sometimes it'd be eleven thirty, and sometimes it would be quarter of twelve, and sometimes it'd be twelve o'clock. I was commuting back and forth to Lenox. I had my work to get up for my class. I had my housework to do. I had my husband. I had all the things that women had to do, so hours were essential to me; but having grown up in a Christian family with a high spirit, and believing in God, so it was harder for me, having grown up the way I did. At the college, you start on time and you quit on time. Because that was established in me, that's what I expected, and that's what I did not get. It didn't mean that I didn't like it because they were "colored" or "Negroes" or whatever you want to call us. I wanted it for my own good, and so I went there [First Congregational Church]. I liked the music because at Jarvis, when we turned off the highway and onto the campus, you could hear the organ playing. It was just so soothing and everything. I went to the First Congregational Church because I was pushed for time and I wanted to enjoy, spiritually and emotionally, the services. They have a beautiful organ there. They used to have a lot of musicians from Tanglewood in the summer. So it was a wonderful thing, and I was very blessed.

Even when I went through my divorce, the minister who was there went with me to the court, not as a witness, but as a friend. My husband, then, decided that he wanted to throw another block [make things difficult], and he wanted me to have to take out a new mortgage on my home. The minister went with me to the bank. I spoke to the person in charge for an application. And I asked him, "Do I need to take out a new mortgage on my home?" He said, "No." I said, "Forget it!"

We've had wonderful ministers. Some of them have passed on. John Ames. Pastor Charles Van Ausdall is there now. You respect him for his position and all, but he is like a brother to me because when my brother passed, he asked what I was doing for Thanksgiving. He said, "Mae, where are you going?" and I said I was going home. "No," he said, "you're coming to the Van's." A group of us would go to the Van's, and he would cook the turkey, and we would do the potatoes. It's just like a member of the family.

I go to the other churches when they have things going on. It isn't that I have anything against them. It's just that I know what my spirit needs, and I feed it.

I've been accused of trying to be white. Now how can I be white? I was born this complexion. I'm going to die this complexion. It wasn't that I was trying to be anything I wasn't. That's what you gotta do. This is why some people are pushed by the way they're treated, but my mother always told me to hold my head high and get something in my head and nobody can take it away from me. So, that I've had all my life, and I've known wonderful, wonderful, wonderful people. And even when I lived in Boston, my Bible teacher, Mr. Peoples, and his family retired from Jarvis and were living in Indianapolis, Indiana. I'd take the train out of Boston at three thirty in the afternoon. By noon the next day, they had made dinner at home and would meet me at the station, and I'd go and have dinner with them. They'd take me back. I'd take the train on in to St. Louis, and I'd take the sunshine special out of there. I'd get into Big Sandie, and they'd drop me off 'cause they don't stop there otherwise. And I'd go to the hotel there, and the hotel manager would drive me on home.

A group of us get together and go out together: Beverly Almond, Ruth Beers, Dr. Norma Thompson, and myself. I didn't make it to church last Sunday. There was so much ice I was afraid I would fall. So different ones called to see how I was. We check on each other. It's that friendliness and people working together that I love. 'Cause that's the way I know.

Many a time people would come to our house, because we lived in the country. In those days unless you were a maid in a white family, you didn't stay in a hotel, and there were very few hotels run by Negroes and whatnot, so people would come to our house and my aunt would go to the kitchen and start getting food. I would go to the guest room and get the sheets and things. So we've always been fortunate to be able to accommodate people.

Even hobos. Remember when we used to use that term? One time a man came to our house. Two sisters had adjoining farms, thirty acres each there. So it was one of those things; we always worked together and did things together and looked out for each other. So Aunt Mintie and I were talking, I guess. This young man had been put off the train. We lived close to the Texas Pacific Railroad. Lots of shipping was done by rail, before all the trucks. This was back in the days when they didn't allow people to ride the train, but when the train stopped, sometimes people'd sneak on, getting a lift to another town where there might be some work. And so Bro Rodgers (my mother said that someday he would be my brother in Christ, so I always called him Bro Rodgers)—so Bro Rodgers said: "This young man was put off of a freight train. He's trying to find a job, so he wants to spend the night." So my aunt looked at me and said: "We're both light sleepers. We'll put him in the guest room." So we did.

In my house, we always sat down to breakfast together. So the next morning we all sat down to breakfast; then my aunt made sandwiches and gave them to him. About a month later we got the most wonderful letter from his wife, thanking us for being so wonderful to him. It's those kind of things that—I just tell people that I've grown up with so much love, that's all I know. And I love people, and I enjoy being around people, with people. I guess it paid off, as you can see one of my students there [in a picture of a group of people hanging on the wall] was instrumental in seeing that my house was painted last fall.

You don't always know what's ahead of you. As long as you're prepared, and as long as you're open minded and you love people, you can make a big difference. People say I make a difference. I don't know what difference I make. I just be myself and do what I can do and love people, and if I can help, I help. If I can't, I never hinder anybody. I don't gossip about anybody. I don't let anybody tell me a lot of junk that's going to weigh on my shoulders. I've had some things that've happened that I wasn't guilty of and whatnot, but I told the good Lord, "Lord, you created her and Lord of Angels same as you did me. I cannot reach her. I'll turn it over to you."

You see, I feel like I got a straight line to God and I can talk to him any time of day or night or any place I am—subway, automobile, airplane. One time I got to a place where I couldn't pray, and I knew that wasn't me. A Heifer Plan [a missionary group] was in progress. They were planning to go to the Holy Land. I borrowed money and went for that ten-day journey. I studied the Bible and see people and talk about people at the Wailing Wall. But this cannot have the imprint on the mind the way it is if you actually go there and see that Wailing Wall and see people actually fall down and wail at that wall. And to see Jerusalem the way you studied it in the Bible. The Sea of Galilee . . . to stand by the Sea of Galilee and look out over the Sea of Galilee and to really think about how they used to sink the ships and that's where the big catch was with the fish. It all came alive. At the close of the ten days, somewhere between Paris, France, and New York City, I found myself sitting there with one of the Haddad girls, and the Holy Spirit came upon me, and I found myself silently saying the Lord's Prayer. I knew my prayers had been answered. So, that's why I say . . . in the air, on the train, airplane, anywhere, He's there, and He's always on the job, night and day.

Mae E. Brown

Mae E. Brown was born in Texas in 1914. After living in Boston for a few years, she moved to Housatonic in 1954 and continues to live there. She taught home economics at Lenox High School for twenty-three years and managed the cafeteria for fourteen. A congregant of the First Congregational Church in Great Barrington since 1960, she is a member of the Thursday Morning Club. This essay was compiled from material gathered in an interview in Housatonic on 6 January 2006 and a telephone interview on 26 January 2006 conducted by Ellen Broderick and MaeEllen Scarpa.

Community Guides

The following entries trace the histories and describe life in the major Black communities of the region. The entries also list key extant sites and some no longer extant that were or remain part of African American history and life in these communities. Some of these sites are private property and the privacy of the owners should be respected. Many sites associated with African American history no longer exist and not all of those are included here. The *See also* notations at the end of each guide direct readers to other entries in the volume relevant to that community.

MASSACHUSETTS

Gulf Road/Wizard's Glen

Gulf Road, which passes through Wizard's Glen in Dalton and Lanesboro Gulf in Lanesboro, Massachusetts, has not changed much over the years. It is still narrow and unpaved, the terrain rocky and rugged. Near there, in Dalton, was a cluster of nearly a dozen small cabins, a small community of Blacks that sprang up probably in the 1820s—"for the most part a colony of slaves who had fled from their masters in New York state," according to an article in the *Berkshire Hills* in 1903. It is generally believed the Underground Railroad operated along a corridor from Lebanon Mountain through Pittsfield to Dalton. There was once a cave beneath the road, possibly used by the Underground Railroad. At the Lanesboro end of this road was a house used as an Underground Railroad station, near the Berkshire Mall.

Those who lingered there felt secure from pursuit. "Some of these cabins had their patches for the cultivation of corn and potatoes and fish[;] berries and roots were abundant. On such these colored folks lived comfortably but humbly, but in the enjoyment of the freedom which they had thus isolated themselves to procure. Dalton Historical Commission files indicate that the heads of these thriving families bore the names of their old owners, and among them were the Van Alstynes, Van Burens, Jacobs, Moore, and Jackson, the latter being the slave of Gen. Andrew Jackson." A description in the *Berkshire Hills* in July 1905 describes the kind of life there: "Sambo and Dinah, a colored couple well along in years, had a little shanty of their own construction in the Gulf, to which was attached an ell which was made of white birch poles and thatched with weeds and ferns which they had gathered from the woods. Here they lived in contentment, supporting themselves by selling berries in their season as well as herbs and roots to the White women of the towns for medicinal purposes and for making home-made beer, while for their own use and comfort they raised potatoes and vegetables and were very successful in the growing of watermelons, in which they took especial pride."

The Gulf has even earlier associations with Native Americans. Samuel L. Caesar, a full-blooded Indian who was born in St. Armand, Quebec, in December 1827, lived near there. Caesar went to

The original Indian head painted on a rock in Wizard's Glen by George Hoose of Gulf Road, Dalton, in the 1920s. Photo courtesy of Dalton Historical Commission.

A postcard showing the road through Wizard's Glen, Dalton. Photo courtesy of Gail Pinna.

Dalton after serving in the Civil War in Company G, 5th Regiment, Massachusetts Volunteer Cavalry. He entered the ice business and raised a family with his wife, a Black woman named Hannah Louise Hoose, whose family owned the Hoose Mountain Farm. Known for his strength, both of body and mind, Caesar died in 1929. Hooses, Caesars, and other Black families there found menial employment in farming, laundering, and doing domestic work. In a later generation Archie Caesar operated a landscaping business.

George Hoose painted a large Indian head on a boulder on Gulf Road around the time of the World War I. It has been periodically repainted ever since. Helen M. Madison (1912–2001), Florence Richards (1917–1998), and Hanna Richards (1913–1998) are among Hoose descendants who lived in the Gulf Road vicinity. The home of the late Ellen M. Hoose, a small dwelling at the edge of the Glen at 471 Gulf Road, is believed by members of the Dalton Historical Commission to be one of the last surviving of the old Black community. Hoose acquired her home in 1909, but the building dates to Charles Hoose's purchase in 1868. The property entered tax title in 2004, and Dalton Historical Commission members expressed the hope it might be preserved by the town as an important reminder of a largely forgotten aspect of area history.

Bernard A. Drew, Mary Jane Caliento, and Gail Pinna

See also African American Entrepreneurs, Underground Railroad, Civil War: The 54th Massachusetts Volunteer Infantry Regiment

Sources

Baker, T. Nelson (pastor, Second Congregational Church, Pittsfield). "Samuel L. Caesar, a Wise Man from Youth." Letter. *Berkshire Eagle*, c. 11 Feb. 1929.

Berkshire Hills. Articles January 1901, May 1903, and July 1905.

Caesar, Archie D. "One Soldier's Experience." In *A Bicentennial History of Dalton, Massachusetts, 1784–1984.* Ed. by Bernard A. Drew. Dalton, MA: Bicentennial Committee, 1984.

Dalton Historical Commission. Hoose House Survey Form, Dalton, MA. [Available at Town Hall and the Berkshire County Regional Planning Commission, Pittsfield]

"Grip Claims Civil War Veteran [Samuel L. Caesar]." *Berkshire Eagle*, c. 9 Feb. 1929."

Indian Painting Restored." *Berkshire Eagle*, 13 Aug. 1988.

Pittsfield

The earliest recorded Black presence in Pittsfield dates to 1761, the same year the town was incorporated. According to anecdotal sources, Blacks were present from the beginning of European incursion into the area. Certainly, they were present as early as 1752, when whites settled the town, because "many of the early [white] citizens of Pittsfield held slaves." A slave document shows that one of the town's founders, William Williams, purchased a slave woman named Pendar in 1761. She later gained her freedom, and her family can be traced through historical records for at least four generations.

In Pittsfield's early days, Blacks supported the establishment of the town's agricultural and skilled-labor base. In 1760 the Black population of Berkshire County was 3 percent. Samuel Harrison (1818–1900), a minister and former slave, wrote:

> The old colored settlers in this vicinity came from New York State during the days of slavery, and settled here. Some of them were pursued by their owners, but they were ransomed by some of the citizens. Instances of these were the cases of the Fosters and Potters. Many recollected Old Uncle Tom Brown, who lived upon the Pontoosuc road, and was gate keeper at the cemetery grounds. He was born in Dutchess or Orange County, New York, and was about twenty years old about the time of the Revolutionary war. He had been the father of seven children. He belonged to the Livingston family. He walked away to Pittsfield, and he lived eleven years in the family of old Parson Allen, the first minister of the town. (Harrison 1877, 24)

By 1791, Blacks were included in the poll tax rolls, which meant that they possessed personal or real property as well as knowledge of a skill to be assessed by the town. There were forty-five Black residents in Pittsfield in the 1790 census. Only four were listed as heads of household, maintaining their own separate residences, yet there were more than the four who were assessed taxes. One example was a woman named Hazel Blossom, who was taxed but not listed as a separate head of household. The four heads of households in the 1790 census were Anthony Clever, Titus Grant, Thomas Scheen, and Isaac Gardner. At this time, although a few Blacks had established themselves in the town as independent small farmers, most tilled the soil of others.

Gravestone of Rev. Samuel Harrison, Pittsfield Cemetery. Photo by Pat Cotton. Courtesy of the Samuel Harrison Society, Inc.

In 1827 the town rejected a proposal that would have established segregated schools in the city, primarily because there were not enough Black children to fill a separate school. The population was increasing, however. Pittsfield, in the 1840 census, had 202 Blacks, the largest number of any town in Berkshire County, which had a total of 1,259 Black residents.

In 1846 three women (Catherine Fields, Mary Richards, and Delilah Potter) and four men (Morris Potter, John L. Brown, William Potter, and Davis S. Thomas) founded the Second Congregational Church, a church for persons of color. Before its establishment Blacks attended other churches in Pittsfield, especially the First Congregational Church, yet from the beginning they were assigned to separate, segregated seating and had no role in the management of the church. Discrimination stemming from a refusal of baptism and other privileges prompted the group to organize their own church.

The Pittsfield church was fortunate because it was supported by white citizens, including the Rev. John Todd of the First Congregational Church. They helped the new congregation purchase its first church site on First Street. Three years later the Rev. Samuel Harrison was named the pastor of the Second Congregational Church.

Reverend Harrison was a staunch abolitionist, assisting locals to help fugitive slaves and writing fiery sermons about slavery. In 1850, Blacks called a meeting at the church and pledged that "no fugitive slave should be taken from this town without resistance." When there was a rumor of a slave catcher at the Old Berkshire hotel, Harrison was dispatched to find out about the situation. It seemed that the abolitionist Lewis Tappan had been mistakenly identified. He and Harrison had a fine laugh at that.

Gravestone of the wife of Rev. Samuel Harrison, Pittsfield Cemetery. Photo by Pat Cotton. Courtesy of the Samuel Harrison Society, Inc.

The Reverend Samuel Harrison House in 2005. Photo by Rachel Fletcher.

Some white residents, such as Lyman Warriner of the Berkshire House, gave jobs to fugitive slaves and protected them from slave catchers. Others behaved more shamefully. On one occasion at the American House, the abolitionist Frederick Douglass (1817–1895) was given lodgings but was asked to eat elsewhere. He collected his belongings and removed himself to another hotel. The Black community was incensed at his treatment and talked of initiating a civil rights bill.

Reverend Harrison interrupted his long service at the Second Congregational Church to serve as chaplain for the all-Black 54th Massachusetts Regiment during the Civil War. A number of other Pittsfield natives joined the ranks of that regiment, seeking to defend the Union and bring freedom to their enslaved brethren.

Harrison was also a notable chronicler of Pittsfield's history. In 1874 he wrote, "Pittsfield to-day is far in advance of what Pittsfield was twenty-five years ago." Nevertheless, Pittsfield was still plagued by discrimination. Berkshire mills, while hiring immigrants, did not provide employment to Blacks. The censuses of 1850, 1860, and 1870 report a total of two Black paper mill employees and no Black textile workers. Harrison observed, "As everywhere else, of course, segregation of various sorts persisted in Berkshire after the formal end of slavery.

St. John's Masonic Temple in 2005. Photo by Jenna Turner.

Voting, jury service, free access to public accommodations, transport and schools were banned for Blacks in most of Massachusetts until the 1840s and beyond. These strictures were somewhat less onerous in Berkshire than other places" (Harrison 1876). Harrison and the Black community in Pittsfield continued to work for the equal opportunity and justice that the Fourteenth Amendment guaranteed them.

At the beginning of the twentieth century, many Blacks left Pittsfield for manufacturing jobs in the West. Many of those who remained were employed

Charles A. Persip American Legion Post 68 in 2005. Photo by Rachel Fletcher.

The Christian Center in 2005. Photo by Jenna Turner.

in service jobs, such as at hotels. As the twentieth century wore on, the town became a thriving small metropolis, and the Black population grew once more, especially with an in-migration from a number of southern states. African Americans in Pittsfield supported the abolition of southern Jim Crow laws in transportation, education, public accommodations, and voting, while at home they protested discrimination in jobs and housing.

A countywide chapter of the NAACP was founded in 1918; it functioned until the mid-twenties and was reactivated in 1945. In the 1960s—its most active period—its offices were located at 467 North Street in Pittsfield. Most of the presidents of the chapter were also Pittsfield natives. The NAACP sent residents to participate in the 1963 March on Washington, registered voters during the Freedom Summer of 1964 in Alabama and Mississippi, created affordable housing in Pittsfield, organized sympathy protests at the Woolworth's on North Street, initiated a collection of Black history and literature at the local office, hosted a number of cultural fairs, and was the conduit for communication to the national organization when some citizens of Great Barrington sought to stop the 1969 memorial dedication at the boyhood home of W. E. B. Du Bois.

The West Street neighborhood had several businesses operated by Blacks on both sides of West Street (according to a letter to the editor of the *Berkshire Eagle* in 1992), included the following: John Stevens tailor shop, Henry Walker's garage, Harry West's social club and pool hall, and John Persip's restaurant. A hotel parking lot and Kaybee Toy are now on these sites. Jim Keffred barber shop and the Two-car taxi service owned by Van Dewitt and Charlie Gaulden still operate in the neighborhood.

Frances Jones-Sneed, with the research assistance of Emilie Piper, Sue Denault, Anne Munn, and Ivan Newton

See also Black Entrepreneurs; Sylvanus Grant, Hewer of the Pittsfield Elm; Men's Work 1863–1946; Florence Edmonds, Public-Health Nurse; Henry

Second Congregational Church. Photo by Judith Oleskiewicz. Courtesy of Rev. Carol A. Killian [Towley], Pastor, Second Congregational Church, Pittsfield, MA.

Victory Temple United Church of God in Christ in 2005. Photo by Jenna Turner.

Jenkins Roberts, Physician; Slavery in the Berkshires; Underground Railroad; National Association for the Advancement of Colored People; Activist Orators; Struggles and Achievements; Dorothy Amos, Educator; Margaret Alexander Hart, Educator; Teaching Black History and Culture; American Revolution; Civil War: The 54th Massachusetts Volunteer Infantry Regiment; Civil War: Other Massachusetts Units and Service; World War I; The Persips in World War I; World War II; Berkshire Women in World War II; Religious Institutions; The Second Congregational

Church, Pittsfield; Samuel Harrison, Minister and Activist; Samuel Harrison and Harrison House Photo Essay; Thomas Nelson Baker, Minister and Philosopher; Willard H. Durant, Pastor and Community Leader; Entertainment and Social Life; Sports; Frank Grant, Baseball Player; Billy Hart, Athlete; Larry King, Athlete

Mildred Persip, c. 1940s, Pittsfield. Photo courtesy of Mrs. Frances Persip Duval Collection.

Pittsfield Sites

1. **Margaret Hart Library,** Reid Middle School, located at 950 North Street, was named after the highly regarded Black educator.
2. **Pittsfield Cemetery** at 203 Wahconah Street holds the graves of Rev. Samuel Harrison and his wife.
3. **Berkshire Medical Institute** (BMI; founded in 1823) is at 725 North Street. BMI conferred the first medical degree on a Black student in 1847, the same year that Rush Medical School awarded a degree to a Black man named David Peck.
4. **NAACP Office**, at 467 North Street, was the office of the Berkshire County chapter of the NAACP during the 1960s.
5. **Reverend Samuel Harrison House** still stands at 82 Third Street as of this writing; however, it is in great need of repair. The Samuel Harrison Society's mission is restoration of the house as a museum of African American history. The house was accepted for inclusion in the National Register of Historic Places in 2006.
6. **Persip Park,** above the railroad tracks at the corner of North Street and Columbus Avenue, was dedicated to the Persip family in March 1983.
7. **Woolworth Protest Site** was the scene of a civil rights march. The Woolworth's chain of variety stores refused to serve African Americans at their lunch counters in the South. The Berkshire County NAACP organized a march to support the southern boycott of Woolworth's North Street store in the 1960s.
8. **Park Square,** at the intersection of North and South Streets, is the site of a plaque memorializing a notable elm tree. In 1863 the Town of Pittsfield engaged a skilled woodsman to cut down the most famous tree in town, the Pittsfield Elm. That man was Sylvanus Grant (1844–1927). The tree stood 128 feet tall with a 28-foot circumference.

Price Memorial A. M. E. Zion Church in 2006. Photo by Ivan Newton.

9. **Berkshire Athenaeum,** at 1 Wendell Avenue, maintains the county's major local history collection.

10. **Charles A. Persip American Legion Post 68,** at 41 Wendell Avenue, was eponomously named in honor of the man who was a two-time commander of the American Legion Post 68 and the grandson of Civil War veteran Charles Hamilton, of the 54th Massachusetts Regiment.

11. **Dorothy Amos Park** (formerly the West Side Park), at 310 and 340 West Street, was so-named in 1975 for the esteemed Black educator.

12. **St. John's Masonic Temple,** Eastern Star, is located across from 176 Robbins Ave.

13. **The Christian Center,** at 193 Robbins Avenue, is a community center for inter-denominational worship established in the 1960s.

14. **Dorothy Amos Community Preschool,** 314 Columbus Avenue, was originally founded by Dorothy Reid Amos in 1971 as the Early Childhood Development Center, a day-care facility for low-income families.

15. **Second Congregational Church** is the oldest Black religious organization in the county. It was at first located between 101 and 109 First Street (1846–1940), then at 373 Columbus Avenue (1941–1969; the remains of this building were demolished on 2 April 1981), and as of this writing at 50 Onota Street (1969–present).

16. **Victory Temple United Church of God in Christ,** one of three predominantly African American churches founded in the 1960s, is located at 154 Dewey Avenue.

17. **Price Memorial A. M. E. Zion Church,** the second predominantly Black church founded in Pittsfield, is located at 163 Linden Street.

18. **The Elizabeth Freeman Center in Pittsfield,** at 43 Francis Avenue, is one of three centers with that name in Berkshire County that focus on social services for children and families. The other two are located in North Adams and Lee.

19. **Berkshire Historical Society** is located at 780 Holmes Road.

See map on page 172.

UPPER HOUSATONIC VALLEY AFRICAN AMERICAN HERITAGE TRAIL

PITTSFIELD

1 Margaret Hart Library, Reid Middle School, 950 North Street

2 Graves, Rev. Samuel Harrison and Wife, Pittsfield Cemetery, 203 Wahconah St

3 Berkshire Medical Institute, 725 North Street

4 NAACP, Berkshire County Chapter, 1960s, 467 North Street

5 Rev. Samuel Harrison House, 82 Third Street

6 Persip Park, North Street and Columbus Avenue

7 Woolworth Protest Site, 1960s, North Street

8 Park Square, North and South Streets

9 Berkshire Athenaeum, 1 Wendell Avenue

10 Charles A. Persip American Legion Post 68, 41 Wendell Avenue

11 Dorothy Amos Park, 310-340 West Street

12 St. John's Masonic Temple, 176 Robbins Avenue

13 Christian Center, 193 Robbins Avenue

14 Dorothy Amos Community Preschool, 314 Columbus Avenue

15 Second Congregational Church, presently 50 Onota Street

16 Victory Temple United Church of God in Christ, 154 Dewey Avenue

17 Price Memorial African Methodist Episcopal Zion Church, 163 Linden Street

18 Elizabeth Freeman Center, 43 Francis Avenue

19 Berkshire Historical Society, 780 Holmes Road

KEY

■ Accessible Sites

◆ Inaccessible Sites or Private Residences

⬡ Local Archives and Resources

Please respect the privacy of the owners of these properties today.

Map prepared by Rachel Fletcher. 15 May 2006
GIS datalayers provided by Berkshire Natural Resources Council

MILES

Sources

"Alfred Persip Sr. Dies at Age 87; Was Longtime Leader of Veterans." *Berkshire Eagle*, 6 April 1983.

"Area NAACP to Picket Woolworth's." Berkshire Eagle, 18 June 1963.

"B. C. Robillard Elected Head of NAACP Branch." *Berkshire Eagle*, 12 April 1966.

Berkshire Eagle, 10 July 1980.

Berkshire Medical Institute yearly catalogs [Available in the Local History Room, Berkshire Athenaeum, Pittsfield, MA.]

"Berkshire NAACP to Join Southern Summer Project." *Berkshire Eagle*, 17 April 1965.

Carmen, Linda. "Youths Told of Contribution of Blacks in World War I."

Chapman, Gerard. "Remembering the Persips." *Berkshire Eagle*, 21 May 1994.

"City Elects 1st Negro in School Board Contest." *Berkshire Eagle*, 8 Nov. 1967.

"50 Picket Pittsfield Woolworth's." *Berkshire Eagle*, 21 June 1963.

Harrison, Samuel. *An Appeal of a Colored Man to His Fellow Citizens of a Fairer Hue in the United States.* Pittsfield, MA: Chickering & Axtell, 1877. [Available at the Berkshire Athenaeum, Pittsfield, MA.]

Harrison, Samuel. *A Centennial Sermon Delivered in the Chapel of the Methodist Episcopal Church, July 2, 1876.* Pittsfield, MA: Chickering & Axtell, 1877. [Available at the Berkshire Athenaeum, Pittsfield, MA.]

Harrison, Samuel. *Pittsfield: Twenty-Five Years Ago.* Pittsfield, MA: Chickering & Axtell, 1876. [Available at the Berkshire Athenaeum, Pittsfield, MA.]

Harrison, Samuel. R*ev. Samuel Harrison, His Life Story, as Told by Himself.* Pittsfield, MA: Privately printed, 1899. [Available at the Berkshire Athenaeum, Pittsfield, MA.]

Katz, Judy. "Blacks Boycotted Berkshire Community Action Council Election." *Berkshire Eagle*, 9 Feb. 1979.

Katz, Judy. "Blacks in the City Pull Together." *Berkshire Eagle*, 18 June 1979.

King, Nick. "NAACP Establishing Library of Black History and Literature." *Berkshire Eagle*, 28 Dec. 1972.

Larson, Neil. "Existing Conditions and Historical Analysis of the Samuel Harrison House, 80 Third Street, Pittsfield, MA." Prepared for the Massachusetts Historical Commission.

"NAACP Area Field Secretary Coming to Outline Plans." *Berkshire Eagle*, 7 May 1965.

"NAACP Pickets Woolworth in Mild Demonstration Here." *Berkshire Eagle*, 28 March 1960.

"Negro Riots Not Expected Here by Area NAACP Head." *Berkshire Eagle*, 29 July 1967.

"Obtained Justice in Civil War Days for Pittsfield Man." *Berkshire Eagle*, 6 June 1925. [Available at the Berkshire Athenaeum, Pittsfield, MA.]

O'Conner, Gerald. "Black Pittsfield: Notes of Hope, Notes of Despair." *Berkshire Eagle*, 21 May 1984.

Overmeyer, James E. "Persip, U.S. Black Soldier in World War I, Questions Move That Put Him in French Army." *Berkshire Eagle*, 15 Sept. 1977.

Peuser, Richard W., and Budge Weidman, comps. *Compiled Military Service Records of Volunteer Union Soldiers Who Served with the United States Colored Troops: 54th Massachusetts Infantry Regiment (Colored).* Ed. by DeAnne Blanton. College Park, MD: National Archives Microfilm Publications, 1996. [Available on microfilm at the Silvio O. Conte National Archives, Pittsfield, MA.]

"Reverend Samuel Harrison." *Berkshire Eagle*, 11 Aug. 1900. [Available at the Berkshire Athenaeum, Pittsfield, MA.]

Rollin H. Cooke Collection, Master Index of Persons. Vols. 1–66 [Available at the Berkshire Athenaeum, Pittsfield, MA.]

Sass, Samuel. "Sylvanus Grant and the Pittsfield Elm." *Berkshire Eagle*, 18 Oct. 1984.

Scheer, Peter. "Thousand Attend Black Festival." *Berkshire Eagle*, 22 July 1974.

Smith, J. E. A. *The History of Pittsfield, Massachusetts.* Springfield, MA: C. W. Bryan & Co., 1876. [Available at the Berkshire Athenaeum, Pittsfield, MA.]

Taylor, Richard H. *Historical Directory of the Congregational, Christian and United Church of Christ Congregations in Berkshire County, Massachusetts: 1734–1979.* Dalton, MA: Berkshire Association of the United Church of Christ, 1979.

White, Mark. "The March Remembered." *Berkshire Sampler*, 28 Aug. 1983.

Lenox

Blacks first resided in Lenox in the 1770s, when land given to the original proprietors was sold to their heirs and others. In 1772 a man identified as Titus Negro bought one of these lots, but nothing else is known of him. The 1790 U.S. Census shows seventeen "Other Free Persons" living in Lenox. Eight were members of two Black households—six in the Simon Bow household and two in the Samuel Boyd household. Not named in the census, the other nine individuals lived in white households. The Black population began growing in the 1840s as Black men moved over from New York state to take jobs helping to build the estates and then working in them as cooks and butlers. Women worked as domestics and provided services such as washing clothes and dressmaking. Newcomers from New York often maintained ties to their old communities, and there was apparently much movement back and forth for a number of years.

The 1860 census shows an increase to seventy Black individuals, including seven young men in the House of Corrections. Most of the people had been born in either Massachusetts or New York state. Those born in New York were often older, suggesting that they had arrived earlier in the century. The 1860 population consisted of thirty-eight females and thirty-two males, fifteen under the age of sixteen. Most lived in their own homes. The occupations were quite varied compared with those of other towns: laborer (thirteen), farm laborer (four), farmer (one), cook (three), hostler (one), washerwoman (five), dressmaker/seamstress (three), domestic/housekeeper (five), and beer maker (one).

Seventeen individuals are listed as being illiterate, a high number compared with other towns at the time. Nearly all so listed were older people, born in New York state. As time went on, the number of illiterate persons decreased, since children learned to read in school and their parents learned from them.

One resident was Lena Grant, aged sixty-seven, the widow of Jacob Grant who owned real estate valued at $700 and personal property worth $150. Lena's daughter Adeline had a dressmaking shop in her parent's home on Main Street with Helen Pilcher. Pilcher's daughter, Emily, did seamstress work in the shop. Lena was the aunt (by marriage) of the professional baseball player Frank Grant of Williamstown and also grandmother of Sylvanus Grant, the man who cut down the storied Pittsfield Elm.

The leading Black family at the time was that of Joseph Scermahorn (also Schermerhorn, Schurmhorn, or Schermahorn). According to the census the family was in Lenox in 1840, and probably earlier. Joseph was born in New York state in 1795 or 1796. He established a farm in Lenox and in 1860 owned land valued at $1,500 and personal property valued at $300, making him the wealthiest Black in town. In 1850 his real estate had been valued at $800. He and his wife at one time also worked for Judge William Walker in town. In 1860 the household included his

The James VanDerZee home in Lenox before the demolition. James's room is to the upper left and his grandmother's house is to the right. Photograph by James VanDerZee. Copyright Donna Mussenden VanDerZee.

The David Osterhout House on Hubbard Street in 2006. Photo by Rachel Fletcher.

wife Charlotte, aged sixty-one; Lucy Keeling, aged fifty-one; and Richard W. and Charles B. Dodge, aged seven and two, respectively. The three adults were listed as illiterate. Joseph is listed in 1870 as Joseph Schermerhorn, aged seventy-six, and Charlotte is listed as seventy-four years old. No longer listed as illiterate, he is now eligible to vote. His property is given as $1,000/$500 (real estate/ personal property). The only Black Schermerhorns known in the county, they do not appear in subsequent censuses.

Another old Lenox Black family (or families) was that known as Prince, Prime, or Pruyn. Occasionally the same person is called by one of these surnames and then later by another. All three names have at one time or another belonged to Black people, but *Prime* only to this family in Lenox. *Prince* was a classic name among free Blacks in the north. There was a Peter Prince in Lenox in 1830, and his demographics resemble those of a Peter Prime in Lenox in the 1840s. A man identified as D. Prince had a house on the 1841–1842 map drawn by William Bartlett. In later years most Prince families were white.

Prime was considered one of the descriptive or occupational names of freed slaves in the north, signifying honor or quality (in England it sometimes meant "slender"). Peter Prime, who would have been forty-one or forty-two years old in 1841, lived on the northwest side of Cliffwood Street. At first no one in the family could read, but by 1860 both Anna Prime and her and Peter's son, John, a hostler,

could do so. In 1865 John, then in his sixties, began receiving help, mostly firewood, from other citizens. As was common in the region, individuals would provide care and supplies for the poor and sick, keeping track of their expenses, and would be reimbursed by the town at the end of the year. Another who received help was (Mrs.) Patience Williams, who was brought firewood and food and had repairs made to her home between 1862 and 1871.

James Prime and his wife, Wealthy Ann, were born in Connecticut, so they may not have been directly related to Peter. As shown in the town records of childhood deaths, they experienced much tragedy. Their son Robert died of dysentery on 20 January 1850, and five-and-a-half-year-old Horace of a blow to his head on 11 December in the same year. A daughter, Mary, also died in 1850, and another child, Richard, in 1851. But by 1860 they had six children living (four boys, two girls), with the oldest four in school.

The name *Pruyn* has referred mainly to whites. One of the Black Pruyns was a Revolutionary War soldier from Great Barrington. A Peter H. Pruyn of Lenox was a private in the 54th Regiment and was wounded in action in the Civil War.

Twelve men from Lenox served in the 54th Massachusetts Regiment in the Civil War: Jacob Adams, Henry J. Carter (wounded), John Hall (died of sunstroke), Thomas Jackson (died of disease), Charles F. Patterson, George G. Peters, Edward Porter (transferred to 55th Regiment; killed), Peter H.

Pruyn (wounded), Charles Van Allen (killed by friendly fire), John E. Vosburgh (died of tuberculosis), George F. Waterman (missing in action; presumed dead), and Samuel Weever (wounded). Six Black soldiers died in the war, a surprisingly large number given that they came from a local Black population of only about one hundred.

Lenox's most famous Black son is James VanDerZee, who was born in Lenox in 1886 and died in Washington, D.C. in 1983, after receiving an honorary degree (one of several so received) from Howard University. He is best known for the thousands of pictures he took in the 1920s in Harlem. VanDerZee's photographs showed the people and life of the Harlem Renaissance—photographs that recorded with pride and clarity Blacks' achievements in music, art, and literature during this important period.

VanDerZee's father, John VanDerZee, came from New Baltimore, New York, in the late 1870s and married Susan Elizabeth Egbert of Lenox. He was another in the long line of Black migrants from New Baltimore who moved to Lenox. The couple relocated to New York City and worked as butler and maid to Ulysses S. Grant before moving back to Lenox, where John was the sexton at Trinity Church and Susan ran a bakery. James attended the local school with his sisters and brothers. When he left for Harlem in 1906, he was an aspiring violinist and was equally skilled at the piano. After he landed a job in 1915 as a darkroom technician, however, his career as a photographer superseded that of musician. He opened his own portrait studio on 135th Street just two years later. By then he had met and married his second wife, Gaynella Greenlee, the love of his life.

One of VanDerZee's famous photographs is of Hubert Butler of Lenox, in his army uniform, taken in VanDerZee's studio in Harlem in 1943. Butler was raised in Lenox by VanDerZee's aunts the Osterhouts, who ran a laundry from their home and were neighbors of the VanDerZee's. An altar boy at the Trinity Episcopal Church, Butler was also vice president of his senior class at Lenox High School. On entering the military in World War II, he was stationed in Alabama, where he encountered segregation and discrimination for the first time. The experience was evidently personally devastating; he later lost contact with friends and family in Lenox.

The VanDerZee property, situated between those of the Egberts and the Osterhouts, was taken by eminent domain by the state, which paid the family. But James VanDerZee did not want the money; he wanted to keep the family enclave intact, while the other members wanted the money and persuaded him to sign the pact. The house was eventually torn down.

Perhaps the most visible Black in Lenox during much of the twentieth century was Simon M. James, who worked for the Lenox Savings Bank for seventy-two years. He was born Simon Jaynes in June of 1888, son of Nellie Malone, who was Irish, and Simon Jaynes of New York City. The young boy grew up in Lenox on Stonover Farm, where his father was a teamster, in charge of the horses. His father had changed their name to James by the 1910 census. The younger Simon, who worked as a servant in the house of Edward Hale, married Minnie in the late 1920s, and together they had six children—Simon III, Almeda, Minnie, Edna, Grace, and Herbert. James had begun to work for the bank in 1905. In later years, when he knew nearly every resident of the town, he was so well trusted that customers of the bank who met him on the street would often hand their banking over to him and go on their way. He and Minnie owned an eight-room house on Jaynes Road with a beautiful garden, which was widely admired.

Lenox can claim a special place in Berkshire Black sports history. David Gunn Sr. of Stockbridge, who operated Van Allen's Trucking in Lenox, coached the Lenox High School baseball and basketball teams in 1943 and 1945 and at Lenox School in 1945. The Lenox teams had only white players. Gunn was the first Black coach of a white team in the county and likely one of the first in the entire nation. He was both successful and popular. George Darey, a member of one of the teams, recalls school superintendent Floyd Newport, when Coach Gunn was called aside, telling the team they were making history by playing for the first Black coach of a white team in the county, and perhaps even in the country. In 1985 Gunn was the first coach elected to the Lenox High School Hall of Fame.

From 1949 to 1960 the town was home to the Lenox Merchants, an integrated semipro basketball team. The team was founded and managed by Butch Gregory of Lenox and played in a league of eastern semipro teams. Unlike most teams that were all white, the Merchants had several regular Black players, including Williamstown's Billy Hart and Stockbridge's St. Clair Gunn.

By the end of the century, Blacks were a small minority in town. They numbered only 76 in the 2000 census total population of 5,077 in Lenox.

Elaine S. Gunn, Barbara Bartle, Eve Perera, Ann-Elizabeth Barnes, Claudette M. Webster, and David Levinson

See also David Lester Gunn Sr., Coach and Community Leader; American Revolution; Civil War: The 54th Massachusetts Volunteer Infantry Regiment; Civil War: Other Massachusetts Units and Service; World War II; Kinship; Guest Homes for African Americans; Entertainment and Social Life; The Harlem Renaissance; James VanDerZee, Photographer; Sports

Lenox Sites

1. **Grave of Anna Kneeland Haggerty** (Mrs. Robert Gould Shaw) is in Cemetery at Church on the Hill, Main Street and Greenwood Street.
2. Site of the **James VanDerZee Boyhood Home** is located under the Route 7 bypass.
3. **Osterhout House** is on the northeast corner of the Route 7 and Hubbard Street intersection.
4. **The Museum of the Gilded Age** is at Ventfort Hall, 104 Walker Street.
5. **Wheatleigh** (former home of the Music Inn) is on Hawthorne Road (the property is actually in Stockbridge).

See map on page 178.

Sources

Bartlett, William. "Map of Lenox Village: Berkshire C. Mass as It Was in the Years of 1851, and 1842."

Bellow, Daniel O. "Glory, a Story of Berkshire Blacks." *Berkshire Eagle*, 8 Jan. 1990.

Darey, George. Personal communication with Rachel Fletcher, 2005.

"David Gunn Sr." Obituary in a Service of Worship to Celebrate the Life of David L. Gunn. 27 March 1986.

1860 Census of Berkshire County. Unpublished manuscript.

Ancestry.com. http://ancestry.com (accessed 28 April 2006).

Gunn, Elaine, Barbara Bartle, and Eve Perera. "African Americans in Lenox, Talk at the Lenox Community Center, February 9, 1997." Unpublished manuscript.

RootsWeb. Lenox, Massachusetts, 1790 Census Sorted by Head of Household. http://www.rootsweb.com (accessed 28 April 2006).

Shaw, Robert Gould. *Blue-Eyed Child of Fortune: The Civil War Letters of Robert Gould Shaw*. Ed. by Russell Duncan. Athens: University of Georgia Press, 1992.

Walsh, Susan B. "Old Timer at Lenox Bank Has Held Job 72 Years." *Berkshire Eagle*, 26 July 1977.

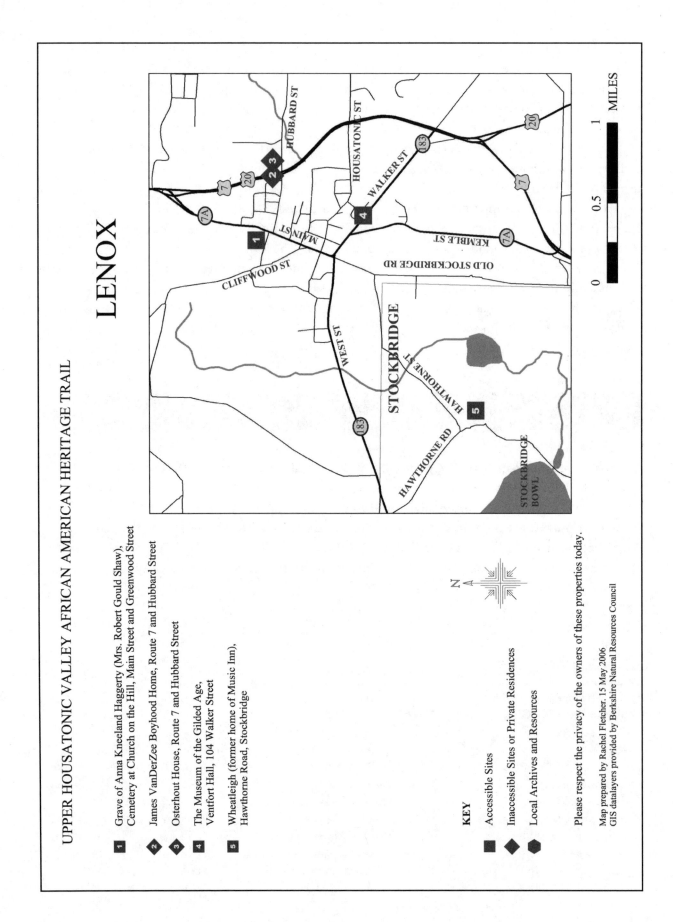

UPPER HOUSATONIC VALLEY AFRICAN AMERICAN HERITAGE TRAIL

LENOX

1   Grave of Anna Kneeland Haggerty (Mrs. Robert Gould Shaw),
Cemetery at Church on the Hill, Main Street and Greenwood Street

2   James VanDerZee Boyhood Home, Route 7 and Hubbard Street

3   Osterhout House, Route 7 and Hubbard Street

4   The Museum of the Gilded Age,
Ventfort Hall, 104 Walker Street

5   Wheatleigh (former home of Music Inn),
Hawthorne Road, Stockbridge

KEY

◼   Accessible Sites

◆   Inaccessible Sites or Private Residences

⬢   Local Archives and Resources

Please respect the privacy of the owners of these properties today.

Map prepared by Rachel Fletcher. 15 May 2006
GIS datalayers provided by Berkshire Natural Resources Council

Lee

Compared with other towns in southern Berkshire County, Lee was the home of few Blacks in its early history, since the town was not incorporated until 1777, later than other southerly settlements. But there were a few Black families before 1830. Those who are known from documentary sources are Peter (surname unknown), Daniel and Betsey (Betty?) Santie (or Santee), Frank Francis, Robert Brigs (Briggs?), Peter Ranney, Frederic Brewster, Harvey Miller, and Edward Hurlbut. In the census some are listed as individuals living with white families, and others are classified as "all other free persons" and later as "persons of color."

The first documented Black resident of Lee was a Revolutionary soldier named Peter, who was engaged in town for three years. He joined Captain Chadwick's company of Colonel Brewer's regiment. Town folklore has it that during the Revolutionary period a small number of Blacks, Native Americans, and whites lived in the northern part of town along Washington Mountain Brook Road.

The 1790 census shows three "other free persons" in town. On 11 November 1792 Daniel Santie (Santee) and Betsey (or Betty), his wife, were admitted to the Congregational Church. They are not listed as "colored" in the church records. In June of the following year, Daniel "publicly confessed his wickedness in deceiving Mr. Jeremiah Wormer, and violating a covenant engagement entered into with him, and asked the forgiveness of the church, on which the church voted to forgive him, and restore him to their charity and fellowship." Jeremiah Wormer had settled in the Hoplands section of Lee in 1774. Whatever the offense, it was not serious enough to be taken up in the Court of Common Pleas. Gale's 1854 history reports that Daniel, "the Negro," and Betty (Betsey) his wife were gatekeepers of the meeting house, so to speak, sitting on each side of the entrance. Daniel had a long cane, with which he "faithfully kept the unruly dogs out of the church, and became the terror of all the roguish boys within." Daniel, Betsey, and two others are the only "other free persons" listed in the 1800 census.

Memorial Hall in Lee in 2005.
Photo by Zachary Mino.

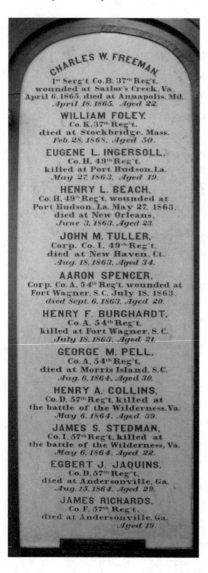

One of the memorial plaques in Lee's Memorial Hall in 2005. Photo by Zachary Mino.

CHARLES W. FREEMAN.
1st Serg't Co.B. 37th Reg't.
wounded at Sailor's Creek. Va.
April 6.1865. died at Annapolis. Md.
April 18.1865. Aged 22.

WILLIAM FOLEY.
Co. K. 37th Reg't.
died at Stockbridge. Mass.
Feb. 28. 1868. Aged 50.

EUGENE L. INGERSOLL.
Co. H. 49th Reg't.
killed at Port Hudson. La.
May 27. 1863. Aged 19.

HENRY L. BEACH.
Co. H. 49th Reg't. wounded at
Port Hudson. La. May 27. 1863.
died at New Orleans.
June 3. 1863. Aged 23.

JOHN M. TULLER.
Corp. Co. I. 49th Reg't.
died at New Haven. Ct.
Aug. 18. 1863. Aged 34.

AARON SPENCER.
Corp. Co. A. 54th Reg't. wounded at
Fort Wagner. S.C. July 18. 1863.
died Sept. 6. 1863. Aged 20.

HENRY F. BURGHARDT.
Co. A. 54th Reg't.
killed at Fort Wagner. S.C.
July 18. 1863. Aged 21.

GEORGE M. PELL.
Co. A. 54th Reg't.
died at Morris Island. S.C.
Aug. 6. 1864. Aged 30.

HENRY A. COLLINS.
Co. D. 57th Reg't. killed at
the battle of the Wilderness. Va.
May 6. 1864. Aged 39.

JAMES S. STEDMAN.
Co. I. 57th Reg't. killed at
the battle of the Wilderness. Va.
May 6. 1864. Aged 22.

EGBERT J. JAQUINS.
Co. D. 57th Reg't.
died at Andersonville. Ga.
Aug. 15. 1864. Aged 29.

JAMES RICHARDS.
Co. F. 57th Reg't.
died at Andersonville. Ga.
Aged 19.

By 1810 the population had increased to include eighteen "free persons" and an unknown number of Blacks living with white families. A free Black named Frank Francis bought a total of 9.5 acres of land in 1813 and 1821, said to be in the Washington Road area in the north part of town. He purchased a house and more land in 1834 and 1837 and is listed as a yeoman and husbandman in these deeds. Born in New York, he married and had a family and died at the age of ninety-eight in March 1862 at the Town Farm.

By the 1820s manufacturing employed most Lee residents, rather than agriculture or commerce, thus limiting opportunities for Blacks, although some did work in the mills later in the century. Only twelve were employed by white families. Robert Brigs had a household of four. Ten years later, traces of a larger Black presence began to emerge. Harvey Miller with a household of three lived next door to U. F. (Frederic) Brewster, who had a household of seven. Not far from them was Frank Francis with a family of five, and his adjoining neighbor Edward Hurlbut with a family of seven. Down the road was Peter Ranney. He was born in the West Indies, and his estimated age was fifty-five. Also living there were his wife Fanny, born in Virginia, and possibly a married daughter and son-in-law—Mary and Lewis Burnet, in their thirties, with a daughter Lucy, age ten, all born in Massachusetts. These Ranneys are not to be confused with the white-Indian Rannys in Connecticut, some of whom came to the Berkshires.

The Black population of Lee grew over the next decades. The 1860 census shows fifty-seven Blacks; twenty-nine females and twenty-eight males. Twenty were under the age of fourteen. Almost all were born in Massachusetts or New York. Their occupations were listed as servant (eleven), laborer (five), farm laborer (five), housekeeper (five), washerwoman (two), and one each for butcher, shoemaker, basket maker, and "whiteworker." One of those listed in the census was Aaron Spencer, then eighteen years old. He joined the 54th Massachusetts regiment in 1863 and died on 5 September 1863 in the siege of Fort Wagner, South Carolina.

By 1875 the Black population had increased to 105, with the town population at 3,900. An article in the *Lee Gleaner* on 15 May 1901 complained about a Black "carnival" held in Northrup's Hall. Lee was by now a center of the Black community in the region, and such festivals—held two or three times a year—attracted Black people from surrounding towns and New York state. School records show that the Black population was dispersed around town and not concentrated in any one neighborhood. In 1910 the population began a permanent decline, since the lack of jobs drove Black men to look for work in the shade tobacco industry near Hartford and in factories in Yonkers,

A portion of the memorial plaque in Lee's Memorial Hall which lists three Black men killed in the Civil War. Photo by Zachary Mino.

New York. The population has remained small ever since. Among families who remained were the Wards, Stallings, and Bassetts. The 2000 census shows 40 Black residents.

The community was large enough that it attracted Black preachers by the 1840s. In 1844 the Rev. Albert Marie began the work of the African Methodist Episcopal Church in town, and in 1852 the members built a church on High Street. There were twenty-four members in 1877. The county atlas for 1876 shows two Black churches, one on High Street and the other on Prospect. The origin of the second church is unknown, but it was probably an African Methodist Episcopal Zion Church, since there was an A. M. E. Zion pastor, Cyrus Oliver, in town in 1870. What came of the second church is also unknown. In 1882 the church community split when the Rev. Charles Ackworth began holding prayer meetings (possibly Baptist) in the town hall and then in homes. He failed to take control of the A. M. E. church building, and in 1883 it was sold, with services held in a building on High Street. The A. M. E. pastor at the time was Robert Jeter, who was assisted occasionally by his son Clifford. Jeter also owned a restaurant and five homes on "Prospect Heights" (built in 1906), which he sold. After his death, in Georgia in 1925, the High Street church building was torn down. In the 1890s the Rev. Dr. Frank Freeman was the spiritual leader of the Black community, centered on his large home at the top of Prospect Street. As the Black population declined in the twentieth century, so, too, did the churches.

Two white men who grew up in Lee played a role in the Black fight for equality, although on opposite sides of the issue. The writer Albion Winegar Tourgee (1838–1905), of Lee parents but born in the Midwest, spent some of his youth living with an aunt and uncle in Lee. He was also an attorney and judge in the South, who advocated Black equality through education. Tourgee lost the case of Homer Adolph Plessy in Louisiana and went on to take the case before the U.S. Supreme Court as *Plessy v. Ferguson*. When the court found against Plessy and upheld the concept of "separate but equal," it was Justice Henry Billings Brown (1836–1913), also of Lee, who delivered the ruling. One of the seven judges who concurred with Brown was Stephen J. Field, who was raised in Stockbridge. *Plessy v. Ferguson* was the landmark Supreme Court decision that locked racial segregation into place for decades.

Emilie Piper, David Levinson, and Barbara Allen

See also American Revolution; Civil War: The 54th Massachusetts Volunteer Infantry Regiment; Civil War: Other Massachusetts Units and Service; Religious Institutions

Lee Sites

1. **Black Church** site, east side of Prospect Street
2. **Jeter House** site, west side of Prospect Street
3. **African Methodist Episcopal Church** site, west side of High Street
4. **Lee Library,** 100 Main Street, houses a local history collection.
5. **Memorial Hall,** 32 Main Street, has a plaque listing three 54th Massachusetts Regiment soldiers from Lee killed during the Civil War.

See map on page 183.

Sources

Adams, C. C. *Middletown Upper House … and a Full Genealogy of the Ranney Family.* New York: Grafton Press, 1909.

Berkshire County Registry of Deeds, Pittsfield, MA. Grantees 1761–1830. 1860 Census of Berkshire County. Unpublished manuscript.

"The Colored Carnival." *Lee Gleaner,* 15 May 1901.

Consolati, Florence. *See All the People; or, Life in Lee.* Lee, MA, 1978.

"Frank Francis." *Berkshire Courier,* 27 March 1862.

Gale, Reverend A. *History of the Town of Lee.* Lee, MA: French and Royce, 1854.

Gooding, James Henry. *On the Altar of Freedom: A Black Soldiers Civil War Letters from the Front.* Amherst: University of Massachusetts Press, 1991.

Heads of Families at the First Census of the United States, Taken in the Year 1790. Massachusetts. Washington, DC: Department of Commerce and Labor, Bureau of the Census, 1906.

Hyde, C. M., and A. Hyde. *The Centennial Celebration and Centennial History of the Town of Lee, Mass.* Springfield, MA: Charles W. Bryan and Co., 1878.

Knurow Collection. Vol. 42, 165. Pittsfield, MA, Berkshire Athenaeum.

Records of the Town of Lee from Its Incorporation to 1801. Lee, MA: Press of the *Valley Gleaner,* 1900.

Secretary of the Commonwealth, comp. *Massachusetts Soldiers and Sailors in the War of the Revolution.* Boston: Wright and Potter, 1896–1908.

Smith, R. W. *Town Talk.* New York: Vantage Press, 1976.

United States Census, Lee, MA, 1796–1850.

Wilson, Walter. "Famed Fighter for Rights Was Lee Resident." *Berkshire Eagle,* 14 Feb. 1975, 14.

Woodson, C. G. *Free Negro Heads of Families in the United States in 1830.* The Association for the Study of Negro Life and History, 1925.

UPPER HOUSATONIC VALLEY AFRICAN AMERICAN HERITAGE TRAIL

LEE

1. Black Church, Prospect Street
2. Jeter House, Prospect Street
3. African Methodist Episcopal Church, High Street
4. Lee Library, 100 Main Street
5. Memorial Hall, 32 Main Street

KEY

Accessible Sites

Inaccessible Sites or Private Residences

Local Archives and Resources

Please respect the privacy of the owners of these properties today.

Map prepared by Rachel Fletcher. 15 May 2006
GIS datalayers provided by Berkshire Natural Resources Council

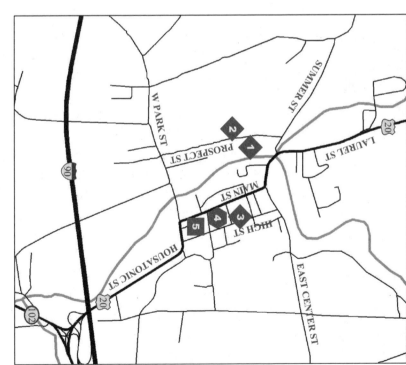

Stockbridge

Early Stockbridge's population included a rainbow array of native Mohicans, Dutch fur traders, English homesteaders, Mohawk students at the mission school, and enslaved and free Blacks—a blend found nowhere else in Berkshire County, if even in all of New England then. Dutchmen Johoiakim Van Valkenburgh and Elias Van Schaack came from Kinderhook, New York, and were among the first whites to make contact with the native Mohicans here, the former bartering cookware and other goods for furs from the latter. Indian Town (later, Stockbridge) was permanently settled by the English in 1734. Several Dutch individuals disdained trade rules and swapped liquor for goods. Only reluctantly accepted by the English, most of the Dutch were forced to resettle in the Upper Parish of Sheffield, which became Great Barrington. The use of slaves and bonded house servants dates from the earliest years of the town.

The Rev. John Sergeant, after a winter in Great Barrington, settled on Prospect Hill in 1739, where he built the Mission House to serve the population of Mohicans. (The building was moved to Main Street in 1926 and later became a house museum, operated by the Trustees of Reservations). Timothy Woodbridge taught at the mission school. Sergeant's successor, the Rev. Jonathan Edwards, arrived in Stockbridge in 1751 with a Black house slave, Rose, to whom he soon granted freedom. She married Joab Benny, a free Black man who had accompanied the Edwardses to town.

The first documented Blacks in Berkshire County are Cuffee and Nana Negro, manumitted by Van Schaack in 1746, though they very likely had lived in town a decade or more by then. A modest population of Blacks emerged in town, some receiving their freedom there, others coming as free Blacks, primarily from Northampton and vicinity. Agrippa Hull came to Stockbridge as a free youth in 1765. At the same time, there remained enslaved Blacks whose freedom came only after Mum Bett's celebrated court case in 1781. Bett, who came to be known as Elizabeth Freeman, settled in town in the Sedgwick household, where she helped raise the children and prepare the meals. Some Blacks were able to acquire property, and they clustered around Agawam Pond, just south of the village. Joab and Rose Benny, for example, bought 50 acres from John Skushawmn in 1755 on Evergreen Hill. Freeman purchased her own home, on Cherry Hill Road, in 1803, with a view of the northern face of Monument Mountain, and five years later moved there permanently.

Gravestone of Agrippa Hull in Stockbridge Cemetery in 2005. Photo by Zachary Mino.

The mission closed in 1776, and the English settlers by 1785 had nudged the Mohicans out of town. Blacks, however, remained, and their relatively stable settlement predated and had distinct characteristics from those that would form in neighboring Sheffield and Great Barrington. Sheffield's population of free Blacks emerged only after Bett's court case and was far more transient than Stockbridge's, reflecting the town's proximity to Connecticut and New York, which were much later in granting freedom to Blacks and from which there came a constant flow of runaways. Great Barrington's Rosseter Street came later still, after the arrival of the railroad.

Stockbridge's small Black population almost from the start showed modest entrepreneurial spirit. Joab Benny, for instance, was by various reports a blacksmith and tanner. Agrippa Hull and his second wife, Margaret (or "Peggy"), had a catering business. Three quarters of a century later, Charles Allen ran a small hotel for African American guests just beyond the Red Lion Inn.

With tenacity, the researcher finds bits and pieces of the story of African Americans in Stockbridge in marriage, birth and death records, probate materials, cemetery listings, real estate transactions, and court of common pleas proceedings. In early church records, the words *nigra* or *niger* or *coloured* were sometimes used to identify persons of African descent; these designations were not consistently used. When Blacks joined the Congregational Church, they sometimes came with letters from the previous community or church that they had attended. In the church records from 1776–1819, a few people of African descent are listed as having a first name but no last name. An example of this is "Edward, negro man and Priscilla, negro woman; baptized and received into the church Dec. 25th, 1785." The following persons of African descent were members between 1827 and 1844: Agrippa Hull, Mary Slocomb Jackson, Betsey Jackson, Sherman Mars, Mary Hull Way, and Mary E. Howell. As with all people, the church was a community in which births, deaths, and marriages were celebrated. In the 25 August 1819 church record, the following names are listed as "Heads of Household": Horace Weston, Thomas Dunkins, Agrippa Hull, Enoch Humphrey, Rose Salter, Thomas Kellis, Betty Freeman (Elizabeth's daughter), and Richard Cady.

Early town records indicate residents were assessed four taxes for which different books were kept: state tax, school and highway tax, minister tax, and meeting house or church tax. Elizabeth Freeman appears on the tax records in Stockbridge for the first time in 1811. Also listed are Agrippa Hull and Enoch Humphrey. She paid $.29 in taxes. Humphrey and Hull paid $.50 and $.75 respectively. They are mixed in with all other resident taxpayers in 1810 and 1811.

Gravestone of Elizabeth Freeman in Stockbridge Cemetery in 2005. Photo by Zachary Mino.

Starting in 1799 and ending in 1836, however, they are separated out from the rest of the taxpayers, appearing at the end of the record under the heading "People of Colour." From 1811 to 1821 Freeman, Hull, and Humphrey are consistently found on the tax records, joined by others who come and go, and the three pay on an average of \$.22 to \$1.09 in taxes on their property and personal income. Freeman is the sole female to appear on the records under "People of Colour," and she could vote and therefore did not pay a poll tax.

In the 1790 U.S. federal census, there were four headings, or designations, for determining the makeup of its residents: "Free white males of 16 years and upwards including heads of families," "Free white males under 16 years," "Free white females including heads of families," and "All other free persons." Slaves were also a heading, but this column is empty for the entire state of Massachusetts. The Stockbridge census lists 65 "all other free persons," which could include both Native Americans and people of African descent. The total population of Stockbridge in 1790 was 1,336, making "all other free persons" under 5 percent of the population.

There were ten families whose "head of household" were Black, and seventeen families who were listed as having between one and five "all other free persons" living with them. Theodore Sedgwick is listed as having three free white males of sixteen-plus years; four free white males under sixteen years, and six free white females as well as three free persons. Two of these free persons could have been Elizabeth Freeman and her daughter, Betty.

In the earliest years, church members of African descent often had no last names in church record books, such as one found in this entry in the Congregational Church records of 1776–1819: "Tamar, negro woman, was received into the church June 18th, 1809." Other Black members, who were fully named, were Agrippa Hull, Mary Slocomb Jackson, Betsey Jackson, Sherman Mars, Mary Hull Way, and Mary E. Howell. It should be noted that membership was not a prerequisite for attending church. For example, Joab and Rose Benny (not listed as members), who married in 1756, raised three daughters, one of whom, Clarisa, was baptized in the Congregational Church on 4 March 1782. Another daughter, Almira, married Nicholas Rich in the church on 18 February 1830.

Stockbridge Blacks showed the same patriotic vigor as their white neighbors during wartime. Frank Duncan, William Erving, Festus Prince, Caesar Freeman, Agrippa Hull, Negro Humphrey, Cato Mumford (also recorded as Mumfrey or Muffy), Titus Pomp, and Prince Wanton served in the American Revolution. Charles H. Piper, John Clow, John Q. Williams, Valorous W. Williams, and Charles T. Way wore blue uniforms during the Civil War.

Alice McNiff, an associate professor at New York University and a cottager in Stockbridge, conducted a thorough assessment of the Black population during the mid-1960s. McNiff's research unearthed general comfort in living in Stockbridge, though Blacks' small numbers brought feelings of isolation. There was evident disgust with some housing practices and generally a lack of educational opportunity seen beyond the public school level.

Since the 1960s, Blacks have become full participants in the educational system. An example is Stockbridge resident Homer L. ("Skip") Meade, a former English and Black studies teacher at Monument Mountain Regional High School, who as of this writing is senior area director for National Evaluation Systems. Meade, who also taught at Simon's Rock College and the University of Massachusetts, organized the 1979 dedication of the Du Bois Homesite in Great Barrington as a National Historic Landmark.

While it is entrenched in white theater tradition, Stockbridge's Berkshire Theater Festival has cast Black performers, such as Louis Gossett Jr. in *Waiting for Godot* in 1966. In 2003 the play, *The Hill: The Life and Times of W. E. B. Du Bois*, written by Great Barrington resident Mickey Friedman, was staged at the Berkshire Theater Festival. The role of Du Bois was played by Tony Award-winner Chuck

Copper, and more than 1,600 people attended the six performances. The play was the culmination of Berkshire Country Day School's W. E. B. Du Bois Centennial celebration.

There were fewer African Americans in Stockbridge in the early 2000s than there were in 1790. In the latter year, sixty-four Blacks were counted, while the 2000 census recorded only twenty-eight.

Bernard A. Drew, with information from Emilie S. Piper, Claudette Webster, Barbara Allen, Ann Elizabeth Barnes, and Ellen Broderick.

See also Cuffee and Nana Negro, Pioneer Blacks in Berkshire County; Mum Bett (Elizabeth Freeman), Anti-Slavery Pioneer; American Revolution; Agrippa Hull, American Revolution Veteran and Caterer; Civil War: The Massachusetts 54th Volunteer Infantry Regiment; Civil War: Other Massachusetts Units and Service; Guest Homes for African Americans; Entertainment and Social Life; Local Black Children as Norman Rockwell Models

Stockbridge Sites

1. **Normal Rockwell Museum** on Route 23 houses examples of Rockwell's work which used local Black children as models.
2. **Graves of Elizabeth Freeman and Agrippa Hull** are in the Stockbridge Cemetery, on Route 102. Hull is buried in the southwest corner of the cemetery, in row 22 from Church Street. Freeman is buried in the Sedgwick Pie in the northeast corner of the cemetery.
3. **Sedgwick House,** 22 Main Street, is a private residence.
4. **Stockbridge Library,** Main Street, has a large local history collection.

See map on page 188.

Sources

Drew, Bernard A. *If They Close the Door on You, Go in the Window: Origins of the African American Community in Sheffield, Great Barrington and Stockbridge.* Great Barrington, MA: Attic Revivals Press, 2004.

First Congregational Church. Records [HC1972.005]. Stockbridge Library Historical Collection. Stockbridge, MA.

Piper, Emilie. "The Family of Agrippa Hull." In *Berkshire Genealogy.* Vol. 22, no. 1, 3–6.

Sedgwick Sarah C., and Cristina Sedgwick Marquand. *Stockbridge 1739–1939.* Stockbridge, MA: Berkshire Traveller Press, 1974 [Originally printed by *Berkshire Courier*, Great Barrington, MA, 1939.]

Silvio Conte National Archives. Pittsfield, MA. (Census information, provided by Pat Walsh and staff.)

Stockbridge, Massachusetts, and a Key to Its Record. N.p.: Berkshire Historical Society, 1998.

Stockbridge Tax Record [HC1972.004]. Stockbridge Library Historical Collection. Stockbridge, MA.

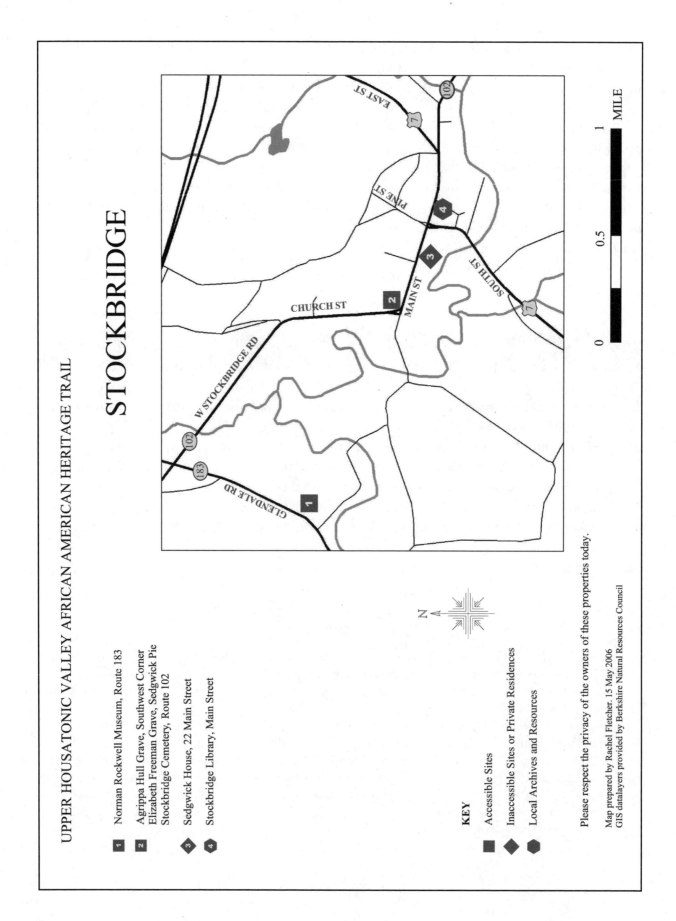

STOCKBRIDGE

UPPER HOUSATONIC VALLEY AFRICAN AMERICAN HERITAGE TRAIL

1 Norman Rockwell Museum, Route 183

2 Agrippa Hull Grave, Southwest Corner
Elizabeth Freeman Grave, Sedgwick Pie
Stockbridge Cemetery, Route 102

3 Sedgwick House, 22 Main Street

4 Stockbridge Library, Main Street

KEY

■ Accessible Sites

♦ Inaccessible Sites or Private Residences

⬢ Local Archives and Resources

Please respect the privacy of the owners of these properties today.

Map prepared by Rachel Fletcher. 15 May 2006
GIS datalayers provided by Berkshire Natural Resources Council

Great Barrington

The first recorded Black resident of Great Barrington is a man known only as "Simon, a Negro," who joined the Great Barrington Congregational Church on 25 May 1746. The first known Black taxpayer appeared in the tax roll for 1772; he was listed as Cato Negro. Three Black men are known to have served in the American Revolution—John Adams, York Kilburn, and Negro Morton. Whether Tom or Jack Burghardt, an ancestor of W. E. B. Du Bois, served or not remains a matter of debate. The first United States census in 1790 shows forty-six individuals counted under the category "All Other Free Persons." Twenty-five are shown as living in white households and are not listed by name. Those named as having their own households are Jacob (Negro), household of two; Moses Rogers, household of two; Cuffee (Negro), household of seven; Caeser Joy, household of seven; and Silas Glasgo, household of two.

The Burghardt, Piper, Van Allen, Ray, Jacklin, Bunker, Ferris, and Freeman families were all residing in town before 1850. Many members of the Burghardt, Piper, and Van Allen families were related through marriage. Most families are best described as homesteaders, in that they owned small amounts of land and had gardens and a few animals but earned most of their income by working for others.

The 1860 county census records 131 Blacks in Great Barrington. The population was fairly young, with 76 females and 55 males, 43 of whom were children under the age of 14. Almost all were born in Massachusetts, Connecticut, or New York. Most lived in their own homes, although some individuals and families lived in the homes of the white families for whom they worked. The occupations were laborer (26), servant/domestic (25), housewife (17), barber (2), coachman (1), and Methodist clergyman (1).

During the Civil War twelve men from Great Barrington served in the all-Black 54th Massachusetts Regiment. These were John Ferris, Ralph Gardner, Franklin Gover, Abraham Jackson, Francis Jackson, James Jackson, Levi Jackson, William Stevens, Jacob Thomas, Charles Thompson, David Van Allen, and Edward Williams.

By the mid-1800s, Blacks were routinely buried in Mahaiwe Cemetery. The cemetery has two Black plots with at least fifty graves, most of them unmarked. The oldest known grave is that of Louisa M. Burghardt, who died on 9 October 1849 at age twenty-four. Among the burials are at least five men who served in the Civil War. The most interesting burial announcement in the *Berkshire Courier* was for Jane A., who died on 19 April 1877 at age eighty-eight, and her husband, Pompey Phillips, who died on 13 May 1880, at age ninety-five. "Born and died slaves, in the state of New York. They found refuge and friends, here." The couple farmed on land in the Seekonk section of town. Nearly all graves date from the 1860s to the 1890s. After 1895 most Blacks in Great Barrington were buried in Elmwood Cemetery, off Route 7.

An influx of people from the South led to the founding of the African Methodist Episcopal Zion Society in the 1860s. Prior to then, Blacks who

Eloise Brinson Woods and William Woods at the Great Barrington Post Office, 1 February 1992, at the issue of the W. E. B. Du Bois 29-cent stamp. Photo by Donald B. Victor.

attended church did so at the Congregational and Episcopal churches in town and the Congregational Church in Egremont. Some continued to do so even after the founding of the Zion Society. The society was the first and remains the oldest Black institution in town. It provided schooling for children, a literary society, debates, and musical and dramatic entertainment for its members and the town. In 1887 the society became the Clinton A. M. E. Zion Church and its building on Elm Court was dedicated. Joseph G. Smith, who served from 1885 to 1887, was the first pastor. The church was a regular contributor to the church-based social life in the southern Berkshires, with suppers, ice cream parties, dramatic readings, plays, concerts, and speakers providing entertainment and also much-needed income for the church. The most spectacular event took place in 1890, when the church sponsored a New England dinner, attended by over four hundred people.

The market town and government seat for the southern Berkshires farming region, Great Barrington began to change in the mid-nineteenth century as textile and paper mills and then tourism replaced farming as the main economic activities. With the decline of farming and with employment discrimination in the mills, a considerable number of Black men and women had to look elsewhere—including outside the region—for work, and many found work in the growing tourism industry as domestics, butlers, and cooks. A few entrepreneurs, such as Jason Cooley, Manuel Mason, and George Jackson, opened restaurants, catering operations, and boarding houses. By the late nineteenth and the early twentieth century, the town's Black population was composed primarily of older women.

From the 1860s into the 1890s, the population fluctuated seasonally, expanding in the summer as Blacks came to work in tourist facilities or accompanied summering white families. New members of the community often came first in the summer and then decided to stay on. Leading members of the community in the late nineteenth and the early twentieth century were, respectively, pastors J. F. Waters and David Overton, and pastors George Jackson, Lena Wooster, and Edward Wooster.

After the Clinton A. M. E. Zion Church opened in 1887 on Elm Court in Great Barrington, Black members of the church began to settle on Elm Court and neighboring Rosseter Street. As African Americans migrated north from 1910 to 1920, Great Barrington's Black population grew, and by the 1930s the Rosseter Street neighborhood had become the town's "Black" neighborhood, with sev-

Diversity of Black Folk

In his 1968 Autobiography W. E. B. Du Bois recalled the diversity of the small Black population in the southern Berkshires.

My family was among the oldest inhabitants in the valley. The family had spread slowly through the county intermarrying among cousins and other black folk, with some, but limited infiltration of white blood. Other dark families had come in and there was intermingling with local Indians. In one or two cases there were groups of apparently later black immigrants from Africa, near Sheffield, for instance. Surviving also was an isolated group of black folk whose origin was obscure. We knew little of them but felt above them because of our education and economic status.

Source: Du Bois, W. E. B. *The Autobiography of W. E. B. Du Bois. A Soliloquy on Viewing My Life from the Last Decade of Its First Century.* New York: International Publishers, 1968, 83.

eral Black families owning homes on the street and adjacent ones. The neighborhood was actually integrated, there always being a mix of Black and white families. Because houses were inexpensive and available, unlike rental housing in town, the neighborhood was desirable. Not all Blacks lived in the neighborhood, however; it was not uncommon for single women to live in the homes of their employers, and some families lived on the east side of the Housatonic River.

By the 1940s the neighborhood had expanded to include several houses on Railroad Avenue, Castle Lane, the east side of Main Street, and lower Cottage Street. The larger and more stable community formed several institutions of its own: the Clinton church expanded, and the Macedonia Baptist Church (1944) and Moorish Science Temple (1944–1949) were founded; two Black socialclubs (Jolly Club No. 12 and the Progressive Club) attracted several dozen members; and the Sunset Inn on Rosseter Street provided accommodations for visitors. In 1925, local residents had formed the Colored Giants baseball team. Brinson's Cleaners had opened in 1925 on Main Street, and in the 1940s Martha Crawford opened an inn, tearoom, and employment agency on Elm Court. Another entrepreneur was Warren Davis, who ran a lumber business and speculated in land from about 1910 until the late 1950s.

The condition of some of the housing was not the best, and in 1943 Rev. H. W. Morrison of the Clinton Church went before the selectmen to complain that "housing conditions for colored people in Great Barrington . . . are for the most part unfit for human habitation." He further noted "that when the present war is over, America faces a new problem, which is involved with the general improvement in the national attitude towards people of different races and creeds" (*Berkshire Courier* 1943).

The former home and office of Warren Davis and Maybelle Gunn at 11 Rosseter Street, in 2004. Photo by Anne Munn.

Since the 1980s the town's African American population has declined, and the Rosseter Street neighborhood has begun to gentrify.

Several Black men from the town served in World War II, including Joseph Gunn, Albert Brinson Jr., Elliot White, Isaac Crawford Sr., Benjamin Carter, James Madison, Julian Hamilton, Clarence Gunn, and Joseph Coffin. By the 1940s college education and professional employment for women in teaching and nursing opened up and employment at General Electric—and later at other manufacturing facilities—became available to both men and women. Evelyn Haile and Mattie Bowens worked as nurses at Fairview Hospital. In the 1960s and 1970s Homer Meade, Elaine Gunn, Martha

The Macedonia Baptist Church on Rosseter Street in 2005. Photo by Zachary Mino.

The Clinton African Methodist Episcopal Zion Church on Elm Court in 2004. Photo by Rachel Fletcher.

W. E. B. Du Bois mural in the Taconic parking lot in 2003. Photo by Erik Callahan.

Pierce, Earl Bean, and George Taylor taught in the schools. Active in the community during these years were (Mrs.) Pinkie Brooks, (Mrs.) Sinclara Gunn, Wray Gunn, Rev. H. W. Morrison, Rev. Raleigh Dove, Martha Crawford, and Albert and Susie Brinson. On 13 October 1949 Edna Dixon Hardy became the first Black woman to have her photo accompany her marriage (to Willie J. Wilks) announcement in the *Berkshire Courier*.

In the 1950s some members of the community became active in the civil rights movement; with other members of the Pittsfield NAACP, they fought for their rights through the 1960s. Maybelle Gunn, Elaine Gunn, and Ruth D. Jones were much involved, and the Clinton A. M. E. Zion pastor Rev. William Durante represented the community when race relations became tense in the mid-1960s. In 1968 the Du Bois boyhood homesite on Route 23 received national recognition and created local controversy when the newspaper and others objected to a public marker designating it as his home. In the late 1950s and early 1960s, women from the Clinton and Macedonia churches joined with women from churches throughout the county to form a branch of the Council of United Church Women to work for social justice. Mrs. Pinkie Brooks served as chair of the South County chapter.

Since the 1960s the community has decreased in size, with many young African Americans (along with their white peers) having left for college or employment after high school and not returning. The 2000 census placed the African American population at 157, only 2.09 percent of the town population.

In the 1990s, appreciation of W. E. B. Du Bois became more public. Markers were placed at his birth site on Church Street and, as mentioned earlier, at the graves of his wife and son in Mahaiwe Cemetery. Simon's Rock College initiated an annual Du Bois lecture by a visiting scholar, and the Clinton Church in 2001 began an annual Du Bois program as well. In 2002 the Du Bois River Garden, a park adjoining

W. E. B. Du Bois River Park and Garden on the Housatonic River Walk in 2005. Photo by Rachel Fletcher.

Du Bois on the Housatonic

In the extract below, W. E. B. Du Bois paints a quaint portrait of his childhood surroundings—while eloquently taking industrial polluters to task. Today, his longing to see the Housatonic River restored is honored by the W. E. B. Du Bois River Garden, a park along the Housatonic River Walk (www.gbriverwalk.org/riverwkDuBoisGarden.html).

> I was born by a golden river and in the shadow of two great hills, five years after the Emancipation Proclamation. The house was quaint with clapboards running up and down, neatly trimmed, and there [were] five rooms, a tiny porch, a rosy front yard, and unbelievably delicious strawberries in the rear. . . . That river of my birth was golden because of the woolen and paper waste that soiled it. The gold was theirs, not ours; but the gleam and the glint was for all.

Source: Du Bois, W. E. B. *Darkwater: Voices from Within the Veil.* New York: Harcourt Brace, 1920, 3, 6.

the Housatonic River Walk, was constructed and a walking tour of fifty Du Bois sites published. A large mural honoring Du Bois was painted in the Taconic parking lot by members (Natalie Hill, Nathaniel Ivory, Fionn McCabe, Brett Parson, Theo Pulfer-Terino, and Rebecca Weinman) of the Railroad Street Youth Project in 2003.

Finally, it should be noted that several leading African Americans have been Dowmel Lecturers at Monument Mountain High School in Great Barrington. These include the politician Jesse Jackson in 1998, educator Marion Wright Edelman in 2000, radio talk-show host and politician Alan Keyes in 2002, and former surgeon general Dr. David Satcher in 2003. In 2005 longtime resident (since 1931) Moses Haile was named Citizen of the Year by the Rotary Club. Also in that year, in May, the town voted by a substantial margin to have signs erected at each end of town noting Great

Jason and Almira Cooley House on East Street in 2005. Photo by Zachary Mino.

Gravestones of Nina Gomer and Burghardt Du Bois in Mahaiwe Cemetery, c. 1999. Photo by Erik Callahan.

Barrington as the birthplace of W. E. B. Du Bois and in June the selectboard authorized six signs to be put up. Signs were erected early in 2006. That year saw, as well, the opening of the Du Bois Center of American History on South Main Street and the formation of the Friends of the Du Bois Homesite.

David Levinson

See also Black Entrepreneurs; Warren Davis, Entrepreneur; May Edward Chinn, Physician; Underground Railroad; W. E. B. Du Bois, Scholar and Activist; James Weldon Johnson, Essayist and Activist; W. E. B. Du Bois Memorial Committee;

W. E. B. Du Bois Homesite Photo Essay; Ruth D. Jones, Preserver of the Legacy of W. E. B. Du Bois; David Graham Du Bois, Scholar and Activist; Teaching Black History and Culture; American Revolution; Civil War: The 54th Massachusetts Volunteer Infantry Regiment; Civil War: Other Massachusetts Units and Service; Religious Institutions; Women as Religious Leaders; Clinton A. M. E. Zion Church, Great Barrington; Guest Homes for African Ameri- cans; Entertainment and Social Life; African American Literary Societies; W. E. B. Du Bois, Native Son; Du Bois Williams, Professor and Sole Granddaughter of W. E. B. Du Bois; Elaine Gunn; Mae Brown

Gravestones in the Black burial plot at the south end of Mahaiwe Cemetery in 2005. Photo by Zachary Mino.

The National Historic Landmark sign at the W. E. B. Du Bois Homesite on Route 23 in 2003. Photo by Erik Callahan.

Great Barrington Sites

1. **John Nail Summer Home** is on Alford Road. John Nail was James Weldon Johnson's brother-in-law and a New York City real estate developer.

2. **James Weldon Johnson Summer Home** is on Alford and Seekonk roads (private residence). The shed he wrote in is no longer standing.

3. **Simon's Rock College Library,** 84 Alford Road, houses the Du Bois Collection of African American history and culture. The college also sponsors an annual Du Bois lecture.

4. **Rosseter Street/Elm Court** neighborhood has since the 1920s been home to many Black families, although the neighborhood has always been integrated. Warren Davis lived at number 11.

5. **Macedonia Baptist Church,** 9 Rosseter Street, founded in 1944, was the second Black religious institution in Great Barrington. The church moved into this building in 1954.

6. **Clinton African Methodist Episcopal Zion Church,** 9 Elm Court, was dedicated in 1887 and is the oldest Black institutional building in continual use in the county.

7. **Mason Library,** 231 Main Street, was used by James Weldon Johnson and houses a special local history collection.

8. **W. E. B. Du Bois Mural,** Taconic parking lot, off Railroad Street, was painted by the Railroad Street Youth Project in 2003.

9. **W. E. B. Du Bois Birth Site,** east end of Church Street, is identified by a historical marker.

10. **W. E. B. Du Bois River Park and Garden,** at the River Walk, east end of Church Street, was dedicated in 2002 and acknowledges Du Bois's lifelong love of the Housatonic River and Berkshire environment.

11. **Jason and Almira Cooley House,** East Street, is one of the first homes built in the late 1800s on the east side of the river (private residence). Cooley was one the first Black entrepreneurs, and the couple founded the Clinton A. M. E. Zion Church.

12. In front of **Town Hall on Main Street** was the courthouse where Elizabeth Freeman filed her "suit for liberty" in 1781.

13. **Mahaiwe Cemetery** is on South Main Street (Route 7), at the corner of Silver Street. The larger Black plot in the Mahaiwe Cemetery is located in the lower level of the north end of the cemetery. It is the open area to the right of the historic marker of the graves of W. E. B. Du Bois's son Burghardt (died 1899) and wife, Nina Gomer Du Bois (died 1950). A small, white cross with the name Burghardt now marks Burghardt's grave, although he was buried in an unmarked grave. Du Bois's daughter, Yolande, was buried here as well in 1961. Her grave is unmarked. The smaller plot, which contains a cluster of markers, is at the south end of the cemetery. The stones mark the graves of members of the Piper, Burghardt, Jackson, Suma, and Lewis families.

14. **The Du Bois Center of American History,** 684 South Main Street, houses a collection of books and manuscripts relevant to Du Bois and other prominent African Americans.

15. **W. E. B. Du Bois Boyhood Homesite National Landmark** is located on Route 23, 0.25 mile past the junction with Route 71 heading west from Great Barrington. The site is marked by a bronze marker but is not accessible to the public.

16. **Mary White Ovington Cottage,** is located on Route 71, Alford (private residence).

See map on page 196.

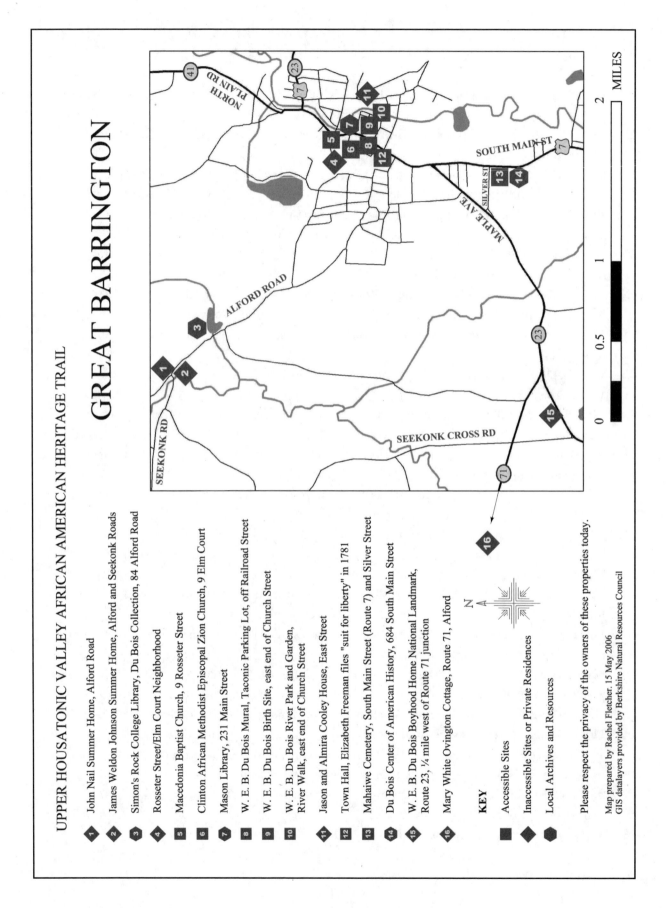

GREAT BARRINGTON

UPPER HOUSATONIC VALLEY AFRICAN AMERICAN HERITAGE TRAIL

1 John Nail Summer Home, Alford Road

2 James Weldon Johnson Summer Home, Alford and Seekonk Roads

3 Simon's Rock College Library, Du Bois Collection, 84 Alford Road

4 Rosseter Street/Elm Court Neighborhood

5 Macedonia Baptist Church, 9 Rosseter Street

6 Clinton African Methodist Episcopal Zion Church, 9 Elm Court

7 Mason Library, 231 Main Street

8 W. E. B. Du Bois Mural, Taconic Parking Lot, off Railroad Street

9 W. E. B. Du Bois Birth Site, east end of Church Street

10 W. E. B. Du Bois River Park and Garden,
River Walk, east end of Church Street

11 Jason and Almira Cooley House, East Street

12 Town Hall, Elizabeth Freeman files "suit for liberty" in 1781

13 Mahaiwe Cemetery, South Main Street (Route 7) and Silver Street

14 Du Bois Center of American History, 684 South Main Street

15 W. E. B. Du Bois Boyhood Home National Landmark,
Route 23, ¼ mile west of Route 71 junction

16 Mary White Ovington Cottage, Route 71, Alford

KEY

■ Accessible Sites

◆ Inaccessible Sites or Private Residences

⬡ Local Archives and Resources

Please respect the privacy of the owners of these properties today.

Map prepared by Rachel Fletcher. 15 May 2006
GIS datalayers provided by Berkshire Natural Resources Council

Sources

"Charges Negroes Are Ill-Housed Here." *Berkshire Courier*, 15 Feb. 1943.

Clinton African Methodist Episcopal Zion Church. Records, 1936–2006. Great Barrington, MA.

Doughton, Thomas L. "Men Listing Massachusetts Towns as Their Place of Residence, Who Enlisted in the 54th Regiment" (1999). http://www.geocities.com/afroyankees/Military/54mass2.html (accessed 14 Nov. 2004).

Drew, Bernard A. *Fifty Sites in Great Barrington, Massachusetts, Associated with the Civil Rights Activist W. E. B. Du Bois.* Great Barrington, MA: Great Barrington Historical Society, 2002.

Drew, Bernard A. *Great Barrington: Great Town/Great History.* Great Barrington, MA: Great Barrington Historical Society, 1999.

Drew, Bernard A. "Willoughby's Sunset Inn." *Berkshire Eagle*, 22 May 2004.

Du Bois, W. E. B. *The Autobiography of W. E. B. Du Bois.* New York: International Publishers, 1968.

Du Bois, W. E. B. "Early Writings: Columns from the New York Independent." Reprinted in *The Seventh Son: The Thought and Writings of W. E. B. Du Bois.* Vol. 1, 1883–1885. Ed. by Julius Lester, 154–69. New York: Vintage Books, 1971.

Du Bois, W. E. B. Personal communication to George P. Fitzpatrick, 13 June 1961.

Du Bois, W. E. B. "Speech of W. E. B. DuBois '84 at the Annual Meeting of the Alumni of Searles High School, July 21, 1930." *Berkshire Courier*, 31 July 1930. [Text of the speech available at http://www.gbriverwalk.org/riverwkDuBoisCourier.html.]

"Early Records of the Congregational Church." Typed manuscript. [Available at the Mason Library, Great Barrington, MA.]

"1860 Census of Berkshire County." Unpublished manuscript.

First Resistance Chapter, National Society of the Daughters of the American Revolution. "Tombstone Inscriptions, Great Barrington, Massachusetts" (1935–1938). Typed manuscript. [Available at the Mason Library, Great Barrington, MA.]

Great Barrington Land Conservancy. "W. E. B. Du Bois River Garden." http://www.gbriverwalk.org/riverwkDuBoisGarden.html (accessed 15 Nov. 2004).

Gunn, Wray. Personal communication with the author, 2004.

"Heads of Families at the First Census of the United States, Taken in the Year 1790." (See Massachusetts.) Washington, DC: Department of Commerce and Labor, Bureau of the Census, 1906.

Hoog, Cynthia T. "Cemetery Inscriptions in Great Barrington, Massachusetts." Unpublished report, 1987. [Available at the Mason Library, Great Barrington, MA.]

Hoog, Cynthia T. "Death Notices from the Berkshire Courier, 1834 through 1890." Unpublished report. [Available at the Mason Library, Great Barrington, MA.]

Levinson, David. *Sewing Circles, Dime Suppers, and W. E. B. Du Bois: A History of the Clinton African Episcopal Zion Church.* Great Barrington, MA: Berkshire Publishing Group, 2006.

Muller, Nancy L. "W. E. B. Du Bois and the House of the Black Burghardts: Land, Family, and African Americans in New England." Diss., University of Massachusetts, Amherst, 2001.

New England Historical and Genealogical Society. "Vital Records of Great Barrington, Massachusetts, to the Year 1850." Boston, MA: New England Historical and Genealogical Society, 1904. http://www.rootsweb.com/~maberksh/towns/greatbarr/grt_barr_birth.html (accessed 15 Nov. 2004).

"Records of Deaths, Kept by Rev. Sylvester Burt, of the Congregational Church." Typed manuscript. [Available at the Mason Library, Great Barrington, MA.]

Taylor, C. A. *History of Great Barrington: Part I, 1676–1882,* Great Barrington, MA: Town of Great Barrington, 1928. [First published 1882.]

Honoring W. E. B. Du Bois in His Hometown Photo Essay

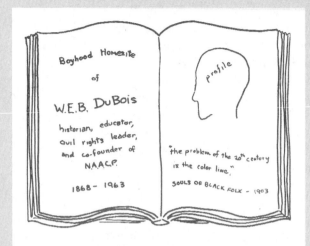

Sketch of plaque, which was to be placed on a boulder at the Du Bois Memorial Park dedication in 1969. Courtesy of Ruth D. Jones Collection, W. E. B. Du Bois Memorial Committee.

The National Historic Landmark sign dated 1979, at the W. E. B. Du Bois Boyhood Homesite on Route 23 in Great Barrington in 2003. Photo by Rachel Fletcher.

An historic marker placed by the Great Barrington Historical Society in 1994 noting the graves of Nina Gomer and Burghardt Du Bois in Mahaiwe Cemetery, Great Barrington, in 2005. Photo by Zachary Mino.

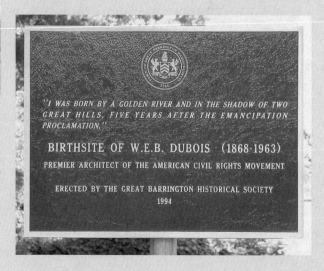

An historic marker placed by the Great Barrington Historical Society in 1994 at the W. E. B. Du Bois birth site on Church Street in Great Barrington in 2004. Photo by Rachel Fletcher.

The dedication stone placed in 2002 marking the W. E. B. Du Bois River Garden park on the Housatonic River Walk in Great Barrington in 2005. Photo by Rachel Fletcher.

A portion of the W. E. B. Du Bois Mural painted by Railroad Street Youth in 2003 in the Taconic parking lot in Great Barrington in 2005. Photo by Zachary Mino.

One of the W. E. B. Du Bois road signs placed by the Town of Great Barrington in 2006, looking south, entering Great Barrington from Egremont on Route 71. Photo by Rachel Fletcher.

Sheffield

The Ashley House in 2005. Photo by Rachel Fletcher.

Sheffield was gradually settled, beginning in the 1730s, largely by English coming from Westfield and by Dutch from Livingston Manor in New York state. While the Dutch held slaves in other Berkshire towns, it was largely the English in Sheffield who kept Black people in servitude. When the first Blacks came to the town is undocumented.

The Massachusetts Tax Valuation List of 1771 carries the names of a dozen Sheffield families with at least one "servant for life" in the household. The John Ashleys, father and son, colonel and general, had eight slaves between them, three of whom resorted to legal challenge in 1781 to obtain their freedom. Zack Mullen sued Colonel Ashley in the spring of 1781, alleging mistreatment the previous winter. His court case was delayed as Mum Bett and Brom—former slaves of the Ashleys, the latter probably from General Ashley's household—brought forward their case, seeking acknowledgment of their freedom under the recently written Massachusetts constitution. Or at least that was Bett's version, while the only document in the case asserted a claim under property rights. We are not privy as to what Bett's skilled lawyer, Theodore Sedgwick, argued that day, but the two Blacks won their cases. Ashley eventually abandoned his appeal and settled with Mullen out of court.

With Bett and Brom's court victory, it was a gradual route to emancipation. Sudden freedom left most former slaves economically helpless, thus few were ready to embark on their own. The only resident of African descent to own land prior to 1800 in Sheffield, according to deed records, was Jupiter Rogers, who purchased 5.5 acres on the county highway for $11 in 1797. Harmon Cooley in 1834 owned 160 acres valued at $2,109. He raised hops and had a hops press and kiln, as well as seven head of cattle and twenty-seven sheep.

But ownership records do not tell the full story. Blacks in large numbers flowed through Ashley Falls and Sheffield in the decades before the Civil War. Initially these were runaways from New York state, which did not abolish slavery until 1827, forty-six years after Massachusetts abolished it. Only a few of the newcomers could afford to purchase land; most rented or squatted. Names come and go in the Ashley account books (the family operated a small store in addition to grist- and sawmills in Ashley Falls), suggesting a temporary residency. None paid in cash; it was a barter economy. Many gravitated to a section called New Guinea, on Berkshire School Road, a likely conduit for the Underground Railroad in the years leading up to the Civil War. While the neighborhood was known for its isolation and the belligerence of some inhabitants, it was also home to Union Army veteran Edward Augustus Croslear, perhaps the most successful Black farmer in town in his generation. Through the establishment of a small church and district school, the community attempted to overcome the poverty and illiteracy of the neighborhood.

The New Guinea section is at and around the junction of Berkshire School Road and Bear's Den Road. The area was evidently first settled by Blacks around 1800 and remained a Black section of town until the early 1900s. The name New Guinea was an insulting one given to the area by white residents of town. Not all of the town's Black population lived in the area, and most of those who did were evidently poorer and less well educated than those who lived elsewhere. In 1885 a chapel was built on Bear's Den Road on land given by G. H. Andrus and used on and off until it burned down, around 1915. An article in *The Berkshire Courier* in 1904 described the chapel as follows: "They have a little Methodist chapel of their own and all attend services. No shanty is so humble but it has a picture of Abraham Lincoln and some scriptural quotations on the wall."

In 1903 the town sought to segregate area Black children in their own school on Sheffield Plain, an effort that failed when the residents objected and the school burned one night. While educators couched their efforts in noble terms, as of this writing there were still Black residents in Sheffield in 2006 who saw it as simple Jim Crowism. The town's school board opened a new school in New Guinea and staffed it for a dozen years before the student population there became so diminished it grew impractical to keep open. Later the school building, near the west entrance to the Mount Everett Regional School campus, was made a private residence.

Milo Freeland was the first Black to answer the Civil War call to arms after Lincoln's Emancipation Proclamation of January 1863. He joined the famed all-Black 54th Massachusetts Regiment, as did David Addison, Edward Croslear, John C. Harris, George Jarvis, William Jones, Nathaniel H. Johnson, Norman Johnson, Edward Moore, Henry J. Tucker,

Historic marker on the green in Ashley Falls recognizing Mum Bett in 2005. Photo by Rachel Fletcher.

and Ira Waterman. Blacks from Sheffield served in later conflicts as well.

The African American population largely lived and worked on the land, tending their own small farms but often working on neighboring white farms for adequate income. Warren H. Davis of Great Barrington, an indefatigable "landjobber" from the 1910s until his death, in 1960, was active in Sheffield. He acquired rights from Berkshire School headmaster Seaver B. Buck in 1913 to set up a portable sawmill on campus to cut up chestnut trees killed by the blight. Davis was sufficiently successful at acquiring timber rights in the Beartown section of Great Barrington that in 1928 he purchased a former Berkshire Street Railway car barn in Sheffield and established a sawmill, which he operated for more than a decade.

Sheffield's Black population has remained relatively stable. Back in 1790 there were thirty-seven Blacks; in the 2000 census there were thirty-five. But the figures overlook a large nineteenth-century peak. In the early 2000s many of the Black families in town have ties to early generations: Gladys Grady said it was traditional understanding in her family that there was a link with Elizabeth "Mum Bett" Freeman, and Minnie Golden's family reckoned way back. Wray

Gunn, president of the Sheffield Historical Society and chairman of the Planning Board, was descended from Mary Gunn, the adopted daughter of Agrippa Hull, who settled in Stockbridge before the Revolution. Wray Gunn was also active in Great Barrington in the 1970s and 1980s as head of the Clinton African Methodist Episcopal Zion Church Trustee Board, the Lions Club, and Construct, Inc. Characteristics of the Black community have also changed. Wray Gunn is a chemist. John James of Ashley Falls is an architect specializing in historic restorations; he served as the town's first Black selectman from 1991 to 1994. Dennis Watlington is an award-winning filmmaker and author. William Greaves, who lived in Sheffield in the 1980s, also is an award-winning filmmaker.

Bernard A. Drew

See also Slavery in the Berkshires; Mum Bett (Elizabeth Freeman), Anti-Slavery Pioneer; Underground Railroad; Struggles and Achievements; American Revolution; Civil War: The 54th Massachusetts Volunteer Infantry Regiment; Edward Augustus Croslear, Civil War Veteran and Farmer; Civil War: Other Massachusetts Units and Service; Religious Institutions

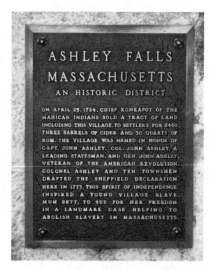

Plaque on the Ashley Falls historic marker recognizing Mum Bett. It reads: "This sprit of independence inspired a a young village slave, Mum Bett, to sue for her freedom in a landmark case helping to abolish slavery in Massachusetts." Photo by Rachel Fletcher.

Sheffield Sites

1. **Sheffield Historical Society,** 159–161 Main Street, has a large collection on town history and material on local African American history.
2. **New Guinea neighborhood, Berkshire School and Bear's Den Roads** are sites of private residences.
3. **Ashley House,** 117 Cooper Hill Road, is maintained by The Trustees of Reservations and is open for tours seasonally. It is dedicated to the study of Elizabeth Freeman and South County African Americans.
4. **Historic District marker, Ashley Falls,** is located on the green in front of the post office. The last third of text on the marker reads, "This spirit of independence inspired a young village slave, Mum Bett, to sue for her freedom in a landmark case helping to abolish slavery in Massachusetts."

See map on page 203.

Sources

"Degenerate New Guinea." *Berkshire Courier*, 17 Dec. 1903.

Drew, Bernard A. *If They Close the Door on You, Go in the Window: Origins of the African American Community in Sheffield, Great Barrington & Stockbridge.* Great Barrington: Attic Revivals Press, 2004.

Miller, James R. *Early Life in Sheffield, Berkshire County, Massachusetts.* Sheffield, MA: Sheffield Historical Society, 2002.

Preiss, Lillian. *Sheffield, Frontier Town.* Sheffield, MA: Sheffield Bicentennial Committee, 1974.

"Sheffield School Trouble." *Berkshire Courier*, 10 Dec. 1903.

UPPER HOUSATONIC VALLEY AFRICAN AMERICAN HERITAGE TRAIL

SHEFFIELD

1 Sheffield Historical Society, 159-161 Main Street

2 New Guinea neighborhood, Berkshire School and Bear's Den Roads

3 Ashley House, 117 Cooper Hill Road

4 Historic District Marker, the Green, Ashley Falls

KEY

⬡ Accessible Sites

◆ Inaccessible Sites or Private Residences

■ Local Archives and Resources

N

Please respect the privacy of the owners of these properties today.

Map prepared by Rachel Fletcher, 15 May 2006
GIS datalayers provided by Berkshire Natural Resources Council

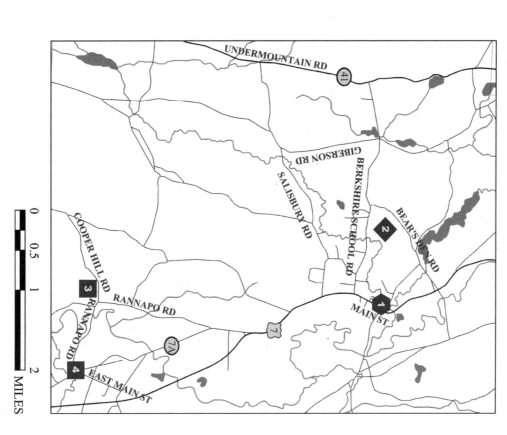

Mum Bett and Ashley House Photo Essay

Portrait of "Mumbet," watercolor on ivory by Susan Anne Livingston Ridley Sedgwick, 1811. Copyright Massachusetts Historical Society, Boston, MA.

Ashley House in Ashley Falls, in 2005. Photo by Jay Gouline.

Ashley House in Ashley Falls, in 2004. Photo by Anne Munn.

The Col. John Ashley House, in its original location on the west bank of the Housatonic River, c. 1929. The house was just one part of an extensive farm, with many outbuildings. The Ashley family owned thousands of acres of farmland and woodlots in Sheffield. The land was worked by both white tenant farmers and enslaved African Americans until slavery was ended in the early 1780s. Photo courtesy of The Trustees of Reservations Collection.

The front façade of the Ashley House, when it faced Rannapo Road. This photograph was taken 1929 or 1930, shortly before the house was moved to its current location, ¼ mile west on Cooper Hill Road. The house was built in 1735, the doorway visible in this photograph was added 1770–1810. Photo courtesy of The Trustees of Reservations Collection.

Tearing down the ell, south side, c. 1930. The original rear ell of the Ashley House was added sometime after 1810. It replaced the original c. 1735 lean-to that probably housed the several enslaved African Americans, including Mum Bett. Photo courtesy of The Trustees of Reservations Collection.

CONNECTICUT

Northwest Connecticut

The lives of people of African ancestry in northwest Connecticut differed from that of people just to the north in Berkshire County in two important ways. First, some remained slaves for a longer period of time, as slavery ended later in Connecticut than in Massachusetts. Laws against slavery first appeared in Connecticut in 1784, and slavery then slowly disappeared and was finally abolished fully in 1848. Massachusetts ended slavery much earlier, in 1781, through judicial interpretation of the state constitution. (Summaries of these two state histories of slavery open the chapter on civil rights in this volume.) Second, work opportunities were different, with the colonial and even postcolonial economy of northwest Connecticut being different from that of the Berkshires. In northwest Connecticut the economy rested heavily on the iron industry. Northern Litchfield County and nearby towns in Dutchess and Columbia counties in New York and southern Berkshire County had been the heart of the colonial iron industry. The iron industry prospered there because the region had the four key requirements for colonial-era iron production—iron ore, limestone, wood to burn into charcoal, and water power. Blacks as well as whites were employed in the iron industry, with Blacks especially working as producers of charcoal from wood for heating the forges and as laborers.

The six town surveys that follow—Salisbury, Norfolk, Sharon, Cornwall, Kent, and Warren—focus on Black history from the colonial era through the Civil War. This represents the first attempt to systematically document the early Black residents of the region.

Following the Civil War the Black population of northwest Connecticut declined, as did the white population in several towns. Several developments explain the decline. One was the Civil War, which resulted in more than half the Black men who had served from the region either being killed or wounded. And others chose not to return. A second development was the decline of the iron industry in the region in the nineteenth century as new technology and the use of anthracite coal in place of charcoal moved the industry farther south. The last iron operation in the region—Beckley Furnace in East Canaan—closed in 1923. A third development was the decline of small farms that lacked enough acreage to grow crops like corn to sustain themselves as dairy farms, the primary form of farming in the region. In addition, consolidation of the industry meant that farmers needed the capital, which they rarely could amass, to pay for transportation of milk to bulk dairies like Borden's in Amenia/Wassaic, New York. For African Americans there was little reason to stay and more opportunity in cities such as Hartford and New Haven. The 2000 federal census shows the total African American population in the seven towns of Warren, Kent, Sharon, Salisbury, Canaan, Norfolk, and Cornwall as only 143, less than 1 percent of the total population.

David Levinson and Jonathan Olly

See also Slavery in Northwest Connecticut; James Mars, Community Leader and Activist; Underground Railroad; Eugene Brooks, Educator; American Revolution; Milo J. Freeland, First to Fulfill His Term with the 54th Massachusetts Regiment; Civil

War: The Connecticut 29th and 31st Volunteer Infantry Regiments; Freeborn Garretson and "Black Harry" Hosier in Northwest Connecticut; Lemuel Haynes, Pioneer Minister.

Sources

Felton, Harold W. *Canaan, a Small New England Town during the American Revolutionary War*. Falls Village, CT: The Bramble Co., 1990.

Greene, Lorenzo Johnston. *The Negro in Colonial New England*. New York: Atheneum, 1942.

Kirby, Ed. *Echoes of Iron in Connecticut's Northwest Corner*. Sharon, CT: Sharon Historical Society, 1998.

Mars, James. *Life of James Mars, a Slave Born and Sold in Connecticut*. 6th ed. Hartford, CT: Case, Lockwood & Co., 1868.

History of Litchfield County, Connecticut, with Illustrations and Biographical Sketches of Its Prominent Men and Pioneers. Philadelphia: J. W. Lewis & Co., 1881.

Salisbury

After Sharon, Salisbury had the largest Black population in Connecticut's upper Housatonic Valley. In 1774 there were 1,936 white settlers and 44 people of color. The 1790 census unfortunately does not give totals for all towns in Litchfield County. Searching by person, however, one well-known resident stands out: Joshua Porter, head of a household of twelve that included four slaves. During the American Revolution he was a colonel in the militia and was put in charge of the Salisbury Furnace, casting cannons for the Continental Army. He was also a medical doctor, town selectman, justice of the peace, and county judge. Frequently away on business, he doubtlessly had the slaves help run his household and farm.

The size of Salisbury's eighteenth-century slave population is unknown, but the town had the largest number of runaway slaves advertised in the *Connecticut Courant* of any town in the region—more likely indicating a larger slave population than a harsher form of slavery. Four runaway advertisements appear between 1767 and 1798:

Run away from the Subscriber of Salisbury, on the Night of the 13th Instant, a Negro Man named Thomas, about 24 Years of Age, he had on a double breasted Bearskin Jacket of a mix'd Colour, over the other, with Matthew Man Buttons; said Negro is about Five Foot Eight Inches high. Whoever takes up said Negro, and secures him, or returns his [sic] to the Subscriber, shall have Two Dollars Reward, and all reasonable Charges paid by

JONATHAN MOOR, junr.

N. B. All Masters of Vessels are forbid carrying off said Negro, or concealing of him upon the Peril of the Law.

Salisbury, April 15th, 1767.

A runaway slave ad for "a Negro or Mulatto Girl, named Hannah" from the *Connecticut Courant and Weekly Intelligencer* of 17 August 1784. Courtesy of American Antiquarian Society.

A runaway child ad for "a Negro Boy named Mark" from the *Connecticut Courant and Weekly Intelligencer* of 13 July 1795. Courtesy of American Antiquarian Society.

Run away from the subscriber, a Negro or Mulatto Girl, named Hannah, but assumes the name of Hannah Watson, had on a calico bonnet, and other thin cloths, midling size, with long black hair, was the property of Thomas Philips of Salisbury; from whom she pretends emancipation in writing, but it is an illegal one. It is supposed she intends to reside in Farmington, or to press on to Rhode-Island where said Philips bought her. Whoever will secure said Girl, so that the subscriber can get her, shall be entitled to Three Dollars reward and reasonable charges, paid on notice where she is secured.

ADONIJAH STRONG
Salisbury, August 12, 1784.

Run away from his father last Sunday evening, a Negro Boy named Mark, 19 years old, slim built; had on a grayish coat, jacket and trowsers, goes a little lame. All persons are forbid harboring, employing, or carrying off said boy on penalty of the law.

MARK COLEMAN
Salisbury, June 23 [1795].

TEN DOLLAR REWARD
Run away from the subscriber on the night of the 24th of April last, a mulatto boy, named JACK, about 17 years old, calls himself John Andre; he was born a slave and lived with the subscriber from an infant, & has been treated with kindness and attention—is a good reader and writes a good hand, and has been promised his freedom when of age—has been brought up to the farming business; said boy may be known by a large scar on one of his arms about his elbow by being scalded when a child; took with him one suit of homemade cloaths, mixed with black and white, and a great coat of the same kind, and also stole and carried with him a new coat and overalls London smoke with yellow metal buttons, and a broadcloth coat lead colour and a number of other articles of cloathing. Whoever will apprehend said boy and return him to his master, or give information so that he may be recovered, shall receive Ten Dollars reward and reasonable expenses paid.

SAMUEL LEE
Salisbury, May 8 [1798].

The ads reveal details of their otherwise unknown lives. Hannah, or Hannah Watson as her master identified her alias, took an unusual route to possible freedom in August of 1784. Subscriber

208

Adonijah Strong thought she might be heading to Farmington or Rhode Island, where she was purchased. Rhode Island figured prominently in the slave trade, with Newport as its center. There men arrived from all over New England to purchase slaves imported from Africa and the Caribbean. With her forged emancipation letter from Thomas Philips in hand, Hannah may have been searching for separated family or friends. Her well-dressed appearance of "a calico bonnet, and other thin cloths . . . with long black hair" hints at her possible job as a domestic servant in Philips's home.

Not all runaways were slaves. Just as today, children often left home for reasons varying from adventure to escaping hardship. Such was the case of Mark, a nineteen-year-old Black man who fled Salisbury in June of 1795. His father, Mark Coleman, took out the ad a week after he left, using a line ironically also found in runaway slave ads: "All persons are forbid harboring, employing, or carrying off said boy on penalty of the law." Though not appearing in the 1790 census, Mark is listed in the 1800 census as the head of a household of five "all other free persons" in Salisbury.

Despite the years of "kindness and attention," seventeen-year-old Jack or John Andre was unwilling to wait another eight years until his promised manumission. Besides the large wardrobe he took with him, he left with something more valuable than just Samuel Lee's new clothes: an education. Many literate slaves put their knowledge to work right away during their escape, forging letters of manumission. As with all of the runaway slaves it is unknown if he successfully escaped.

Entering the nineteenth century Salisbury had twenty-seven "all other free persons" and three slaves. Federal census reports show the free population, predominantly if not exclusively African American, increased over the decades, from 48 in 1810 to 77 in 1830 and 106 by 1860. The slave population dropped to one in 1830. His identity is unknown except for his age of between fifty-five and ninety-nine years. He belonged to John Russell, a sixty-eight-year-old farmer and war veteran.

Of the fifty-two Black men in Salisbury in 1860, eleven enlisted in December and January of 1863–1864 into the 29th Connecticut Volunteer Infantry. A twelfth man instead joined the 31st Connecticut Volunteer Infantry in April of 1864. Half would be killed or injured by war's end.

A short time earlier, a Black man named Henry Hector joined the U.S. Navy in May of 1862. Born in Salisbury, he was living in New York at the time of his enlistment. For three years he worked as a waiter aboard the ships *Huntsville* and *San Jacinto* before being discharged in 1865. New York City, especially after it outlawed slavery in 1827, became one of the largest free Black communities in the nation, attracting many rural Blacks in search of jobs, equality, and social opportunity.

Jonathan Olly

Sources

Church, Samuel. *A Historical Address Delivered at the Commemoration of the One Hundredth Anniversary of the First Annual Town Meeting of the Town of Salisbury, October 20, A.D. 1841.* New Haven, CT: Hitchcock & Stafford, 1842.
Connecticut Courant and the Weekly Advertiser. 20 April 1767, 3; 17 Aug. 1784, 3; 29 June 1795, 3; 14 May 1798, 3.

Norfolk (Canaan)

The early Black history in Norfolk before the American Revolution is largely unknown, but later events still present a rich heritage. Much of what is known derives from the region's most famous African American, James Mars. His story is similar to the lives of many Blacks in the region at the time but unusual in that he wrote down and published that history in his autobiography in 1864. Born a slave in 1790 in Canaan, he, along with his family, fled to Norfolk when their owner, Amos Thompson, decided to return to the South. For several weeks, residents of Norfolk hid the family in houses and barns, until the slave owner relented, and agreed to a deal. In exchange for his parents' and sister's freedom, Mars and his brother were sold as indentured laborers to two local men in 1798. Older brother John went to Banajah Bingham of Salisbury, and James was bound to William Munger of Norfolk.

Unlike their children, Jupiter and Fanny Mars (James's parents) were exempt from the gradual abolition law, so the deal was their only legal chance for freedom, except for fleeing to another town or state. Consequently, James Mars worked for Munger, until he was nearly twenty-five, having to pay Munger $90 to be freed before that age. But James maintained a cordial relationship with the family after his indenture and was present at the deathbed of William and, later, of William's daughter. Mars is discussed elsewhere in this volume, but it is important to note that even in 1864, New England slavery was not universally known or acknowledged.

Less than twenty years after final emancipation of Connecticut's slaves, Mars had to remind people of an institution that had existed in their native land for two centuries. As in the contemporary Fitz-Greene Halleck poem "Connecticut," the public had largely forgotten part of its own history.

Gravestone of Milo Freeland in North Canaan in 2005. Photo by Zachary Mino.

210

Gravestone of James Mars in Center Cemetery, Norfolk, Connecticut, in 2005. His grave is part of Connecticut's Freedom Trail. Photo by Christopher Callahan.

Part of that history survives in Mars's book. His father, Jupiter, was born a slave in New York and later "was General Van Rensaeller's slave in the time of the Revolution, and was a soldier in that war." Eventually the Rev. Amos Thompson purchased Jupiter, who soon married one of Thompson's other slaves, Fanny.

Discounting the case of James Mars, who was a slave in all but name only, the practice was gone by 1800 in Norfolk, when the census records a free Black population of twenty-eight. In the next sixty years the population remained small at seventy-two. In the interim Mars started a family in Norfolk and became a deacon in the Congregational Church before eventually moving to Hartford and then Massachusetts. Eventually he returned to Norfolk, where he died in 1880; his grave is in the Center Cemetery. Years before, his brother John had become a minister, and according to the writings of one resident, Mary Oakley Beach, "My father said that Rev. John Mars . . . made the best prayer he ever heard. He preached in this church in April, 1872, at Dr. Eldridge's request, giving two most excellent sermons" (Crissey 1900, 370).

The Rev. Joseph Eldridge was also a town historian. At some point he asked James Mars to write up some recollections of the town. Eldridge then used the information to write an early history of the community, which was posthumously published in part in Theron Wilmot Crissey's history of Norfolk (1900).

While the Black community in Norfolk remained small, the town started showing antislavery sentiments in the 1840s. Individuals voted for abolitionist candidates in the 1840 and 1844 presidential elections. The latter year also saw the founding of the Norfolk Anti-Slavery Society, an auxiliary to the Connecticut Anti-Slavery Society, founded in 1790. Congregational Church records of the 1840s and 1850s record numerous attempts to protest slavery, though many were unsuccessful. A vote in 1850 to condemn slavery and censure church members who supported it was defeated twenty-five to six. One of the six yes votes belonged to Deacon Amos Pettibone. Strongly abolitionist, he did not wait for public opinion to match his own. His house became a stop on the Underground Railroad, one of supposedly many stations in town.

On Sunday, 17 February 1861, the town's respected Congregational minister, Joseph Eldridge, delivered a sermon demonstrating that the Bible did not condone slavery. By this point his congregation was largely in agreement. A year before, in 1860, a Black man named John M. Pierce, born in Norfolk but living in Philadelphia, joined the U.S.

Navy; he served as a steward until 1863. That winter, in November and December, five more Blacks from Norfolk joined the military, in their case the 29th Connecticut Volunteer Infantry. Two additional Norfolk Blacks had joined the 54th Massachusetts that spring. One man from each regiment, Ensign Prince of the 29th, and Edward Hines of the 54th, died during the war, the latter missing after the famous assault on Fort Wagner on 18 July 1863. He was never found. In remembrance of their sacrifice and the thirty-three other soldiers from Norfolk who died during the war, the town erected a granite monument on the town green, listing the names of the fallen.

Jonathan Olly

Norfolk Sites (including Canaan)

1. In East Canaan (about 6 miles west of Norfolk) **Milo Freeland's grave** is in Hillside Cemetery on Route 44. It is in Lot B8 to the rear of the cemetery, immediately to the right of the center driveway.
2. In North Canaan, **Mountain View Cemetery** has a special section for Blacks with unmarked graves.
3. **Center Cemetery**, on Old Colony Road off of Litchfield Road, Route 272, is a stop on the Connecticut Freedom Trail. The grave of James Mars is at the rear of the cemetery and is identified with an informative marker. Nearby are the graves of his father, Jupiter Mars, and those of other eighteenth- and nineteenth-century Blacks. Follow Freedom Trail markers once in the cemetery gate.
4. **Village Green.** A granite monument in the center of the green lists the names of thirty-five Civil War soldiers killed during the war, including Black soldiers Ensign Prince and Edward Hines.
5. **The Congregational Church** built in 1813 is across the street from the green. It was the locale of Rev. Joseph Eldridge's 17 February 1861 sermon demonstrating that the Bible did not condone slavery.

See map page 222.

Sources

Crissey, Theron Wilmot, comp. *History of Norfolk, Litchfield County, Connecticut.* Everett, MA: Massachusetts Publishing Co., 1900.

Mars, James. *Life of James Mars, a Slave, Born and Sold in Connecticut.* Hartford, CT: Case, Lockwood & Co., 1868.

Sharon

Blacks were among the first to settle in Sharon, predominantly as slaves. Peter Pratt, Sharon's discredited first minister, mortgaged his slave Pegg to two men from Dutchess County, New York, on 25 May 1748 to settle debts. In Hartford's *Connecticut Courant* newspaper on 10 November 1766, one Simeon Smith of Sharon advertised a farm for sale, adding at the bottom, "A likely Negro Man, well skill'd in Farming, and the Pot-Ash Business, to be sold by said Smith." The anonymous man demonstrates that slaves were valuable skilled workers, in this case in the manufacture of soap, glass, and other products from wood ashes.

Treated as pieces of property to be bought and sold, many slaves escaped. Two examples from Sharon are known:

TWENTY DOLLARS REWARD.

Run away from the subscriber in October last, a Negro Wench named ZIL, about 15 years old, small of her age, pretends she is free, the last she has been heard of she was going to Lenox. Whoever will return her to her master shall receive the above reward; or if any person will send word or inform her master so that he can get her again, shall be well rewarded for their trouble.

    REUBEN HOPKINS.

    Sharon, January 25, 1779.

Reuben Hopkins waited four months before advertising the escape of Zil. Interestingly, Hopkins mentions that she is probably going to Lenox. She demonstrates that slaves as well as free Blacks moved over the porous borders separating the northeastern colonies. While her reasons for heading to Lenox are unknown, Massachusetts would outlaw slavery within a few years, starting a long tradition of flights northward to freedom. Also, Hopkins's reward of $20 was unusually large in comparison with the $5 rewards military companies offered for deserters at the time.

FIVE DOLLARS REWARD.

Ran away from the subscriber, living in Sharon, about the 20th of June last, a NEGRO MAN, named DARBY, about five feet six inches high, 25 years of age, speaks broken; had on when he went away, a tow cloth shirt and trowsers only; he formerly belonged to Canterbury, and is supposed to have gone that way; and as he had an inclination to enter into the service, it is likely he will attempt to enlist—Whoever will take up said Negro and secure him in any gaol in the United States, so that the owner may have him again, shall be entitled to the above reward, and necessary charges paid by

    LEMUEL BRUSH.

    Sharon (State of Connecticut) July 16, 1782.

TWENTY DOLLARS REWARD.
RUN away from the subscriber in October last, a Negro Wench named ZIL, about 15 years old, small of her age, pretends she is free, the last she has been heard of she was going to Lenox. Whoever will return her to her master shall receive the above reward; or if any person will send word or inform her master so that he can get her again, shall be well rewarded for their trouble.
REUBEN HOPKINS
Sharon, January 25, 1779.

A runaway slave ad for "a Negro Wench named ZIL" from the *Connecticut Courant and Weekly Intelligencer* of 9 March 1779. Courtesy of American Antiquarian Society.

Five Dollars Reward,
RAN AWAY from the subscriber, living in Sharon, about the 20th of June last, a NEGRO MAN, named DARBY, about five feet six inches high, 25 years of age, speaks broken; had on when he went away, a tow cloth shirt and trowsers only; he formerly belonged to Canterbury, and is supposed to have gone that way; and as he had an inclination to enter into the service, it is likely he will attempt to inlist.----Whoever will take up said Negro and secure him in any goal in the United States, so that the owner may have him again, shall be entitled to the above reward, if necessary charges paid, by
LEMUEL BRUSH.
Sharon (State of Connecticut) July 16, 1782.

A runaway slave ad for "a NEGRO MAN, named Darby" from the *Connecticut Courant and Weekly Intelligencer* of 30 July 1782. Courtesy of American Antiquarian Society.

Joining a military company would have provided a means of escape as well as financial or patriotic reward for Darby. Whether he eventually enlisted is unknown. The only identified Black Revolutionary War soldier from Sharon is a man known only as Negor, who served from 1777 to 1779.

A better-known veteran, who settled in Sharon after the war, was Robin Starr. Tradition records that he was brought as a slave from Guinea, on Africa's west coast, to Danbury, Connecticut, some time before the Revolution. When the war broke out, Robin was a slave in the household of Josiah Starr of Danbury. With Josiah's consent, Robin enlisted in the Continental Army in 1777, eventually fighting in seven battles from Lake Champlain to Yorktown, Virginia. By 1781 he had earned enough money to purchase his freedom and continued fighting as a free man until 1783. George Washington signed his discharge certificate. For his six years of service, Starr received the Badge of Merit. Around 1790 he and his wife Lilly moved to Sharon, settling near the village of Ellsworth in an area eventually known as Guinea. Their son Abel was born in 1791.

By the 1800 census, slavery had ended in Sharon, and a free Black population of 39 grew to 91 in 1820 and 135 by 1860. Town records of the 1850s and 1860s record many marriages and births of African American residents. At least 14 different white lawyers, town clerks, ministers, and justices of the peace performed marriages for Blacks in town, hinting at positive relations between the Black minority and white majority. The records often listed the occupations of each spouse and included laborer, housekeeper, farmer, soldier, stonecutter, sailor, and basket maker. There was also at least one family with one spouse listed as "white" and the other "colored," though it is impossible to clarify often-arbitrary definitions of race.

During the Civil War sixteen Black men from Sharon enlisted in the 29th, 31st, and 14th Connecticut Volunteer Infantry Regiments—the latter being an ostensibly all-white unit. The soldier in the 14th, William Bush, either may have been light-skinned enough to pass as white or simply no one cared about his skin color. Eleven of the sixteen men were killed or wounded, the highest toll for any town in the region. Two of the wounded men were Josiah and Lewis H. Starr, sons of Abel Starr and grandsons of Revolutionary War veteran Robin Starr.

In a sign of respect for the fallen soldiers of Sharon, Black and white, the town erected a soldiers' monument in 1885. Included on the north, west, and east faces are names of four of the seven Blacks who died: William H. Gaul, Charles

Treadway, Charles Reed, and Henry Bush. The stone memorial continues to perpetuate the "noble deeds and sacrifices" of Sharon's citizens. The graves of the Bush brothers are together with their parents in nearby Hillside Cemetery.

Jonathan Olly

The Soldier's Monument in Sharon in 2005. It lists the names of four Blacks killed in the Civil War— Henry Bush, Charles Reed, William Gaul, and Charles Treadway. Photo by Constance Brooks.

Sharon Sites

6. **Hillside Cemetery** on Cemetery Hill Road holds graves of the Bush brothers who served in the Civil War.

7. **The Soldiers' Monument** erected in 1885 lists four of seven Black casualties in the Civil War— William H. Gaul, Charles Treadway, Charles Reed, and Henry Bush. Located on the west side of Main Street, where it meets Cemetery Hill Road.

8. A boulder marks the site of the eighteenth-century **Congregational Church** that was the locale of the trial of "Black Harry" Hosier in June 1777. It is across the street from Hotchkiss Library, on the town green.

9. **Guinea** neighborhood, where the Starr and other families lived, no longer extant, was located in the southeast part of town marked by Guinea Road and Guinea Brook.

See map on page 222.

Sources

Connecticut Courant and Weekly Intelligence, 10 Nov. 1779, 1.

Connecticut Courant and Weekly Intelligencer, 2 March 1779, 2.

Connecticut Courant and Weekly Intelligencer, 16 July 1782, 1.

Goodenough, G. F. *A Gossip about a Country Parish of the Hills and Its People.* Amenia, NY: Times Press, 1900.

Sedgwick, Charles F. *General History of the Town of Sharon, Litchfield County, Conn.* Amenia, NY: Charles Walsh, 1898.

Town of Sharon Vital Records, 1739–1855/1867. http://www.rootsweb.com/~ctlitch2/towns/sharon/sharon.htm (accessed 5 April 2005).

Tucker, Adeline Jackson, and Alene Jackson Smith. *Live, Labor, Love: The History of a Northern Family, 1700–1900.* Westminster, MD: Heritage Books, 2005.

Van Alstyne, Lawrence. *Burying Grounds of Sharon, Connecticut, Amenia and North East New York: Being an abstract of Inscriptions from Thirty Places of Burial in the Above Named Towns.* Amenia, NY: Walsh, Griffen & Hoysradt, 1903.

White, David O. *Connecticut's Black Soldiers. 1775–1783.* Chester, CT: Pequot Press, 1973.

Cornwall

The first record of a Black person in Cornwall is possibly 1759 or 1767, when Cele Jackson "belonging to Dea.[con] Abbit" was baptized on either 8 July 1759 or 12 November 1767 (Starr 1926, 477). Joseph Essex had his "negro servant" Peter baptized on 6 June 1779. The first federal census of the town records four free Black households: one headed by Jack Freedom (four members), two Samuel Greens (four and five members), and a Jacob Green (six members). Additionally, twelve white households owned a total of nineteen slaves and employed eight individuals only identified as "all other free persons," meaning Native or African Americans. The Freedom family is identified in Starr's (1926) history of the town as having "lived on the Canaan and Washington Turnpike, below the old Corban place, and were quite respected."

Despite the kind treatment some received, slaves still desired freedom. The following ad appeared on page three of the *Connecticut Courant and Weekly Hartford Intelligencer* on Tuesday, 7 June 1774:

> Runaway from the Subscriber in Cornwall, in Litchfield County, a Negro Man named Prince, about 27 Years old, about five feet high, this Country born, he is thin faced, with a large Pimple or Wart on one Side of his Nose, speaks good English, is a good Fidler. Had on and took with him a coarse brown kersey Coat, with smooth yellow Buttons, one Pair Leather Breeches, one Pair brown ribb'd worsted Stockings, one ditto white Linen, ribb'd, has a small Foot, and wears yellow Metal Buckles in his Shoes: He is supposed to have a forged Pass with him. Whoever will take up said Negro, and return him to his Master, or secure him so that he may have him again, shall have five Dollars Reward, and all reasonable Charges paid by me,

STEPHEN ROYCE.
Cornwall, May 24, 1774.

The advertisement provides a glimpse at a slave's life: his dress, musical interest, and limited education. The possible forged pass hints at either Prince's literacy or a friendship with someone who could write.

Even within the bounds of slavery, families managed to survive. Peg, the only slave of the Rev. Joseph W. Gold in the 1790 census, was eventually freed by Gold's heirs, and married Cesar Afric from Litchfield on 29 November 1792. Heman Swift, a Litchfield County judge and retired Revolutionary War general, owned the family of James and Patience, which eventually included their two children, Edward or Ned, born 9 March 1789, and Peony, born 6 October 1791. Essex and Dinah, were Black servants of Samuel Barrett and had three children, Nancy, Amos, and Rachel, born in the 1780s. An unusual adoption took place on 27 January 1797, when John Sedgwick's wife took from his sister in Vermont a Black girl named Omia. "She is adopted as my child and entitled to the same freedom at the same age as my children are," he testified in a record filed with Cornwall's town clerk on 5 October 1801 (Gold 1904, 400).

By this point the town's population of "all other free persons" had increased to thirty, while the slave population had dropped to four. The group of thirty was not solely of African descent. In a description of the town written in 1801 by Elijah Allen (and published in 1985 as *Cornwall in 1801*), Allen records eleven "free Africans in this Town," along with one family of five Native Americans, and "one or two Squaws [who] live with the Negroes as their Wives." Intermarriage was not uncommon between African and Native Americans.

During the American Revolution four Blacks enlisted from Cornwall: (Samuel?) Heth (? –1776), Samuel Green (1776), Thomas Sackett (1778), and

Jack Freedom (1781). It is difficult to tell who served as a freeman or a slave. In his 1926 history listing Revolutionary War soldiers, Starr notes for Jack Freedom that "the town had 30 pounds for enlisting him." Whether Freedom or the town received this bounty is unclear from the brief detail. Freedom and Green are the only free Black families listed in the 1790 census of Cornwall, so possibly Samuel and Jack were already free or won their liberty through their military service. In the same town history, Heth is identified as a slave belonging to Patrick Hindman, and "Of three Heths probably this was Samuel, in Parson's 6th Continentals; sick at Stanford; disch. Nov. 1776. He and [Tom] Warrups gave Mr. Hindman trouble by their quarrels." Tom Warrups was a Native American who lived with Hindman as a servant or slave, along with Heth, on East Street in Cornwall.

Thomas Sackett's story is more complete. While a slave he enlisted into Stephen Hall's Company of the Connecticut 7th Regiment on 25 March 1778. His master, Joseph Wadsworth, freed him on 4 April, presumably in return for Sackett's enlistment. His freedom was short lived, since he died in the army on 1 November 1778. Apparently, in 1793 another resident of Cornwall, John Sedgwick, petitioned the state and won Sackett's unclaimed pay. His relationship to Sackett is unknown.

In the years following the American Revolution, the Black population remained small: seventeen in 1810, thirty-two in 1830, forty-six in 1850, and thirty-eight in 1860. Despite the small population on the eve of the Civil War, four of the only twenty-one Black men in Cornwall enlisted in the 29th Connecticut Volunteer Infantry Regiment in November and December of 1863. Two of the men, George H. Green and Peter Howard, died in service, while the other two, John Lepyon and John L. Watson, were both demoted from sergeant to private on 1 May 1865 in unknown but presumably related circumstances. George Green was probably a descendant of the Revolutionary War veteran Samuel Green. In his will George left $100 to the First Church Sunday School. The detail would be inconsequential except that in an earlier period in the church's history, it had disciplined a successful Black farmer named Prince for not sitting in the "negro pews" segregated in the gallery and main floor. Green's bequest to the church hints at improved relations within the church and in Cornwall.

Jonathan Olly

Cornwall Site

10. **Calhoun Cemetery** holds the remains of four Black Civil War veterans—John Lepyon and John L. Watson of Cornwall and Josiah Starr and David Hector of Sharon. The cemetery is located in the southwest part of Cornwall known as Calhoun Corners. It is located at the intersection of Routes 7 and 45, on the west (river side) of Route 7. See map on page 222.

Sources

Allen, Elijah. *Cornwall in 1801*. Cornwall, CT: Cornwall Historical Society, 1985.

Connecticut Courant and *Weekly Hartford Intelligencer*, 7 June 1774, 3.

Gold, Theodore Sedgwick, ed. *Historical Records of the Town of Cornwall, Litchfield County, Connecticut*. Hartford, CT: Case, Lockwood & Brainerd Co., 1904.

Starr, Edward C. *History of Cornwall, Connecticut: A Typical New England Town*. New Haven, CT: Tuttle, Morehouse & Taylor, 1926.

Kent

Little is known of Kent's early Black history. In the town's vital records the town selectmen bound Timothy Fuller, a ten-year-old Black boy, to Julius Caswell on 9 January 1786 for eleven years—until Fuller turned twenty-one. It was not legally slavery, since the 1790 census for Kent shows two servants but no slaves in Caswell's household. Five households owned a total of seven slaves, while six other families employed a total of seven servants, who were white, Black, or Indian, and bonded for usually a maximum of twenty-one years. A similar arrangement existed for James Mars in nearby Norfolk in 1798, when he became an indentured servant to William Munger, remaining so until reaching adulthood.

As with slaves, not all indentured servants accepted servitude. The following ad appeared in the *Connecticut Courant* for 23 September 1807:

> Ran away from the subscriber on the 29th of August last, a Negro BOY, named Elid, thirteen years old. Whoever will return said boy to his master at Kent, Ore-hill, shall be entitled to twelve and half cents reward and no charges.
>
> All persons are forbid harboring or trusting said boy on penalty of the law.
> PHILONUS BEARDSLEY

Because no census after 1790 lists slaves in Kent, presumably Elid was indentured to Beardsley. After waiting a month for his return, Beardsley's meager reward of "twelve and half cents" indicates his indifference to the boy's return.

One free Black family of four lived in town in 1790, that of Call Freeman. Thirteen years before, he was the only Black man from Kent to fight during the Revolution. He enlisted in September of 1777 and served through January of 1783.

In December 1863 another African American, Henry H. Fitch, also became the sole Black soldier from his town to go to war, enlisting with the 29th Connecticut Volunteer Infantry Regiment. By then the town's Black population comprised forty-five people, down from a high of seventy-seven in 1810. He survived the war but was demoted from corporal to private in unknown circumstances in July of 1864.

Jonathan Olly

Sources

Atwater, Francis. *History of Kent, Connecticut.* Meriden, CT: Journal Publishing Co., 1897.
Connecticut Courant. 23 Sept. 1807, 2.
"Vital Records from the Barbour Collection as Found at the State Library in Hartford" (1739–1832). Kent, CT. http://www.rootsweb.com/~ctlitch2/towns/kent/kent.htm (accessed 5 Apr., 2006).

Warren

The 1790 census for Warren lists five families owning a total of six slaves. In addition, there were two free, probably Black, households: those of Ceasor Beaumont, with four members; and Zadock Wicks, living by himself. Despite the small Black population, William James enlisted during the American Revolution on 19 May 1777. He served a three-year term, being discharged in May of 1780, and later claimed a pension.

Between 1777 and 1801 a town history records twenty-nine slaves born in the town, with seven remaining after 1800. This is probably an error, since census records show slavery extinct there by 1800 as well as six free Black residents; from then on, the free Black population remained small, peaking at twenty-four in 1840 and dropping to eight in 1860. Reflecting the ending of slavery in the town, John Brownson freed his two slaves, Joel and Jinney, in 1796: "Now from motives of Humanity, and at their Mutual Request, I do hereby emancipate my s^d

Slaves and hereby record them free from all Claims and Demands that I, my Heirs, Executors or Assigns, might ever have to them or either of them" (Curtiss 1956, 63).

In the early nineteenth century many of the townspeople were antislavery and several were involved in the Underground Railroad, including town minister Harley Goodwin in the 1830s and 1840s and church deacon Gustavus Rouse. During Goodwin's ministry, abolitionist speaker Abby Kelley addressed a crowd in the church, whom Goodwin had limited to women in an attempt to prevent a riot. Proslavery sentiment was still strong in the community, and in the region, in the 1830s and 1840s. Unfortunately, a mob, "augmented by demonstrators from nearby towns," turned the meeting into a shouting match between the two opposing sides (Curtiss 1956, 65–66).

Jonathan Olly

Warren Site

11. **The Old Cemetery** holds the grave of Ned, who died the child of slaves at the age of nine years on 13 April 1793. The stone is located in the far corner. The stone says:

In Memory of Ned
Who died April 13th 1793 AE 9 years
This stone is erected by his Master J. Talmadge
Pleasant and faithful in life
And in Death lamented

Located in the center of town on the right side of Cornwall Road (Route 45) heading north. See map on page 222.

Source

Curtiss, Lucy Sackett. *The Congregational Church, Warren, Connecticut, 1756–1956.* N.p.: Breewer-Borg, 1956.

Barkhamsted Lighthouse

Barkhamsted Lighthouse is the name given to a triracial (tri-racial) isolate community that existed in Barkhamsted from the mid-1700s to the early 1860s. *Triracial isolate* is the generic label used by social scientists for outcaste communities of whites, Native Americans, and Blacks that formed in colonial America. Some of these communities, such as the Lumbee in North Carolina and the Ramapo mountain people in New Jersey and New York have survived into the twenty-first century. The remains of the Barkhamsted community are located within People's State Forest on the west side of Ragged Mountain off of East River Road. Set forth most fully in Lewis Mill's 115-page poem, the legend of the Lighthouse has been part of Connecticut lore for 200 years.

The Lighthouse is located to the east of the upper Housatonic River valley but is included in this volume because it is significant in regional African American history, for several reasons. First, some of the early inhabitants of the Lighthouse and their descendants moved to other communities, including Canaan, Kent, and Sharon. Second, the Lighthouse is on the Connecticut Freedom Trail and is listed on the National Register of Historic Places. Third, because the site has been well studied, it gives us insight into the way of life in poor, rural New England communities in the eighteenth and the early nineteenth century. It is likely that the way of life at the Lighthouse was not dissimilar from the way of life of people of the New Guinea neighborhood in Sheffield when it was first settled around 1800.

The Lighthouse community was founded by a white woman, Molly Barber (died 1818), and a Narragansett Indian man, James Chaugham (died c. 1790), sometime between 1740 and 1770. Barber came from a wealthy family in Wethersfield, Connecticut, and Chaugham was from Block Island, Rhode Island. He had moved to Wethersfield to work as a laborer, and according to the legend,

A small, unmarked gravestone in the community cemetery. The American flag indicates that the person buried there is a veteran. Photo by Patricia Andreucci.

Barber married him to spite her father, and the couple then fled north to escape her father's wrath. The two had eight children, several of whom stayed in the settlement and took spouses who moved there. One of these was daughter Mercy (died 1842), who married a Black man, Isaac Jacklin (died 1835), in West Hartland Second Congregational Church on 22 January 1785. According to the story, Molly and James objected to their daughter marrying a Black man. It is not clear whether Isaac Jacklin was a free man or a runaway; he had been a servant of George Wyllys Jr., secretary of state of Connecticut in the mid-eighteenth century. In 1784 Jacklin had purchased 49 acres of land in the settlement from Samuel Chaugham, a son of Molly and James. Jacklin's arrival turned the community from one that was biracial (Indian and white) to one that was now triracial (Indian, white, and Black). Moreover, race was evidently an issue, since in 1788 Jacklin was arrested for assault, which had been his reaction to being called a "mulatto man." By the end of century Isaac and Mercy had sold off their land and moved to Winsted, where they lived until their death. Several of their children (who were of Black, white and Indian ancestry) moved to other towns, including Sharon, Canaan, Litchfield, Winchester, and New Milford, in the first three decades of the nineteenth century. A daughter, Betsey Jacklin, may have moved to Great Barrington. The town records show her as intending to marry an Isaac Miller on 18 October 1803. Both are listed as mulattoes.

Archaeologist Kenneth Feder, who studied the settlement, suggests that the Lighthouse community went through three phases of occupation. The first phase lasted from the settlement's founding by Barber and Chaugham until 1789. During this period the community was largely isolated from white society. Descriptions of the settlement in its early years suggest that the houses were crude log cabins covered by bark, that the residents used stone tools, and that the families subsisted by growing vegetables and hunting. None of the residents could read or write, and they saw themselves as Indian (Narragansett) rather than as white. In 1789 the Farmington River Turnpike, which passed by the village, opened to stagecoach traffic, and phase two, which lasted until about 1815, began. Turnpike traffic put the residents in more frequent contact with whites, and so many residents moved into neighboring communities. This period also gave the village its name, because according to legend, stage riders would point to the light from the cabins on this desolate stretch of road and refer to it as the Lighthouse. The third period began about 1815 and ended when the village was abandoned in the early 1860s. During this phase the town of Riverton, a mile to the north, grew rapidly as a small industrial center and the Lighthouse people were now in regular contact with white society. Children went to public schools, land was sold to whites, and the community quickly assimilated into white society.

Archaeological study shows that the settlement covered 70 acres and contained ten houses built on crude stone foundations or over a cellar hole, a quarry, small gardens, a stone mortar, and a cemetery with about fifty graves, some marked with blank stones. The absence of stonewalls separating house sites and the central stone mortar suggest that while the land was owned by individuals, the way of life was communal. The remains of most of these elements are still visible.

David Levinson

Barkhamsted Lighthouse Site

The Jessie Gerard Trail (yellow) in People's State Forest runs through the remains of the Lighthouse settlement. The trail starts at East River Road, and the right trail fork goes through the site. Cellar holes and foundations are clearly visible to the north and east of the trail, and the trail swings south and runs through the cemetery, whose stone markers are visible.

Sources

Connecticut State Library. "Litchfield County Court African Americans and Native Americans Collection." http://www.cslib.org/Litchfield MinoritiesRes.asp (accessed 4 April 2006).

Feder, Kenneth. *A Village of Outcasts: Historical Archaeology and Documentary Research at the Lighthouse Site.* Mountain View, CA: Mayfield, 1994.

Mills, L. S. *The Legend of the Barkhamsted Lighthouse.* Hartford, CT: L. S. Mills, 1952.

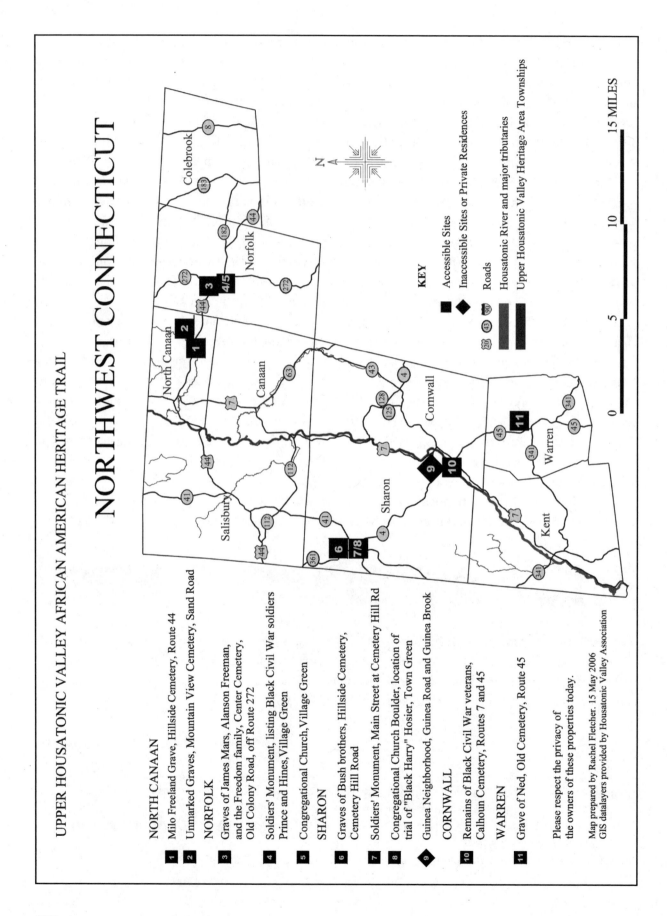

UPPER HOUSATONIC VALLEY AFRICAN AMERICAN HERITAGE TRAIL

NORTHWEST CONNECTICUT

KEY

■ ◆ Accessible Sites

● Inaccessible Sites or Private Residences

Roads

Housatonic River and major tributaries

Upper Housatonic Valley Heritage Area Townships

NORTH CANAAN

1 Milo Freeland Grave, Hillside Cemetery, Route 44

2 Unmarked Graves, Mountain View Cemetery, Sand Road

NORFOLK

3 Graves of James Mars, Alanson Freeman, and the Freedom family, Center Cemetery, Old Colony Road, off Route 272

4 Soldiers' Monument, listing Black Civil War soldiers Prince and Hines, Village Green

5 Congregational Church, Village Green

SHARON

6 Graves of Bush brothers, Hillside Cemetery, Cemetery Hill Road

7 Soldiers' Monument, Main Street at Cemetery Hill Rd

8 Congregational Church Boulder, location of trial of "Black Harry" Hosier, Town Green

◆ 9 Guinea Neighborhood, Guinea Road and Guinea Brook

CORNWALL

10 Remains of Black Civil War veterans, Calhoun Cemetery, Routes 7 and 45

WARREN

11 Grave of Ned, Old Cemetery, Route 45

Please respect the privacy of the owners of these properties today.

Map prepared by Rachel Fletcher. 15 May 2006
GIS datalayers provided by Housatonic Valley Association

Local Resources for the Study of Regional African American History

The institutions listed on the following pages house collections of primary and secondary sources pertaining to African American history and life in the Upper Housatonic Valley. Other resources such as tax and land records and annual town reports can be found in town halls in regional cities and towns.

Massachusetts

Ashley House, Ashley Falls
117 Cooper Hill Road, Ashley Falls, MA 01222
http://www.thetrustees.org/ashleyhouse.cfm
413-298-3229

Berkshire Athenaeum, Pittsfield
One Wendell Avenue, Pittsfield, MA 01201-6385
http://www.berkshire.net/PittsfieldLibrary/
pittsref@cwmars.org 413-499-9488

Berkshire Historical Society, Pittsfield
780 Holmes Road, Pittsfield MA 01201
http://www.berkshirehistory.org/index.html
info@berkshirehistory.org 413-442-1793

**The Du Bois Center of American History,
Great Barrington**
684 South Main Street, Great Barrington, MA 01230
413-644-9596

Friends of the Du Bois Homesite
P. O. Box 1018, Great Barrington, MA 01230
http://www.DuBoisHomesite.org 413-528-3391

Great Barrington Historical Society
PO Box 1106, Great Barrington, MA 01230
http://www.greatbarringtonhistoricalsociety.org
gbhs@bcn.net 413-528-5490

House of Local History, Williamstown
David and Joyce Milne Public Library
1095 Main Street, Williamstown, MA 01267
http://www.williamstown.net/house_
of_local_history.htm
nancywb947@aol.com 413-458-2160

Lee Library Association
100 Main Street, Lee, MA 01238
http://leelibrary.org/
lee@cwmars.org 413-243-0385

Mason Library, Great Barrington
231 Main Street, Great Barrington, MA 01230
http://www.gblibraries.net/ 413-528-2403

**Massachusetts College of Liberal Arts,
Freel Library, Local History Archives**
375 Church Street, North Adams, MA 01247-4124
http://www.mcla.mass.edu/Academics/Academic_
Resources/Library_and_Media/

North Adams Pubic Library
74 Church Street, North Adams, MA 01247
413-662-3133

Samuel Harrison Society
http://www.harrison.lsw.com/

Sheffield Historical Society
159–161 Main Street, P.O. Box 747
Sheffield, MA 01257
http://www.sheffieldhistory.org/
shs@sheffieldhistory.org 413-229-2694

Simon's Rock College Library
Alford Road, Great Barrington MA 01230
http://library.simons-rock.edu/
library@simons-rock.edu
413-528-7370

Stockbridge Library
Main Street, P. O. Box 119
Stockbridge, MA 01262
ballen@cwmars.org 413-298-5501

**Upper Housatonic Valley
African American Heritage Trail**
113 Division Street, Great Barrington, MA 01230
http://www.uhvafamtrail.org
afamtrail@hotmail.com 413-528-3391

**W. E. B. Du Bois Resource Collection
and Directory**
http://www.duboisweb.org

**W. E. B. Du Bois Library,
University of Massachusetts, Amherst**
Special Collections and Archives
W. E. B. Du Bois Library
University of Massachusetts–Amherst,
Amherst, MA 01003
http://www.library.umass.edu/spcoll/spec.html
askanarc@library.umass.edu   413-545-2780

Williams College
Sawyer Library, Chapin Library, and Williams
College Archives
Williamstown, MA 01267
http://www.williams.edu/library/faculty/index.php
413-597-2505

Connecticut

Connecticut Historical Society, Hartford
One Elizabeth Street at Asylum Avenue,
Hartford, CT 06105
http://www.chs.org/index.htm
860-236-5621

Connecticut State Library
231 Capitol Avenue, Hartford, CT 06106
http://www.cslib.org
860-757-6500

Cornwall Historical Society
7 Pine Street, Cornwall, CT 06753
http://www.cornwallhistoricalsociety.org/
860-672-0505

Falls Village-Canaan Historical Society
44 Railroad Street, P.O. Box 206,
Falls Village, CT 06031
http://www.betweenthelakes.com/canaan/
hist_society.htm   860-824-8226

Kent Historical Society
PO Box 651, Kent, CT 06757
http://www.kenthistoricalsociety.org/
860-927-4587

Litchfield Historical Society
P.O. Box 385, 7 South Street, Litchfield, CT 06759
http://www.litchfieldhistoricalsociety.org/
860-567-4501

Norfolk Historical Society
13 Village Green, Norfork, CT 06058
http://www.norfolkhistoricalsociety.com
860-542-5761

Salisbury Association Local History Room
The Academy Building, P.O. Box 553,
24 Main Street, Salisbury, CT 06068
860-435-0566

Scoville Memorial Library
38 Main Street, P.O. Box 374, Salisbury, CT 06068
salisburyhistory@yahoo.com
860-435-1287

Sharon Historical Society
18 Main Street, Sharon, CT 06069
http://www.sharonhist.org
860-364-5688

Index

A

Abolition of slavery, 16–18, 20–22
Abolitionists, 19–22, 23–24, 26–27, 105–106, 167, 211–212
Activist orators, 48–49
Activists, civil rights. *see* Civil rights activists
Adoptions, 216
African dance, 138
African Methodist Episcopal (A. M. E.) Zion Society, Great Barrington, Massachusetts, 65, 96, 97, 111, 126, 189–191. *see also* Clinton A. M. E. Zion Church, Great Barrington, Massachusetts
African Methodist Episcopal churches, 95–96, 181
African American heritage sites. *see* sites, African American heritage
African American studies, 58, 65–67
Agricultural fairs, 2, 6
Ailey, Alvin, 139
Alford, MA, 32
Allen, Charles H., 121
A. M. E. Zion Society. *see* Great Barrington, Massachusetts
American Colonization Society, 11
American Indians. *see* Native Americans
American Legion, 86
American Revolution. *see* Revolutionary War
Amos, Dorothy Reid, 58, 60–61, 171
Antislavery activists. *see* Abolitionists
Architects, 154
Archivists, 45–46
Ashley, John, 200
Ashley Falls, Massachusetts, 200
Ashley House, 200, 202–205
Athletes, 142–146
Authors, 33–35, 59–60, 130

B

Baker, Thomas Nelson, Rev., 101–102, 110
Bank tellers, 176
Bankole-Wright, Simeon, Rev., 102
Barber, Molly, 220
Barkhamsted Lighthouse community, Connecticut, 220–221
"Bars Fight" (ballad), 59
Baseball players, 142–146
Basketball and baseball coaches, 63–64, 178–179
Basketball players, 142–143, 145, 177
Beartown, Massachusetts, 4
Becket, Massachusetts, 138
Bed and breakfasts, 3–4
Berkshire Country Day School, 65
Berkshire County
        slavery in, 20–22
        Underground Railroad, 26–29

wildlife, 127–128
Berkshire Medical Institute, 11, 57
Bett, Mum (Elizabeth Freeman), 23–24, 184, 204
Black studies, 58, 65–67, 153
Bolin, Gauis Charles, 57
Bond, Julian, 38
Boynton, Nehemiah, Rev., 152
Brewster, William, 127–128
Briggs, George N., Governor, 48
Brinson, Albert and Susie, 3
Brooks, Eugene, 61
Brown, Harrison Morgan, 57
Brown, Henry Billings, 181
Brown, Mae E., 157–162
Brown, Sterling, 57
Burghardt family, 118–119
Businesses, 2–4
        Great Barrington, Massachusetts, 154
        Pittsfield, Massachusetts, 169
        Stockbridge, Massachusetts, 185
Butler, Hubert, 176

C

Caterers, 2
Ceasar, Samuel L., 164–165
Census data. *see* Population statistics
Chadwell, George Montgomery, 57
Charcoal producers, 208
Chinn, May Edward, 9, 57–58
Church school, 56, 65
Churches, 94–96. *see also specific churches*
        African Methodist Episcopal churches, 95–96, 181
        Great Barrington, Massachusetts, 189–191
        Lee, Massachusetts, 181
        Pittsfield, Massachusetts, 167, 171
        social and entertainment sources, 123, 126
        Stockbridge, Massachusetts, 185, 186
City councilwomen, 4
Civil rights activists, 30, 35–36, 45, 49
Great Barrington, Massachusetts, 192
Pittsfield, Massachusetts, 169
Civil War
        54th Massachusetts Infantry Regiment, 72–77, 168, 175–176
        Connecticut regiments, 81–84, 209, 212, 214–215, 217
        Massachusetts other units, 78–80
Clergy, 7, 94–96
        abolitionist, 21–22
        Baker, Thomas Nelson, Rev., 110
        Durant, William H., 114
        Harrison, Samuel, Rev., 105–106
        Haynes, Lemuel, 100
        Methodist itinerate, 98–99
        Price Memorial A. M. E. Zion

Church, 114
        Second Congregational Church, Pittsfield, Massachusetts, 101–110
        women, 98
Clinton A. M. E. Zion Church, Great Barrington, Massachusetts, 95, 111–113, 190. *see also* African Methodist Episcopal (A. M. E.) Zion Society, Great Barrington, Massachusetts
clergy, 95, 98
Clothes cleaning business, 3
Clubs, entertainment and social, 124, 137
Coaches, high school, 63–64, 142, 176–177
Cole, Nat King, 2
College education, 56–57, 60
Colleges, regional, 154–155
Colley, Jason, 2
Comithier, Leonard D., Jr., Rev., 102–104
Community leaders, 19–20, 63–64, 114, 192, 202
Concerts, 123
Congregational Church, First, Great Barrington, Massachusetts, 160–161
Congregational Church, Second, Pittsfield, Massachusetts. *see* Second Congregational Church, Pittsfield, Massachusetts
Connecticut, 206–222. *see also specific towns*
        Civil War regiments, 81–84
        Methodist itinerate clergy, 98–99
        slavery in, 16–18, 206
Cooley, Jason, 6, 121
Cooper, Fannie, 102
Cornwall, Connecticut, 216–217
Crawford, Martha, 3–4, 121, 154
Croslear, Edward Augustus, 77–78
Culture and history, Black, 65–67

D

Dafora, Asadata, 138
Dalton, Massachusetts, 164–165
Dance festivals, 139
Davis, W. Allison, 57
Davis, Warren H., 4–5, 201
Deerfield, Massachusetts, 59
Devore, Gary M. and Maria C., 2
Diplomats, 33
Discrimination. *see also* Segregation
        Brown, Mae E., on, 158–162
        Gunn, Elaine, on, 150–153
        in churches, 94, 97, 167
        in education, 56–57
        in employment, 1, 153, 158, 168, 190
        in hotels, 121, 161

in housing, 150–151, 159, 160
in military pay, 106
on trains, 48, 164
Doctors, medical, 9, 11
Douglass, Frederick, 48
Dozier, Esther, Rev., 98
Dry cleaning business, 3
Du Bois collection, 45–46
Du Bois, David Graham, 47
Du Bois Memorial Committee, 37–45
Du Bois, W. E .B., 30–32, 132–135
    Address to the Nation, 81
    on the Berkshire region, 132–135,
       193
    on Black population of the
       Berkshires, 190
    on churches, 96
    descendents, 136–137
    family employment, 9
    Harlem Renaissance, 129
    land purchase, 5
    legacy, 37–47, 65–66, 113, 150,
       156, 192–194
    NAACP and, 35
    Washington, Booker T., and, 49
    on World War I, 85–86
Durant, Willard H., Rev., 36, 114
Durante, William, Rev., 113, 192
Dusk of Dawn (Du Bois), 134
Dutch settlers, 71, 184, 200

E

Edgerton, Jerome T., Rev., 104
Edmonds, Florence, 10, 57
Education, 56–59
    Black history and culture, 58,
       65–67, 153
    college, 56–57, 60, 154–155
Educators, 57–58, 60–63, 136–137, 153,
    154–155
Edwards, Jonathan, Jr., 22
Elm tree of Pittsfield, 6
Emerson, Edward, 73
Employment
    discrimination in, 1, 153, 158, 168,
       190
    Great Barrington, Massachusetts,
       190
    Lee, Massachusetts, 180
    Pittsfield, Massachusetts, 168–169
    statistics, 6–8, 74–80, 88–90
    white-collar, 153–154
Employment agencies, 3
Enlisted men. *see* Military service
Entertainment, 123–126
Entrepreneurs, 2–4
    Great Barrington, Massachusetts,
       154
    Pittsfield, Massachusetts, 169
    Stockbridge, Massachusetts, 185
Episcopal churches, 95. *see also* African
    Methodist Episcopal churches
Essayists, 33–35

F

Factories and mills, 7–8, 154, 168, 189,
    199
Fairs, agricultural, 2, 6
Falls Church, Connecticut, 61
Family relationships, 118–120
Farmers, 2–3, 6–7
First Congregational Church, Great
    Barrington, Massachusetts, 169–161
Food concessions, 2, 6
Football players, 145, 146
Fowler, Cora, 57
Freed slaves. *see* Slaves, freed
Freeland, Milo J., 76–77
Freeman, Elizabeth (Mum Bett), 23–24,
    184
Fugitive Slave Act, 26
Fugitive Slaves. *see* Slaves, runaway

G

Gardner, Eliza Ann, 98
Garretson, Freeborn, 98–99
Genealogy, 118–119
General Electric, 7
Gilbert, Robert A., 127–128
Goodman, Mary, 59
Gordon, Edmund, 37
Governor of Massachusetts, 48
Grant, Frank, 143, 144
Grant, Sylvanus, 6
Grant family, 176
Great Barrington, Massachusetts, 189–196
    cemetery, 191
    churches, 95, 111–113, 160–161
    dry cleaners, 3
    Du Bois, W. E. B., and, 30–32,
       65–66, 132–134, 192–193
    founding families, 30, 189
    high school, 57
    housing conditions, 151
    inns and guest houses, 121–122
    Johnson, James Weldon, and, 34
    neighbor racism, 152
    neighborhoods, 190–191
    restauranteurs, 2
    sites, African American heritage,
       195–196
    social venues, 123–124
    W. E. B. Du Bois Memorial Park,
       37–44
Greaves, William, 202
Guest homes, 121–122
Guidance counselors, 61
Guilford, Vermont, 60
Gulf Road/Wizard's Glen community,
    164–165
Gunn, David Lester, Sr., 63–64, 141,
    176–177
Gunn, Elaine, 58, 150–156
Gunn, Maybelle, 5
Gunn, Wray, 202
Gunn family, 118

H

Haile, Moses, 193
Halleck, Fitz-Greene, 16
Harlem Renaissance, 129, 130
Harrison, James M., 142
Harrison, Samuel, Rev., 7, 101, 105–106,
    167, 168
    beliefs of, 103
    house of, 170
Hart, Billy, 142–143, 145
Hart, Margaret Alexander, 58, 62–63
Harvard University, 32
Haynes, Lemuel, 100
Hector, Henry, 209
High school Black studies, 65
High school sports coaches, 63
Hill, J.J., 84
History and culture, Black, 65–67
Hoose family, 165
Hopkins, Samuel, 21–22
Hosier, Harry, 98–99
Hospitality industry, 7–8
Hotel guest discrimination, 121, 161
Hotel workers, 7–8
Housatonic Agricultural Fair, 2, 6
Housatonic River, 134, 135, 193
Housatonic Valley Regional High
    School, 61
House warmings, 122
Housing discrimination, 150–151, 159,
    160
Hull, Agrippa, 2, 71, 184

I

Indentured servants, 19, 100, 210, 218
Indians. *see* Native Americans
Inns, 121–122
Iron industry, 206

J

Jacklin, Isaac, 220
Jackson, George, 2
Jacob's Pillow, 27, 138–139
James, John, 154, 202
James, Simon M., 176
Jamison, Alexander, Sr., Rev., 104
Jazz, 124–126
Jenkins, Isaiah, Rev., 102
Johnson, James Weldon, 33–35, 150
Jones, Ruth D., 45–46, 155
Judges, Federal, 12–13

K

Kent, Connecticut, 218
King, Larry, 146
King, Martin Luther, Jr., 49
Kinship, 118–120

L

Laborers, 6–7
Land speculators, 4–5, 23
Landscaping business, 4
Lanesboro, Massachusetts, 164–165
Laundry business, 3

Lee, Massachusetts, 179–183
    churches, 94
    restauranteurs, 2
    sites, African-American heritage, 182–183
Legal challenges to slavery, 23–24, 200
Lenox, Massachusetts, 174–178
    schools, 63
    sites, African American heritage, 177–178
    sports, 142, 143
    VanDerZee, James, 131–132
Lenox Merchants (basketball team), 142–143, 145
Liberia, 11
Librarians, 45–46
Lighthouse community, Barkhamsted, Connecticut, 220–221
Lincoln, Abraham, 84
Litchfield County, Connecticut, 16
Literary societies, 126
Lloyd, Samuel, Augustus, and William, 3
Logan, Rayford, 57
Logging industry, 4–5
Lumber dealers, 4–5
Lynchings, 96

M

Macedonia Baptist Church, Great Barrington, Massachusetts, 95–96, 97, 113
Male occupational statistics, 6–7, 74–76, 79–80
Marot, Helen, 35, 140
Marriage, 119–120
Mars, James, 19–20, 212
Mason, Manuel, 2, 6, 122
Mason, Robert Lewis, Rev., 102
Massachusetts College of Liberal Arts, 58, 62
    Local History Program, 67
Massachusetts governor, 48
Massachusetts slavery, 20–22
McFarland, John, Rev., 104
McKinley, Thomas Jefferson, 119
Meade, Homer B. "Skip", 65, 153, 186
Memorial, W. E. B. Du Bois, 37–44
Methodist churches, 95–96
    itinerate clergy, 98–99
Military officers, 73
Military service, 81–84
    Civil War Connecticut regiments, 81–84, 209, 212, 214–215, 217
    Civil War Massachusetts regiments, 72–80, 168, 175–176, 201
    Revolutionary War, 70–71, 179, 189, 214, 216–217
    World War I, 85–86
    World War II, 87–90
    World War II women, 90
Mills and factories, 7–8, 154, 168, 180, 190
Ministers. see Clergy
Mitchell, Jacob, Rev., 94
Models, Norman Rockwell's, 140–141

Moorish Science Temple, 95
Music Inn, 124–126

N

NAACP
    Berkshire County, 35–36, 62, 64
    founding, 30
    Great Barrington meeting place, 113
    guest speakers, 49
    Pittsfield, Massachusetts, chapter, 5, 169
    published philosophy, 34
Native Americans
    Barkhamsted Lighthouse community, 220–221
    Cornwall, Connecticut, 216
    Du Bois, W. E. B., family and, 190
    Gulf Road/Wizard's Glen community, 164–165
    Lee, Massachusetts, 179
    Raid on Deerfield, Massachusetts, 59
    Stockbridge, Massachusetts, 71, 184
Nature and naturalists, 127–128, 132–135
Navy, Civil War enlistees, 78–79
Negro, Cuffee and Nana, 23
Nevers, Harold Leslie, Rev., 102
Niagara Movement, 30
Nightclub owners, 4–5
Norfolk, Connecticut, 210–212
North Adams Normal School, 58, 62
Nurses, 10, 57, 191

O

Occupational statistics, male, 6–7, 74–80, 88–90
Occupations. see Employment
Officers, military, 73
Orators, visiting activist, 48–49
Ornithologists, 127–128
Ovington, Mary White, 32, 34, 35

P

Pan-African congresses, 30
Pastors. see Clergy
Penn, John Garrett, 12–13
Performing arts, 123, 138–139, 186–187
Persip, Alfred K., 86–87
Persip, Charles, 86–87, 171
Pettibone, Amos, 27
Philosophers, 110
Photographers, 127–128, 129, 130–132, 176
Physicians, 9, 11, 57–58
Pioneer blacks, 23
Pittsfield, Massachusetts, 166–172
    baseball, 142
    businesses, 4
    churches, 94–96, 97, 98, 101–110, 113, 114, 167
    Douglass, Frederick, speech in, 48
    elm tree, 6

    public schools, 58–59, 61, 62
    sites, African American heritage, 170–172
    social venues, 123–124
Pittsfield General Hospital, 57
Plays, 65, 186–187
Plessy v. Ferguson, 181
Poets, 33–35, 59–60
Population statistics
    Connecticut, 206
    Cornwall, Connecticut, 216, 217
    Great Barrington, Massachusetts, 189, 192
    Kent, Connecticut, 218
    Lee, Massachusetts, 179–181
    Lenox, Massachusetts, 174, 177
    Norfolk, Connecticut, 211
    Pittsfield, Massachusetts, 166–167
    Salisbury, Connecticut, 207
    Sheffield, Massachusetts, 201
    Stockbridge, Massachusetts, 186–187
    Warren, Connecticut, 219
Porter, Joshua, 207
Prejudice. *see also* Discrimination
    children and, 31–32, 160
    housing and neighbors, 150–152
Preschools, 61
Pressers, 3
Price Memorial A. M. E. Zion Church, Pittsfield, Massachusetts, 95–96, 97, 113, 114, 171
Prime family, 175
Prince, Lucy Terry, 59–60
Prince family, 175
The Problem We All Live With (Rockwell), 140–141
Professionals, 9–13
Property transfers, 120
Public health nurses, 10

R

Racism. *see* Discrimination; Prejudice; Segregation
Religious institutions. *see* Church school
Restaurant discrimination, 150
Restauranteurs, 2
Revolutionary War, 70–71, 179, 1189, 214, 216–217
Rhode Island, 209
Richmond, Virginia, Civil War capture, 84
Rights, voting, 19
Roberts, Henry Jenkins, 11
Rockwell, Norman, 140–141
Runaway slaves. *see* Slaves, runaway

S

St. John's Masonic Temple, 123–124
Salisbury, Connecticut, 207–209
Sawmill owners, 201
Scermahorn (Schermerhorn) family, 174–175
Scholars, 30–32, 47, 110, 136–137
Scholarships, 45–46, 58, 59, 62, 103

School administrators, 61
School sports coaches, 63–64
Schools, 56–59
    Black studies in, 65
    Sports coaches, 63
Second Congregational Church, Great
    Barrington, Massachusetts, 112
Second Congregational Church,
    Pittsfield, Massachusetts, 101–104,
    167, 171
    clergy, 95, 98, 101–110
    founding, 94, 97
Sedgwick, Theodore, 71
Sedgwick, Theodore, II, 22
Sedgwick family, 23–24
Segregation. *see also* Discrimination
    hotel, 121–122
    housing, 150
    military, 72–73, 81, 86, 87
    Pittsfield, Massachusetts, 167, 168
    school, 57, 167, 201
    sports, 142
Selective Service, 85, 87
Selectmen, 202
Servants, indentured, 19, 100, 210, 218
Sharon, Connecticut, 213–215
Shaw, Robert Gould, 73
Shawn, Ted, 138
Sheffield, Massachusetts, 57, 185,
    200–203
Simon's Rock College, 66
Sites, African-American heritage
    Canaan, Connecticut, 212
    Cornwall, Connecticut, 217
    Great Barrington, Massachusetts,
    195–196
    Lee, Massachusetts, 182–183
    Lenox, Massachusetts, 177–178
    Norfolk, Connecticut, 212
    Pittsfield, Massachusetts, 170–172
    Sharon, Connecticut, 215
    Sheffield, Massachusetts, 202–203
    Stockbridge, Massachusetts,
    187–188
    Warren, Connecticut, 219
Slaves and slavery, 15. *see also*
    Abolitionists
    abolition of, 16–18, 20–22
    Connecticut, 16–18, 206
    Cornwall, Connecticut, 216–217
    Fugitive Slave Act, 26
    Kent, Connecticut, 218
    Massachusetts, 20–23
    Norfolk, Connecticut, 210–212
    Pittsfield, Massachusetts, 166
    Revolutionary War, 70
    Sharon, Connecticut, 213–214
    Sheffield, Massachusetts, 200
    Stockbridge, Massachusetts, 184
    Warren, Connecticut, 219
Slaves, former, 210
    activists, 19–20, 23–24
    authors, 59–60
    clergy, 105–106, 110
    Gulf Road community, 164

scholars, 110
    Sheffield, Massachusetts, 200
Slaves, freeing of
    Connecticut, 17, 19–20
    Massachusetts, 23–24
    Revolutionary War, 70
Slaves, runaway
    Cornwall, Connecticut, 216
    Fugitive Slave Act, 26
    Kent, Connecticut, 218
    into Massachusetts, 20, 27, 185
    Salisbury, Connecticut, 207–209
    Second Congregational Church,
    Pittsfield, Massachusetts,
    167–168
    Sharon, Connecticut, 213–214
    Underground Railroad, 25–29,
    139, 164, 212, 219
Social life, 123–126
social scientists, 30
Soldiers. *see* Military service
Songwriters, 33–35
The Souls of Black Folk (Du Bois), 30,
    49, 96, 153
Speakers, visiting activist, 48–49
Sports, 142–146
Starr, Robin, 214
Statistics, male occupational, 6–7,
    79–80, 88–90
Stockbridge, Massachusetts, 184–188
    colonial period, 71
    community leaders, 63–64
    entrepreneurs, 2
    inns and guest houses, 121–122
    sites, African-American heritage,
    187–188
    Washington, Booker T., speech in,
    48–49
Stowe, Harriet Beecher, 22
Summer-employment agencies, 3
Sunday schools, 56

T

Taxpayers, 166, 185–186, 189
Teachers, 57, 58, 61, 62, 153, 158–159,
    192
Tearooms, 4
Theater, 123, 186–187
Timber dealers, 4–5
Tourgee, Albion Winegar, 181
Tourism industry, 7–8, 190
Towley, Carol, Rev., 98, 104
Tree cutters, 6
Tri-racial isolate communities, 220–221

U

Underground Railroad, 25–29, 139, 164,
    212, 219
United Church of Christ (UCC)
    churches, 101
University of Massachusetts, Amherst,
    67

V

VanDerZee, James, 129, 130–132, 176
Veterans
    Croslear, Edward Augustus, 77–78
    Hull, Agrippa, 71
    Persip brothers, 86–87
Victory Temple United Church of God
    in Christ, Pittsfield, Massachusetts,
    95, 171
Voting rights, 19

W

Wagonmakers, 3
Waiters, 7–8
Warren, Connecticut, 219
Washington, Booker T., 48–49, 59
Watlington, Dennis, 202
W. E. B. Du Bois Memorial Park, 37–44
W. E. B. Du Bois River Park and Garden,
    192–193
White, Walter, 129
Wightman, John G., Rev., 104
Williams, Yolande Du Bois, 136–137
Williams College, 56–57, 60, 66–67
Wilson, Stephanie, 58–59
Wilson, Walter, 37
Wizard's Glen community, 164–165
Women
    activists, 23–24, 35
    authors, 59–60
    educators, 60–61, 62–63
    medical professionals, 9, 10
    military service, 90
    religious leaders, 97–98
Woodsmen, 6
Workers, 7–8
World War I, 85–87
World War II, 87–90
Writers. *see* Authors

Z

Zaccho Dance Theatre, 139

About the Editors

David Levinson is a cultural anthropologist (PhD, SUNY/Buffalo) and president of the Berkshire Publishing Group, which he founded with Karen Christensen in 1998. He was for twenty years on the staff, and latterly vice-president, of the Human Relations Area Files at Yale University, an anthropological think-tank. He is the author or editor of over two dozen major books and reference works. He is the senior editor of *American Immigrant Cultures: Builders of a Nation* and editor of the award-winning Religion & Society series. He is also the author of *Sewing Circles, Dime Suppers, and W. E. B. Du Bois: A History of the Clinton A. M. E. Zion Church*, published in October 2006. David also founded and directs the W. E. B. Du Bois Global Research Collection and Directory Online (www.duboisweb.org). He has lived in Great Barrington since 1996.

Rachel Fletcher is a geometer/theatre designer and restoration planner (MFA, Humboldt State University). She is the curator of museum exhibits on geometry and author of the exhibition catalog *The Golden Mean as a Design Tool*. Her essays have appeared in *Nexus Network Journal*, as contributing editor, *Design Spirit*, as associate editor, *Parabola, Via, Building Design,* the *Lindisfarne Letter,* and *The Power of Place.* A resident of Great Barrington since 1981, she is the former executive director of Housatonic River Restoration and the founding director of the town's Housatonic River Walk and W. E. B. Du Bois River Garden Park. She is a trustee of Upper Housatonic Valley National Heritage Area, Inc. and cochairs the Upper Housatonic Valley African American Heritage Trail.

Frances Jones-Sneed is professor of history (PhD, University of Missouri-Columbia) at Massachusetts College of Liberal Arts in North Adams, Massachusetts. Jones-Sneed has worked for twenty years teaching and researching local history and has lived in Williamstown since 1993. She is the codirector of the Upper Housatonic African American Heritage Trail Advisory Council and is currently working on a monograph about W. E. B. Du Bois. She currently codirects a National Endowment for the Humanities grant entitled, "The Shaping Role of Place in African American Biography" and spearheaded a national conference on African American Biography in September 2006.

Bernard A. Drew (BA, Northeastern University) is a local historian, journalist, and author of popular literature reference books. He is the author of the definitive *Great Barrington: Great Town * Great History* and two recent books on regional African American history: *If They Close the Door on You, Go in the Window* and *Dr. Du Bois Rebuilds His Dream House.* A resident of Great Barrington since 1977, he is past president of the Great Barrington and Berkshire County Historical Societies. He has written for *The Berkshire Eagle's* "Our Berkshires" column for a decade and has contributed scholarly pieces to the Society for Industrial Archaeology's newsletter and the Thoreau Society's *The Concord Saunterer.* His *The 100 Most Popular African-American Authors* will be released in the fall of 2006.

Elaine S. Gunn is a retired teacher from the former Bryant School in Great Barrington. A graduate of the former Williams High School in Stockbridge, Massachusetts, she holds a BA and an MEd from the former North Adams State College (now Massachusetts College of Liberal Arts). Ms. Gunn was a civil rights activist in the 1950s and 1960s, a member of the Berkshire County chapter of the NAACP, and a supporter of the original Du Bois Memorial Committee. She has served on the boards of the Norman Rockwell Museum and the Berkshire County Historical Society and on the Board of Deacons at the First Congregational Church in Stockbridge. Currently, she is a member of the Upper Housatonic Valley African American Trail Guide Committee. She resides in Great Barrington with her husband Clarence.